Can You Find Me

With my father and brother in Devon

CHRISTOPHER FRY

Can You Find Me

A FAMILY HISTORY

Thought this sheep-shearing
photo would interest you.
Can you find me.

*On a postcard from my mother
to her sister Ada, 29 July 1906*

Oxford London New York
OXFORD UNIVERSITY PRESS
1978

1978

Oxford University Press, Walton Street, Oxford OX2 6DP

OXFORD LONDON GLASGOW
NEW YORK TORONTO MELBOURNE WELLINGTON
IBADAN NAIROBI DAR ES SALAAM CAPE TOWN
KUALA LUMPUR SINGAPORE JAKARTA HONG KONG TOKYO
DELHI BOMBAY CALCUTTA MADRAS KARACHI

© Christopher Fry 1978

British Library Cataloguing in Publication Data

Fry, Christopher
  Can you find me.
  1. Fry family
  I. Title
  929'.2'0942   CS439.F/   77–30728
  ISBN 0 19–211751–3

*Printed in Great Britain by
Western Printing Services Ltd., Bristol*

To my brother
Charles Leslie Harris

ACKNOWLEDGEMENTS

The seed of this book was sown during a conversation with John Bell, of the Oxford University Press, in which Jon Stallworthy joined. They asked whether I would write a book about my childhood. But though I could see that the impact of the 1914–18 War on a boy between seven and eleven years old might be worth recalling, I didn't feel there was enough in those early years to fill a book. What did interest me was what led up to those years, the story of my parents and my grandparents, aunts and uncles, the network of events and characters out of which I had emerged. Could I find the reality of them, and in doing so recognize anything in the events and people which lives on in me? On my mother's side I found a mine of material, remarkable considering how often the homes were broken up; on my father's side almost nothing. I am most grateful to all those who have helped in the delving: to my cousins Jack and Nora Harris (Jack for his notes about the Harris family, headed 'The Hindsight Saga'); to Tracey Simpson, descended from the Hammonds of New Zealand, who suddenly appeared on my doorstep from Wellington with a fragment of a letter from my great-grandfather; to Diana (Fry) Britton for the Fry origins; Mrs. Betty Potts for material from her father Archibald Marshall; Mrs. Eileen Manley of Wanganui (Lil's daughter); to May and Eileen Hammond (Hal's daughters) for discovering a box of their father's letters; to my cousins Mary Clifford, Iris Hamlyn, and Shona White; to Alan Phillips for permission to quote the little letter from his grandmother.

Outside the family, I owe much to the Reverend R. H. D.

Acknowledgements

Blake who gave up a great deal of his time taking me round the parish of St. Agnes, and for leading me to its early history. The facts of my father's ancestry were supplied by the Reverend H. Gordon Jones, Vicar of Salcombe, who not only searched the parish registers but entertained me in his home. My thanks to him and to Mrs. Gordon Jones who guided me round Salcombe; to Mrs. Nicky Gridley for the early history of Raven Hall; to Margaret Mullen, who patiently typed and retyped my changing versions, and to Judith Chamberlain of the Oxford University Press who put up with my barrage of last-minute emendations.

I am particularly indebted to Catharine Carver who through all the stages of the book encouraged me and brought a clear eye to the shaping; to Morton Marrian for tracking down the eighteenth-century Hammonds; and to Robert Gittings whose criticism, powers of detection and research, and lively interest in following up what clues I could give him have helped beyond measure. Through all the years the book has been on the stocks, often put aside and taken up again, my wife, who has no cousins at all to bless herself with, has taken over the multitude of mine, both past and present, without a tremor.

C.F.

1977

CONTENTS

ILLUSTRATIONS

Illustrations

Introductory

On Wednesday, 18 December 1907, the steamship *Rockabill*
of London, 1,610 tons, docked at Bristol with one of the
heaviest starboard lists that had ever been seen on a vessel
entering the port. She had been through a fearful battering
in the Bay of Biscay, her engines out of action for part of the
time, and squalls had followed her all the way home to an
England of gales and floods. If another arrival in Bristol
hadn't claimed all my mother's attention on that particular
day, the stormy passage of the *Rockabill* would surely have
carried her thoughts to another storm in the Bay of Biscay,
eleven years before, when she and my father were sailing to
Australia to start a new life; or it may have been when they
were returning home forlorn and defeated eighteen months
later. The storm had laid low all the passengers except my
mother. It was one of her proud memories, and her eyes used
to sparkle each time she told the story. She had been the
only one well enough to sit down to dinner, and the captain
for lack of a medal had cut a button off his uniform and
pinned it to her dress. It was one of the treasures of her
button box. But on the day of the docking of the S.S.
Rockabill she had something else to think about. At 5.30 in
the morning she had given birth to me.

She was already thirty-six, by a month, and my father two
years older. They had been married for nearly fifteen un-
prospering years, the first four in the suburbs of London
where my father was a builder's clerk, and then, after the
Australian débâcle, he had set up as a builder in partnership
with his brother Bert in his home town, Gillingham, Kent.

The business failed. My mother always blamed this on Bert's casual business methods and a dishonest solicitor, but I doubt if my father's heart was much in the enterprise. It took this culmination of failure to jolt him into finding at last his real calling. In the summer of 1904, when he was thirty-five years old, 'our beloved and approved in Christ, Charles John Harris' was given a licence by the Bishop of Rochester to work as a lay reader, or vicar's dogsbody, the nearest he could come to ordination. It had been a slow troublesome road to get to a place where his life could have purpose, but now he had found it. And two years earlier the nine childless years of marriage had ended with the birth of a son, my older brother.

So it was like a late spring of life for him when, early in July 1905, his licence renewed by the Bishop of Exeter, he moved with his family to take up an appointment in a group of fifteen hamlets centred on Marwood in north Devon. All through my childhood the names of Marwood, Muddiford, and Little Silver breathed peace and contentment, a brief halcyon time before I existed, when my father's life had only six more years to run. Those were the most untroubled days of my parents' life together. Nothing was ever said to disturb my faith in their perfection; neither illness nor accident marred the seventeen months they lasted. It was so tranquil a time, in memory at least, that no events came down to me, only a shimmer of nostalgia and a few photographs which, like Dante's flame reflected in a mirror, make me want to turn back and share the reality. I bring a magnifying glass to the fading photographs and try to make out the label on the jam pot used at a picnic in the woods.

They lived in a slate-roofed, whitewashed cottage near a spring which spouted from an old wall, where they collected drinking water in earthenware jugs. There was a pony and trap to carry my father round the sprawling parish, or to take my mother to the fête in the vicarage garden, the prettiest and most elegant woman there. A few other occasions were caught before that quiet world ended: a sheep-shearing competition ('Can you find me', my mother wrote on the back of the picture, a question speaking for all of that vanished time); a visit to watch the new steam harvester at work on Gears' farm, and my mother and brother walking a dusty lane to the Mission Hall. *Perchè t'abbagli per veder cosa, che qui non ha loco?* As far as my own life goes these things never existed, and yet I'm sorry for the mortality of 'Daddy Coles, the village philosopher', spade in hand, his philosophy arrested in a grin, and want to know more of Fred Bindon than the brief account sent by one of my aunts to another after a summer holiday in Marwood. 'This photo taken by C.H.,' she wrote, 'picknicking with their friends Mr. & Miss Bindon at their cottage in Little Silver. Mr. B. is really a very nice looking *young* man of 35. invalided from the army last year. served 14 yrs in India. have seldom met a nicer fellow.' He was to make one last appearance in the family history when he identified my father's body and gave evidence at the inquest.

Two happy summers went by, and then in October 1906 my father decided on a change. He applied successfully for the post of lay reader in a Bristol parish. I have the testimonial given him by his rector. 'More than once', he wrote, 'the whole pastoral work of Marwood – very large and scattered – has been left entirely to Mr. Harris and that work has been done with great care, anxiety and success. Mr. Harris has especial power in addresses to children.' He was now to put his calling to a much severer test. On 13 November, my mother's thirty-fifth birthday, they moved to Bristol.

The parish of St. Agnes, on the north-east of the city, had grown out of the Clifton College Mission. Until the 1870s the district had been a wasteland, a place of squatters' shacks and black ash-heaps flooded in times of heavy rain or melting snows by the river Frome. By 1883 there were 750 cottages, lived in by almost twice as many families of tailors, shoe-makers, plasterers, mason's labourers, and quarrymen. The five-shillings-a-week rent was too high for more than a few families to rent a whole cottage to themselves.

The spiritual charge of this settlement was given to a battling Christian socialist, the Reverend Thomas Harvey. 'We must prove our claim to be doing work for the soul', he said, 'by the evidence, tangible and visible, that we are doing work for the body . . . We must diligently set ourselves to consider the recreations and amusement of the people.' The tangible and visible evidence was provided: a Mission Room, a school, a Working Men's Club, a library and reading room. Once all this had been done Harvey could turn his attention to building a church, 'to be', he told the architect Wood Bethell, 'as beautiful and cheering as possible'. So the finials of the pillars were carved with the heads of apostles, saints, and prophets, from Abraham and Isaiah, by way of Edward the Confessor to Wycliff, Bishop Butler, Wesley, Patteson of Melanesia, and Christopher Wordsworth. The pulpit, where my father was to preach, and the font, where I was to be christened, were decorated with mosaics; the font with the Descent of the Dove appropriately on its eastward face. The painted reredos of the Last Supper had two side panels: a Crusader, a Magus, a Monk, and St. Agnes on one, and on the other Bishop Westcott, a Hospital Nurse, a Footballer, and Lord Roberts on his knees, which brought a protest from the War Office.

British trade was going through a recession in 1886, the year the church was consecrated. There were riots in London, and a march of the unemployed through the Bristol streets. Harvey invited the men into the church and 'thundered' against the evils of society. During the strikes and lock-outs of 1889 he wrote, spoke, preached, demonstrated in the cause of the dockers, gas workers, confectionery workers, and particularly the cotton-factory girls. 'I am here because I am a paid agitator,' he declared at a labour demonstration in 1892. 'I believe that every Christian minister is or ought to be a paid agitator . . . Social revolution is coming, and God helping us it must be without confusion and without blood.'

His curate and successor (in 1904) was a man called Arthur Rashleigh, who held Harvey's opinions with less thunder and became my entirely inoperative godfather.

The house, 65 Sussex Place, where I was born thirteen months after the move to Bristol, was in a late-Victorian terrace, two doors away from a corner shop belonging to Ted Legg, a greengrocer, at the foot of Ashley Down Hill. Two days before I was born a girl riding down the hill on a bicycle lost control of her machine and crashed into a wall opposite. She was carried unconscious into my parents' house, an episode which frightened my five-year-old brother, and shocked my mother into forty-eight hours of labour, or so she believed. If so, it was just as well; I was overdue. This I know from the diary of my mother's eldest sister Ada, nicknamed by her family 'Tiny'. (She was scarcely more than four and a half feet tall.) Alone in her lodgings at Langton Green, near Tunbridge Wells, she kept a day-to-day record of her own ill-health and the births, deaths, and illnesses of her relatives and friends. On the 23rd of May 1907 she had written: 'Heard of Day's expected event in November.' But it had taken the faulty brakes on a poor girl's bicycle to get me into the world even in time for Christmas.

Now the day had come. I breathed the air and tried out my lungs. I weighed seven and a half pounds. The doctor was complimentary about the shape of my head, 'the shape I like to see', a comment my mother never tired of recalling. The temporary nurse, whose name was Snow, was so stout and her lap so shallow that my mother feared I should slide off on to the floor. No other domestic recollection of that day has come down to me, and nothing of historic moment happened in the world either. The gales had subsided. Sir Henry Campbell-Bannerman's Government was enjoying the Christmas recess. Like Miss Twinkleton's establishment the country was undergoing a serene hush. I was born on a plateau of time which looked proudly on to the past and with disquiet into the future. On the first morning of my life two speeches

were being prepared, representative of this divide: one by
Lord Curzon, to be given at a dinner for the five hundred
survivors of the Indian Mutiny (Kipling had written a poem
for the occasion); and the other by Sir Edward Grey who,
withdrawing his mind from the bird-life of Falloden, prepared
his comments on the German naval programme. He was not
wanting to complain, he wrote, but if Germany went on
increasing their naval expenditure we could hardly go on
reducing ours. H. G. Wells was soon to publish *The War in
the Air*, but it was still a fantasy. A few hours after I was
born the wings of the machine which carried Louis Blériot
through the air collapsed and dropped him in a tangle of
wreckage on the earth.

Otherwise it was a day very much like any day in the
twenty years since St. Agnes Church had been built. Edward
VII went out shooting at Windsor, but the spirit of Victoria,
six years dead, was slow to abdicate. The Red Maids and the
Blue Maids, children of two local charity schools, wore straw
bonnets and uniforms which had scarcely changed, if at all,
since the 1840s. Müller's Home for Boys made it a flourishing
neighbourhood for orphans, but the parish itself was very
far from flourishing. My father sometimes snatched his dinner
from the table and carried it to a hungry parishioner.

His particular responsibility was the Lake Street Mission
which served the poorest part of the community. Here he
conducted the services, preached, organized entertainments,
ran a club, and held Sunday night discussions with the men.
But the Mission was only a part of his activities. He was also
assistant organist at the church itself, superintendent of the
Boys' Sunday-school, secretary of the Temperance Society,
chairman of the Band of Hope and Church of England's
Men's Society, and choirmaster of the Children's Mission.
'Into all this work', the parish magazine said, 'he threw
himself with a vigour that was beyond his strength, for he
never spared himself. . . . Those who knew him well could
tell of his deep feeling for the people in their poverty and
distress . . .'

Folded inside the notebook in which he jotted down the outlines of his sermons I found a flimsy yellow handbill:

TRADES COUNCIL RIGHT-TO-WORK COMMITTEE

Fellow Citizens,
13,000,000 English people live on the verge of Starvation. In Bristol last winter 25,000 men, women and children were suffering want and misery, the result of Unemployment.
Is it nothing to you, working men, that so much poverty exists?
Is it nothing to you who have plenty of this world's goods that you raise no hand to mitigate the evil?
Is it nothing to you, Politicians and Ministers of Christ, that you utter no protest against the slow murder of young children through poverty because their fathers are denied the Right to Work?
Ask your City Councillor, your Member of Parliament, What are they doing to solve Poverty? This poverty problem can be solved.
Working men, the establishment of the Principle of the 'Right to Work' means much to you, your wives and your children.

A MEETING will be held on Friday, September 23rd, 1910
Sussex Place, Ashley Road.
Chair to be taken at 7.30 sharp.

I can only guess at my father's political persuasion. He had told my mother, as early as the 1906 Liberal election victory, that Lloyd George was the man of the future, a remark which later impressed her by its perspicacity. Perhaps, like Lloyd George himself, he favoured socialist measures but not the socialist party, or tempered his views out of consideration for my mother whose early life had swung between genteel poverty and middle-class affluence, and to whom socialism was a bogy. The difference in their upbringing was more disruptive than either of them would admit. Long afterwards a family friend told me how one day my mother dressed me in a handsome new coat and proudly showed me off to my father. He looked up from his writing and said, 'Aren't we getting rather above ourselves?'; and though I have found that other memories of this friend of my mother's were fantasy, and always weighted against my father, he may well have been defensive about the luxuries my mother had given up when she married him.

In the brief notes he made for what was probably his last sermon (it is where the notebook breaks off) he wrote in his neat, round hand: 'All things are religious that have to do with human conduct. Building of cities, steamboats, roads, housing and clothing, education, invention, culture are all part of the working out of the Kingdom of God upon earth.'

This was the dedicated, almost saintly figure which, for a while after his death, my mother tried to perpetuate for me, even to celestializing him by teaching me to call the first brilliant star of the evening 'Daddy's star'. But as the years went by and his presence receded she began to disturb the image with long-held resentments and censure, not harshly held but quite bitterly suffered, and I began to know of a marriage for which, at times, the rough Bay of Biscay was a symbol, and of a far more complex, embattled, and ultimately tragic man.

A few of his possessions, which my mother sometimes showed to me when I was little, affected me as solemnly as if they had been holy relics: a stole, a mortar-board, some articles of regalia which represented his position in the Freemasons, a heavy ebony ruler (less sacred: I can remember once using it as a rolling pin), and a pile of early sermons, written out in full to be read from the pulpit, opaque with the conventional vocabulary of the Church. Later on when he gained confidence he used only the guide-lines of notes. Among them is a single sentence of autobiography, one pinpoint of light on to his childhood. The text of the sermon is from Genesis 15: 13: 'And [Hagar] called the name of the Lord that spake unto her, Thou God seest me.' Then he jots down: 'Value of passage depends largely on what is put into word God. If any comfort, largely depends on *what* God sees us, what kind of eyes, etc.', and he adds: 'Passage haunted me as a boy. Afraid of the eyes of God.'

No letters from him have survived, only a picture postcard posted to my brother on 8 August 1907, four months before I was born, a bleak picture of the mouth of Ogmore River, Merthyrmawr, South Wales. He had written in pencil on the back (upside down): 'Isn't this pretty? The camp is close here & it is all very lovely but it has been raining hard all day, & it is not very warm. Hoping you will be a very good boy while I'm away. DAD.'

When I look at these things I feel like Ezekiel in the valley of bones and wonder what breath can make them live. Out of the three years when I existed side by side with my father one single memory is all I have kept of him, and even that a headless one. It belongs somewhere in my first year, probably when I was about eight months old, or so I judge from two of the more cheeful entries in my Aunt Ada's diary. On 23 September 1908 she lay on her sofa in Langton Green (I can't remember her ever sitting at a table, though she may have done) and wrote, 'Heard from Day that baby can stand alone.' Then, as many times I saw her do in the years to come, she wiped the nib on a star-shaped penwiper, made of alternate layers of black and red flannel. On 8 December she recorded, 'Heard from Day . . . that baby was trotting about at 11 months.' But the memory I have of my father is before I could either trot or stand. I was crawling somewhere near the hearthrug; in front of me were my father's legs, his boots, stockings, and Norfolk breeches. By pushing my head back I could see as far as his waist. I had a sudden feeling of perfect contentment, as though a warm benediction had alighted on me. Perhaps I then tried to stand, to pull myself up so that I could see his face. If so the physical effort destroyed the sensitive plate of memory. It was after his death before I remember seeing his head and shoulders, half lost in shadow by the glow of a night-light.

But there is another memory, in opposition to the small security of the hearthrug, the impact of a vaster, less merciful world, which may be where consciousness made its first notch on my mind. I was being wheeled in my pram. Whoever was wheeling me (perhaps the young servant called Teresa) stopped to chat with someone who glanced up at the sky and said, 'We're in for a storm.' I looked where she nodded and saw that the sky was a heavy yellow, the yellow of a bruise. It was threatening and coming towards us. The daylight was full of foreboding.

The Langton Green diary has an entry for 30 May 1908: 'A thunderstorm at Bristol. Struck the cross on St. Agnes church.' Perhaps it was the household excitement over the damaged cross which underscored the memory and made sure that I shouldn't forget the warning in the sky. Two later memories have the same burden of advancing evil: the summer day in 1911 when I saw a man in black walking up to the door bearing news of death, and another summer day three years later, when I sat listening to a brass band on Lowestoft Pier and stared out over a North Sea pregnant with the enemy. It was the first week of August 1914.

I remember nothing else about my first three and a half years. I must have been too pleasantly preoccupied to store anything away, for in spite of whooping cough, bronchitis, and measles, all methodically set down in the diary by my aunt, I was robust and persistently cheerful. But by the spring of 1909 my father had worked himself to a standstill. He was ordered to rest for three months. In the previous year we had moved house twice, first to the top of Ashley Hill and then down the hill again to save my father's heart. My mother always held the unlikely opinion that he had strained his heart as a schoolboy doing gymnastics, and during my own school-days she looked on a gymnasium with mistrust. It suggests, at any rate, that he was never a very strong man; and his activities in the parish, preaching, training the choir, playing the organ, running the men's club, getting up entertainments, arranging camps and outings, visiting the sick, the lonely and the dying, were enough to cripple a Hercules. And, in addition, there was the long-drawn-out battle, in which he was sometimes winning, sometimes losing, against depending on drink.

We spent a month or more of that summer at Woolacombe, my mother recovering from tonsillitis and expecting a third child, my father gradually getting back his strength, sometimes paddling with us in the flat foam as it ran up the beach, or helping to build a tall sand-castle which we topped with a Union Jack. It all looks in the photographs as idyllic as Marwood, but it was really as frail as the sand-castle.

In early October I was taken to see Aunt Ada. She had moved from Langton to lodgings at 25 Monson Terrace, Tunbridge Wells, and put down the day in her diary: 'To the station before 10' (we had come there from a visit to my grandparents in Gillingham) 'to meet Day and baby. On the Common, and sat in the drawing room. Day well but thin. Baby a bonny little chick not quite 1 year & 10 months. Saw them off by the 5.10.'

A fortnight later she was writing: 'Day very ill; miscarriage last week.'

It was when my mother spoke of it years afterwards that I first heard her criticize my father. She blamed him for the miscarriage. 'Your father let me carry you downstairs,' she said, and I was puzzled that such a kind man could be so unfeeling. Only now as I think of it I wonder why she didn't mention my father's bad heart, his recent breakdown, and his likely fear of leaving the family without a bread-winner; and he might reasonably have supposed that at nearly two I could get down the stairs myself, if only on my bottom. They seem to have kept their thoughts and feelings to themselves, which is why there were outcrops of them in my mother so long afterwards. In the year and a half following the miscarriage it became increasingly difficult to hold on to happiness.

1910 began badly. My brother was ill with bronchial asthma; and on through March into early April Aunt Ada was making worried little entries in her diary; my mother not well, my mother overtired, my brother still in bed. He not well enough to win third place in a singing competition judged by the Cathedral choirmaster, but immediately afterwards went down with diphtheria. My father photographed him in convalescence standing proudly beside his collection of lead soldiers formed up in display on the dressing-table of his bedroom. They made an impressive show. Infantry, cavalry, bandsmen, stretcher-bearers (the stretchers could be taken out of their hands), Scotsmen, Zulus with spears, men in the khaki of the Boer War, men in helmeted scarlet – most of the slaughterous campaigns of Empire were there – and even Russians in green uniforms, representatives of the Russo-Japanese war in which, as my aunt noted, the Japanese had destroyed the Baltic Fleet a week before my family moved to Marwood: all now neatly paraded on the lace runner of the dressing-table. I had twice mishandled some of these troops: by decorating the tea-table with them, sticking them in the bread, the cakes, and the butter, clapping my hands and calling, 'Look what me done!'; and by dropping them into a saucepan of jam simmering on the fire, much as I am now playing with the eidolons of people into whose hearts and anxieties I can't completely or perhaps even justly come. They were warm-hearted, unselfseeking, sensitive people, my parents; they had humour – my mother's grey eyes were the liveliest, most dancing eyes I have ever seen. I believe, in spite of strains and friction, they never altogether fell out of love. And yet they lived through their last year together in two separate worlds of trouble. My mother was undemonstrative. She expressed her strong affection in silent devotion, seldom in word or gesture. Her anxieties were borne silently, too; not grimly; but she hated to blame, or to say anything that might hurt or distress. There was a particular irony in the situation. When she was little she had listened at night to her father stumbling drunkenly up the stairs and hammering on the door of the bedroom where she slept with her mother. She grew up vowing never to marry a man who drank; and though my father's drinking was private and its effect rigorously disciplined – 'No one could tell,' my mother said, 'but I could tell' – it would have seemed to her the same old story, not, as we should think now, a psychosomatic disturbance, which may have begun with the death of his first wife when he was twenty-two years old and only eight months married. It would have seemed to my mother simply hypocrisy that he was secretary of the Temperance Society and chairman of the Band of Hope. But to him the vows of abstinence, even though made to be broken, were part of the battle, and a hope for others if not for himself; and there were quite long spells when the vows were kept: at Marwood, for instance, and for at least the first year at Bristol. My mother may not have recognized the giant effort of will it entailed. It only confirmed her in the belief that he could master the weakness if he really tried.

Some failure of sympathy between them may have made him lean too heavily on a quite innocent friendship with a young woman, a church worker and my godmother, Florrie Briggs. My mother was unhappy about it, and it may have caused talk in the parish. In the notes for a sermon at this time my father wrote: 'If any man spends his time in finding out faults – searching out evil – he will discover it where it is not to be found and from being a critic he becomes a slanderer, & the most deadly person in the world is a slanderous person.' It could have been a generalization, but it has the ring of protest. As the year wore on, in spite of all his wrestling to live a godly, righteous, and sober life, he found it harder and harder to keep a foothold.

Their childhood wasn't so many years behind them when they met. Before I tell of that meeting I must go as far back as I can into their origins, what bred them and surrounded them, and follow the intricate pattern of chance events which eventually brought them together and me into the world.

CHAPTER TWO

The Frys and the Hammonds

An afternoon call on a summer's day, 26 June 1849, was the casual beginning of all the chances and changes which brought about the events described in the first chapter; at least, we can call it the beginning, since a start has to be made somewhere. It happened in the quiet community of Peckham Rye, where a few families of professional men who worked in the City had settled near the white posts round the Rye to have the benefit of the country air; and where the young William Blake saw a tree full of angels. On that June afternoon a young woman of twenty-two, Emma Louisa Lowe Fry, took her nineteen-year-old brother Charles, her sixteen-year-old brother John, and her fourteen-year-old sister Ellen, to call for the first time on the children of an auctioneer and appraiser, William Henry Hammond. He and his wife, Ann Smith, produced seventeen children over the years, but how many were there to entertain Emma in 1849 it is hard to say. Eight of the seventeen died in infancy and one or two were not yet born; but what is certain, and most to our purpose, is that Emma met the second boy, Edwin Rowland Hammond, and likely enough his two brothers, Francis William (Frank) and Harry Julius, and two of his sisters, Louisa Antoinette and Henrietta Selina. Edwin Rowland was sixteen, the same age as Emma's brother John, but the visit was evidently no more than a polite social gesture. It was November before Edwin Rowland, with two other children unnamed, returned the call, and two years pass before an old diary records, on 23 August 1851, that 'E.R.H. and the Frys met oftener from this time.' The entry means to convey, as reticently as possible, that Rowland, not quite eighteen, had fallen in love with twenty-four-year-old Emma, and she with him. He was a high-spirited, wayward, charming boy, and strongly sexed (he married three times and was divorced at sixty-eight). Emma was petite, grey-eyed and dark-haired, affectionate, gentle, and humorous; not pretty, her nose was too definite for that, but beguiling; and also, as she later showed, tough and resilient, which in the event she needed to be. Her father, Thomas Homfray Fry, had a law-stationery business in Lincoln's Inn Fields. For centuries his forbears, right up to his own day, had been vigorously populating the gently hilly country in Somerset between the Mendip Hills and the sea. The ground of their springing was the village of Barton and its neighbour Winscombe, and also, as time went on, a hamlet called Compton Bishop, and three miles away, on the other side of the Taunton–Bristol road, the little market town of Axbridge.

It was the Frys, my mother's maternal forbears, rather than her father's family the Hammonds, who were always talked of in my boyhood as the stock from which I had sprung, perhaps because being so faithful to a few miles of Somerset they seemed more homogeneous; and so I came in time to take the name as my own by a kind of right. My Aunt Ada told me, while we were out walking one day, that in 1867, when she was ten, she took tea with 'old Mr. William Fry', then aged ninety-six. By holding her hand I was only one link away from the tenth year of the reign of George III.

This proliferation of life, which in the distaff way I belong to, was first called Fry in 1262. There was a man called Roger de Barton whose son William was a serf or villein owned by Wells Cathedral. In 1262, according to the *Liber Albus*, the Dean and Chapter of Wells noted:

William son of Roger de Barton, a native of our Manor of Wynscombe, has been bought into liberty from us by Thomas Corbyn, Vicar of Wynscombe. He and his are free.

There must, I imagine, have been something promising

about William to encourage the vicar so to spend his money. From that time forward he and his descendants were known as le Frye, the free men. His sons, all tenants of the parish of Winscombe, were called Adam le Frye, Martin le Frye, and William le Frye. Since there is a succession of Williams in every generation of the family from the seventeenth to the twentieth century I take the last of these three to be the true begetter of the line which led to my grandmother Emma.

For the next six centuries they went on being born and buried in Barton, Winscombe, Compton Bishop, and Axbridge. What the earlier generations did for a living there is no way of knowing, but before the middle of the eighteenth century they were well-to-do. Three brothers, William, John, and Peter, were born between 1729 and 1734. William married Elizabeth Fox, one of the Quaker Foxes my Aunt Ada said, which may or may not be true. Peter married Elizabeth Homfray of Bristol, who became known in the family as Madam Fry of Axbridge. She died in 1844, ninety-three years old, leaving legacies amounting to £15,697. 1s. 10d. The middle one of the three brothers, John, became my great-great-great-grandfather. He married Ann Isgar and they had nine children. The eldest of them, another Peter, born in 1768, became an attorney, as at least two of his cousins did, and lived with his wife Joanna Chapman at Compton House on the outskirts of Axbridge; and there they died, within a few hours of each other, on 19 December 1846. The house still stands, looking across the Taunton–Bristol road to a hill, sometimes even now called Fry's Hill, where they had a vineyard. The rooms and passageways and attics, the seventeenth-century plaster-work and eighteenth-century panelling, the elegant string-beading of the window frames, are still as they were when Emma's father, Thomas Homfray Fry, grew up in the house with his thirteen brothers and sisters. There must have been Frys living there before Peter and Joanna raised their brood. On a pane in a window that looks south on to the garden one of these scratched his name: *William Fry Dec 3rd 1767.* He was either the father or grandfather (both were called William) of the old Mr. Fry with whom Ada took tea a hundred years later.

I was brought up believing the Frys were Quakers, and certainly if there is anything I have always 'felt in the blood and felt along the heart' it is this. Perhaps at some time they were. I'm reluctant to deny it after living with the belief so long and so compatibly, but the evidence is slight. There are deeds of 1701 and 1826 relating to the Quakers' burial ground at the east end of Axbridge, and years ago a cousin showed me a letter, since lost, written by one of the Frys in the mid-nineteenth century, which used the second person singular throughout, the 'thees' and 'thous' of the Friends. In one of my Uncle Charlie's sketch-books illustrating the story of his life, he has written underneath a painting of his grand-father's house: 'Winscombe, centre of the Quaker religion'. But Peter and Joanna were buried in Axbridge church, with a plaque on the wall to say so; and their son, Thomas Homfray, has a handsome stained-glass window to his memory in the church at Winscombe. It displays at its centre the coat of arms which this unoffending clan had somehow acquired; and very strange and unexpected it is. The nature of the Frys was steady, God-fearing, kindly, unassuming, and mildly humorous; but the coat of arms shows a mailed arm holding a sword, and on the sword is impaled the bloody head of a Moor. The motto reads: *Virtute et Numine*.

Thomas Homfray Fry, my great-grandfather, was born at Compton House in 1800, number seven of Peter's fourteen children. In his early twenties he left Axbridge for London, set up as a law-stationer, and fell in love with a girl called Emma Mary Cooper Spratt who lived with a widowed mother and a sister called Sophy. Her father and only brother had been drowned while bathing. The father, Francis Spratt, was descended, my Aunt Ada carefully records, from 'the cele-brated Bishop Spratt', Bishop of Rochester in Charles II's reign. John Evelyn describes him in his diary entry for 23 November 1680: 'Then went to St. Paul's, to hear that great wit, Dr. Sprat. His talent was a great memory, never making use of notes, a readiness of expression in a most pure and plain style of words, full of matter, easily delivered.' He was a friend of Abraham Cowley's, and in his early twenties wrote some poems of enough merit to win him a place in Johnson's *Lives of the Poets*. Johnson says: 'After the Restoration he took orders, and by Cowley's recommendation was made chaplain to the Duke of Buckingham, whom he is said to have helped in writing The Rehearsal. He was likewise chaplain to the king.'

Emma Spratt was beautiful, talented, and witty, as I judge from a photograph of her in old age and from the album, begun in 1825, into which she copied her own verses, poems by L.E.L. and Thomas Moore, conundrums, acrostics, and jokes, written in the prettiest of hands and illustrated with a charming painting of lilies of the valley, a butterfly, a beetle, and a bluebottle. One of her own poems is called 'On a Sigh':

> Oh give to sorrow momentary ease,
> Thou gentle tell-tale of a pensive breast,
> For thou when cheating hope no more can please,
> Thou canst afford at least a transient rest.
>
> Oh then ambiguous, joyless, softly rise,
> While the tear trembles on the pallid cheek;
> Severe the virtue which a sigh denies
> To save a breaking heart which dare not speak.

She was still only eighteen when she married Thomas Homfray Fry at Chelsea in August 1826 and set up house with him at Valentine Cottage, Peckham Rye. Their pro-creativity was comparatively moderate: seven children in twenty years, one dying in infancy. When the eldest, my grandmother Emma, took her brothers Charles and John and her sister Ellen to call on the Hammond children in June 1849, they left at home a four-year-old, Tom (later to be a tower of strength to Emma and her children), and two-year-old Jessie Mary, 'dear Jessie', whose sad ghost was still walking the family memory when I was small.

The Frys and the Hammonds

The ancestry of the Hammonds became the subject of family dispute. The three youngest of my great-aunts, Rowland's sisters, thought they had proved a splendidly romantic descent, proper to their station in life, with a very grand coat of arms, including an ostrich feather and the motto *En toute Royale*. My great-aunt Annie gave me a copy of Carlyle's *Life and Letters of Oliver Cromwell* with every mention of Cromwell's friend Colonel Robert Hammond scored heavily down the margin. But my second cousin, the novelist and humorist Archibald Marshall, son of the eldest of the Hammond sisters, when he came to write his life story for the entertainment of his daughter, called the grand ancestry 'unfounded'. And so it has proved to be. The Hammonds, in the eighteenth century, were yeoman farmers in villages near Guildford. One of them, William, had three sons. Two of them, Henry and John, became carpenters in Southwark. W. H. Hammond, my great-grandfather, born in 1802 and christened at St. Saviour's, Southwark, was Henry's son. Archibald Marshall says that at 'a very early age' he went to work as a second-hand furniture dealer in Chancery Lane, before becoming an auctioneer. His sister Sarah went as a nurse to the Crimea with Florence Nightingale and became the matron at Guy's Hospital. His wife, Ann Smith, Marshall adds, 'was the daughter of a blindmaker in the Old Kent Road, a most disagreeable old fellow, my father used to say, who had married a very sweet refined Frenchwoman.'

By 1849 they were established at Prospect Place, Peckham Rye, in comfortable style with a moderate fortune, and an auctioneer's business both in Chancery Lane and in Bell Yard; and on 6 April 1852, on the day that Annie the last of their children was born, Rowland announced his engagement to Emma Fry.

In early July the whole Hammond family set off to their summer home in Yorkshire, taking Emma with them. There was the long journey to Scarborough, and then eleven miles still to be travelled, the grown-ups in the carriage, the children and servants in the waggonette, before they turned into the drive at Raven Hall. Rowland must often have talked to Emma about the wild, high headland known as Peak or Ravenscar (called the raven scaur because here the Danes had set up their standard), where a Roman fortress had kept watch over the sea fourteen hundred years before the Hall was built. I like to think of Emma arriving there on that July evening in 1852. By then the day would have been fading and the lights coming up in the fishermen's cottages at Robin Hood's Bay; and perhaps before the dark came Rowland took her across the lawn to the battlemented terrace, where the garden ended and the land made a tumbling descent to the rocks and the sea a long way below. To their left, beyond Robin Hood's Bay, they could see the lights of Whitby Harbour. To their right, through a wrought-iron gate, the terrace led to what remained of Justinian's fort, where the flame had burned to guide the Roman ships on their way to Flamborough Head.

Only a brief abstract of Emma's diary has survived. Nothing more can be known of her visit or how long it lasted, but she must have been told, if not for the first time, the strange story of how the Hall and the eighteen hundred acres of farm and moorland had come into my great-grandfather's possession.

In 1845, in the course of his business of land-agency, he had foreclosed on a mortgage. The mortgage had been raised by an eccentric clergyman-doctor called R. C. Willis, rumoured to be an illegitimate grandson of George III by one of the unmarried princesses. His paternal grandfather had been awarded £20,000 for flogging the King back to sanity. The Reverend Doctor Willis, inheriting a fortune and the Ravenscar estate, had rebuilt the eighteenth-century Hall, constructed the battlemented terrace at great cost, set up iron trees to the west of the house, with tin leaves (painted green) to tinkle in the wind; and in 1836, when the rebuilding was finished, gave a famous Rearing Supper for all the workmen. The stables were freshly bedded with straw so that guests who became incapable could be laid out in comfort. A servant was detailed to observe whether they were alive or dead. What was left of the Reverend Doctor's fortune he lost by backing the wrong horses at Doncaster, and by louse-racing, a sport he was much addicted to. The lice were placed in the centre of a dish; the first louse to reach the rim was the winner. But, as with the horses, he backed the wrong lice. He was reduced to advertising a hypnotic cure for insomnia at a guinea a time. And to mortgaging his property to my great-grandfather.

In this way the magic and history of Raven Hall came into the family, a summer playground for the nine Hammond children, and presently for the thirty-six grandchildren, invited in relays. There they scavenged in the rock-pools, picked bilberries on the moors, played croquet in the home field ('but it wasn't very nice because the grass was rather too long') and bathed in the sea, the men and boys in one place, the ladies and girls in another. Memories of those times linger on in the neighbourhood to this day, kept alive by descendants of men who worked for my great-grandfather. When in 1885 he died, a Justice of the Peace with a London house on Highbury Hill, the *Scarborough Gazette* sang his praises:

He created farms out of the wild moorland, and changed heather into turnips, corn and pasture. He built a church – open to the services of all Christians, conforming or otherwise – a mill and an inn, a shop and cottages and homesteads, together with a manse for the minister of the church . . . a schoolroom and a lecture hall . . . Above all, Mr. Hammond may be said to have created the Scarborough and Whitby railway . . . Nearly twenty years ago he started the idea, obtaining the opinion of eminent engineers, advancing a large amount of money to make the project known and to set it working . . .

The *Whitby Gazette* enlarges on this:

When he first began the agitation . . . he seemed to be heading a forlorn hope. His scheme was regarded by many, and especially by practical people, as visionary and utopian, owing to the engineering difficulties . . . But Mr. Hammond's faith and patience ultimately prevailed, for his perseverance was literally indomitable.

It was what the Scarborough paper called 'the daily dream of his later life'. One of his grandchildren has an entry in her childhood diary: 'Papa had a telegram from Highbury this morning to tell him to go there at once for something very particular; when Papa got there he found Grandpapa only wanted to talk about the railway.'

But when Emma was shown the wonders of Raven Hall by young Rowland none of his father's teeming projects had got under way; the estate was wild, the roads pot-holed, the Hall almost un-neighboured. Thirty years later, when my mother came to holiday there as a little girl, the farmland was thriving, the roads cared for, the railway nearing completion. In the memories she put on paper towards the end of her life she wrote:

When the railway between Scarborough and Whitby was being made we went freely among the navvies working on the line. They were always gentle to us; and on Sundays we used to get someone to carry the organette, a box-like arrangement worked by turning a handle, which played hymn-tunes: 'Scatter seeds of kindness' and 'Beautiful words of life'. We would sit down near the tents, start our tune and sing away, till the men woke up from their Sunday naps and came out of their tents to listen, the sea glistening below, and fishing smacks drawn in close to the shore, the fishermen leaning over the side to catch the sound of the voices drifting down to them.

The Hall was sold twelve years before I was born, but I have seen the windows still reflecting the sun and storms over that stretch of the North Sea. The battlemented terrace, the wrought-iron gate, the cliff paths where Rowland and Emma went scrambling down to Robin Hood's Bay, are changed so little, I could almost believe as I peered through a white sea mist that when it lifted the Hammonds would be revealed living out their Victorian summers yet.

Half a dozen yellowing photographs, taken in the 1860s,

hung on Aunt Ada's bedroom wall when she lived with us. In my early thoughts the Hall was one with the Taj Mahal and the Acropolis, something then unvisited but revered, a monument to the leisured expansive summer days when God looked as benevolently on the family as my great-grandfather looked on his servants and cottagers; and perhaps too benevolently on his eldest son. By the time my mother was singing hymns to the navvies Rowland was in disgrace, cut out of his father's will and banished to Australia, his thirty years of marriage at an end. Why did he change from Ada's 'Dear Papa' into a man she could hardly bring herself to mention? What was he really like? He can't tell us himself because none of his letters was kept, except a very early one, written about 1840 when he was seven years old, to judge by the handwriting:

> Prospect Cottage
> Blackheath Park

My dear Papa & Mama,
I am very happy to inform you, that our Holydays will commence, on the 19 inst. It will be a joyful day. Mrs. Hill intends, to accompany us home, by the 11 o'clock Coach. Please to give my love to my sisters, Grandfathers, Grandmothers, Uncles, Aunts and Cousins.

I remain your
dutiful son
R. Hammond

Ten years after this letter there came the joyful day when Emma Fry agreed to marry him, and on 1 June 1854, when he was still a minor and Emma nearly twenty-seven, the joyful day of the wedding at St. Giles, Camberwell. Before the summer was over Emma was pregnant, but no joy came of that. On New Year's Day 1855 Rowland went down with what was called 'a slight attack of smallpox', lasting for a week. Whatever it was, Emma seems to have caught it and was seriously ill until, on 16 February, she was delivered of a stillborn child. She kept an invitation to an evening party

('Quadrilles 7 o'clock') and wrote on it 'The night my first baby arrived (dead).'

Her father had already retired from his law-stationery business. He was only fifty-four years old, but he had made his money, enough to give Emma a wedding dowry of £8,000, and now he was ready to return to where he came from, west of the Mendip Hills. A house and cottage had been built for him in the village of Winscombe, on a few acres of ground divided by a stream. He called the house Springfield and went to live there a month after Emma's marriage, with his wife and three youngest children, Ellen, Tom, and seven-year-old Jessie. His mother-in-law Mrs. Spratt and her daughter Sophia were settled into the cottage across the stream. His elder brother, Peter Wickens Fry, was living at Compton House, his two unmarried sisters not far away, and his younger brother Bruges at Hill House, Cheddar. A network of relations covered the length and breadth of Somerset, such as the Vowles, the Phippens, the Seabbins, the Duddens, the Keels, the Arneys, the Winters, the Says, and as many more; and four sisters and a brother lay buried in Axbridge churchyard. He had come home.

By the first anniversary of the wedding Emma had conceived a second time. She had been pregnant for two months when she travelled up to Raven Hall with Rowland in August 1855 for the marriage of his elder brother Frank to Rebecca Bedford. She wrote in her diary that the journey lasted from a quarter to seven in the morning to a quarter to nine at night. My Aunt Ada, now shaping in Emma's womb, would have added 'Dreadfully overtired'. But for Emma tiredness was never important enough to spoil her pleasure.

Her parents came up from Somerset to be with her a week before her lying in. It was leap year, 1856. Ada Louise was born on 29 February, and so took four years (as she used to explain to me) to reach her first birthday. I think she felt slightly cheated; she could never happily decide whether the alternative day should be the 28th or 1 March.

Emma took the baby down to Springfield for the whole of

August and most of September, leaving Rowland in London
to his work as auctioneer in Chancery Lane. He had probably
taken over the business from his father, though a year later
he was free to spend more than two months with Emma and
Ada at Winscombe, as though business could look after itself.
Half-way through that long holiday, on 22 August 1857, the
second child, Bessie Mary, was born. During my school-days
she was known as Aunt B, and Ada was known as Aunt A,
but after that the alphabetical order broke down.

In May 1859 came the first boy, Percy Rowland, and in
1860 another girl, Edith Clara. When Edith was two months
old Percy was lamed by polio. A diary entry for 1863 says
'Percy had a special boot for paralysed leg.' Then in 1862
came my mother's favourite sister, Helen Schabner, more
often known as Lil; and in 1864 Edwin Bertram, the most
buffeted by misfortune and the least equipped to withstand
it, who shot himself when he was forty and took his place in
the diary as 'poor Bertie'.

The first letter of Ada's to survive was written a month
after Bertie was born, a companion piece to the one Rowland
had written to his parents at the same age, twenty-three
years before.

8 Milner Street
July 22nd 1864

Dear Mama.
I am glad the holidays are so near, as I shall have a little more
time to play with dear baby. I hope we shall not give you any
trouble, and that nurse will take us into the fields very often. I
hope dear Mama that you will be pleased with the progress I have
made in my studies this half year. I should like the weather to be
very fine during the holidays.

> With much love
> I remain
> your dear child
> A, L, Hammond.

The commas which appear unexpectedly between the initials

proliferated over the next four years until they showered on to a letter in which she mentions the latest addition to the family: the handsome, dashing Harry Beaumont, to be known as Hal, born two days before Christmas Day 1866.

> 41 Milner Square
> Islington
> [December 1868]

Dear Papa,
Xmas draws near, and school books, are put away, and sons, and daughters, show the progress, they have made, with their tutors, and governesses, during the last half year.

As Mrs. Williams, has only been here three months, we perhaps, shall not know as much, as we should, had she been here the whole six. But next year, if all be well, I hope to be, able to play a piece off flourishingly, before any of your friends; and to answer some of the French questions, you sometimes ask me. I hope we shall pass a happy Xmas day, but I should hail, the approaching Friday, with more delight, if another family circle was perfect.

This time two years ago, our little Harry had just come to us, a little live Xmas present; that was a very happy day, when we knew we had another little one to cuddle and love.

> Farewell,
> With best love,
> I am your, loving
> daughter Ada.

She loved her father and trusted him, and when he betrayed her trust her bitterness and contempt were total. But these were still the happy years, and I have a token of them on my shelves, a copy of Bunyan's *Pilgrim's Progress* – 'Ada with Papa's love. Xmas 1865' – full of engravings by P. Prioli and H. C. Selous, of the Slough of Despond, Giant Despair gnawing his nails, the meeting with Apollyon, the shepherds of the Delectable Mountains . . . I brooded over them for hours when I was little.

Papa's love kept her out of bed to recite and 'play a piece off flourishingly' for his friends after dinner. He made her his companion when he went to the Horse Show, or to Lords for the cricket, or the Velocipede Show at the Agricultural Hall. She wrote to him again, her commas quite used up, on 18 June 1869:

Dear Papa

As all the others have written to Mama I am going to do the same to you. I hope the weather will be finer and warmer in the holidays than it has been for the last week and besides it will not be nice for you to have wet weather on your business trip. I am glad Mama is not going with you as I should live in constant dread till you returned especially if this Revolution realy takes place. . . . You must try to get your business over early as if it is rainy we shall want you to have games with us in the evening. Mrs Williams hopes you will think me improved in French and Music since she came 9 months ago and as I like the latter better every day I hope I shall soon be able to relieve Mama sometimes in the accompaniments to your songs. But now with love

Believe me to remain
your affectionate daughter
Ada Louise

She was now thirteen; intelligent, eager to please, affectionate, and evidently happy; but within a year or two the diary begins to show recognizable signs of the Aunt A of my childhood. Her affections, which later on became so guarded as to be scarcely perceptible, seemed fated to end in tears. I found among her papers a photograph of a little girl called Clara Agnes Lovell. She lived in Milner Square, and died of scarlet fever in December 1868. Ada had written underneath the picture 'My first friend'. Another person she loved very much was her mother's youngest sister Jessie.

A letter of 1858 has survived on which Ada has written 'From dear old Jess when I was a baby and she was a little girl.' (Spelling and punctuation as written.)

Springfield

Dear Ada

I hope you have not quite forgotten your old Aunt Jessie I have not forgotten you I wish I could see your dear little face Do you remember all Ducks Chicken and nums (Pussy) and dear little Mamy Clarke she is quite well and sends six kisses to you and six to Bessie.

I have sent two pictures one for you and one for Bessie It is very wet and cold and so foggy that we can scarcely see the garden I suppose you can talk very nicely now and I hope you have not forgotten What dirty Jack does and Uncle Charlie Nana and Nana papa are quite well and send love and lots of kisses to you and dear little Bessie You must give Mama and Bessie a great many kisses from me and Wiffy I have also sent you a pair of scissars but you must ask Mama to have them cleaned before they go in your pretty workbox, and I hope you will soon be able to work nicely Tata dear Ada and please don't forget old

Aunt Jessie
Saturday November 20th 1858

Ada was never happier than when they were together, and in the letter of 18 June 1869 wrote: 'I am sorry dear Jessie is so dissipated as not to be able to pay us another visit before she goes to Uncle John's and as that is such a long way from here we shall have very few opportunities of seeing her again.'

She counted the days until they should meet in September when the whole family, except Bessie and Papa who had gone to Raven Hall, spent a month at Springfield. Ada wrote in her diary: 'Sept.20. Jessie and I visited the burial ground about 11 p.m. to try our nerves. Moonlight night.'

In 1877, when Ada's fondness for her father had almost vanished, Jessie died. From then on all Ada's love and affection would centre on Emma, and on the baby of the family who became her special care, my mother.

CHAPTER THREE

My Mother Arrives

No family in 1869 could have seemed happier or more fortunate than the Hammonds of 41 Milner Square. They hardly needed friends, though they had them in plenty, for the uncles, aunts, and cousins were a sociable clan, calling, dining, entertaining, meeting together at concerts and exhibitions. A nanny, a nursemaid, Mrs. Hart the housekeeper, and three or four servants looked after them with evident devotion. The housemaid and parlourmaid, Jane Coney and Ann Webb, continued to pay affectionate calls after the family had taken refuge in lodgings when Rowland had steered them all on to the rocks. Their work at 41 Milner Square was lightened by the house having a bathroom, with hot and cold running water, at a time when the maids at the great houses in Mayfair were still lugging pails of water upstairs to fill hip-baths: 'March 9, 1869. Bath overflowed. A cascade down the stairs at prayer time.'

Then there was Mrs. Williams the governess, who gave Ada a copy of Gray's *Poetical Works* for Christmas 1868, and in October 1869 Miss Merryweather joined the household to teach the girls music. Percy was at a boarding-school in Kelvedon, near Colchester.

The year had begun with a flurry of children's parties, which perhaps kept Ada from missing Clara Lovell too much. There were visits to Madame Tussaud's, and to the Christy Minstrels, where they ran into their three aunts, Papa's youngest sisters. In the summer holidays they divided the time between Springfield and Raven Hall.

The eighth child arrived on 15 February 1870. Emma's

brother Charles Edward Fry, his wife Kitty and their sons
Arthur and Fred, had come to supper. Half-way through the
evening Emma withdrew and at 11.25 Charles Edward
Bruges Hammond was born. I think of him as the harbinger
of my mother, born in the year before her birth, and dying
eighty-six years later in the year before her death. During
their lives, though for nearly seventy years of that time they
lived at opposite ends of the earth, they were as close and
kept up as loving a correspondence as if they had been born
twins.

Ada copied out her diaries in later life and destroyed the
originals. Some of the entries therefore are retrospective, like
the one a week after Charlie was born: 'The pain commenced
in face that ended in disfigurement.' The disfigurement was
a deep fissure in her cheek. I have a confused memory of her
telling me how it came about. I understood her to say that
one of her teeth exploded. I imagined it flying through her
cheek like a shot from a gun, perhaps breaking the glass of
a picture on the wall. In whatever way the damage was done
it left her resigned to being the plain one of the family.

1870 slipped serenely by. A new governess, Miss Attwood,
had come in place of Mrs. Williams. In April 'parents, Ada &
Bessie to Putney to see the Oxford crew practise, also
Cambridge & Leander'; and the large coloured photograph
of Emma came, 'intended for an heirloom', which now hangs
in my brother's sitting-room. On 22 June the Hammond
grandparents moved from Peckham Rye to 1 Highbury Hill,
and Rowland took Ada with him when he called that evening
to see how they had settled in. In July the three young
Hammond aunts, with Ada, Bessie, Percy, Edith, and Lil,
saw the Queen and the princesses Louise and Beatrice leave
the Agricultural Hall after the opening of the Workmen's
Exhibition. But Ada loved best her expeditions alone with
Papa, such as the visit they made together to Billingsgate Market at six o'clock one September morning to buy
fish.

There were musical evenings and dinner parties. Ada

played a piano duet with Miss Merryweather at a Penny Reading, and went with Emma and a party of Frys to the first of a series of concerts 'got up' by her Uncle Charles. Life, on the surface at least, was companionable and pleasant. Five of the children had chicken-pox just before Christmas, but they were all downstairs in time for Christmas Day, a day of snow, frost, and bright sunshine. There was church in the morning for those who were well enough, and a basket of presents when the midday feast was over. The celebration lacked only one important ingredient for Ada: Papa. 'Quiet day,' she writes. 'Father away.' Over the next ten years more often than not he slipped off somewhere at Christmas time, as though he had some other attachment. But he was back in time for a family gathering at Highbury Hill on 3 January 1871. The only thing Ada tells us about the party is that four-year-old Hal was wearing a blue silk rep dress. She was evidently proud of the way he looked, and so perhaps was he, as he certainly would be in the eighties when he first put on the dress-uniform of the North-West Mounted Police.

Percy had left the Kelvedon school at the end of the Christmas term and was starting as a day-boarder at a school in Barnsbury. Efforts were still being made to help his lameness. 'Percy had a galvanic battery for his leg,' Ada writes.

The Hammond party was followed a week later by the Fry party. Emma's three brothers were all living in London: Charles, with his family of six; John, with one daughter; and twenty-six-year-old Tom, still unmarried, who spent every Sunday at Milner Square, arriving in time for church and staying on to play with the children in the afternoon. On 29 January, Ada notes, he brought the news that Paris had capitulated to the Prussians.

February continued the promise of the new year. Rowland took Emma to the Honourable Artillery Company Regimental Ball, and they danced into the morning. A few days later my mother was conceived.

Ada's diary was full of 'Papa' and 'parents'. They took her to hear the harpist Ellis Roberts, and George Grossmith lecturing on Dickens, and at the end of June they all went off together to Springfield. It rained almost every day of the holiday, as though to prepare them for August when the year would turn melancholy. Between 21 and 31 August there were three deaths: a baby Marshall cousin, four months old; young Peter Fry (Emma's first cousin); and her thirty-eight-year-old brother John, who had been well and happy at the New Year party. Ada felt the wing of the angel of death lift her hair. In the last months of 1871 her diary entries begin to take on the unmistakable tone of the Aunt Ada I was to know so well. She helped the younger children with their lessons, taught at Sunday-school, took sewing classes at a ragged school; and on 29 October comes another of those retrospective entries: 'I began to be ill from overwork but kept about.' It was the beginning of a nervous obsession with her health which took pride of place in her diaries for the next fifty years. The little girl of 1869 is now, in her sixteenth year, turning into my Aunt Ada. She was taking her position as eldest of the family very seriously, beginning to set herself apart from the other children, even from Bessie, the nearest to her in age. I detect an adult note of disapproval in the entry for 20 October: 'Parents & I to the Olympic to see "The Woman in White". Found Bessie & Edith sitting up on our return at 20 to 12.'

For the first time in her diary there comes that careful recording of Sunday observance which was to become such a constant theme: 'Not at Sunday School in afternoon: 1st time missing – except ill or away – since joining. Edith or Lil nearly always went with me. Percy attended a Bible Class at his school every Sunday.' The next day, Monday, 13 November, she makes the entry: 'Emma Marguerite born, 5.25 p.m.', and four days later: 'Baby began to be called Daisy.'

My mother's eighty-six years of life had begun. It was the end of child-bearing for Emma, and the next year would be the last at Milner Square. Already, a month after my mother was born, there came the first tremor of the upheaval to come. In the middle of December Miss Merryweather left, and four days later she was followed by Miss Attwood. There were to be no more governesses. Ada took their place. On New Year's Eve 1872 she went with Bessie and the two maids, Jane and Ann, to the midnight service at the Memorial Hall, and next morning started giving regular lessons to Edith and Lil. Otherwise life went on as before. There were almost as many parties as there were days in January. The doctor's son, Campbell Searle, organized all the older children into some home theatricals, a dumb show on one evening, *Beauty and the Beast* on another; the first and last time, I think, that Ada acted any part except the invalid.

On the day before her sixteenth birthday she and Bessie walked ten miles round the London streets to see the decorations. The Prince of Wales had recovered from his serious illness, and a thankful nation displayed their loyalty in flags and bunting. 'Dreadfully overtired,' Ada adds. And a week later she notes 'My face broke out.'

By this time my mother had been weaned (being fed, the diary says, on Robb's biscuits) and Emma was free to go on a brief trip with Rowland. She wrote home to Bessie.

Dear Nurse,

You cannot think how often I think of you & my precious little Daisy I long to see her which I hope to do Mon. Evening *about ½ 10.* Mr. Cheyney Smith & his wife are with us here, but he has to be in town by the last train tomorrow & Papa wants to travel with him. they are most charming companions & I am thoroughly enjoying myself. The day is glorious & as hot as summer. Mrs. Smiths baby is enormous & only 10 months old. she is not a bit afraid of me, I think she is almost as big & quite as fat as Charlie, can stand & begins to talk; very fair & almost red hair but a pretty happy face. How I long to know how you sleep with baby. I woke several times in the night & quite awake at six altho' did not get up till the chamber maid brought me a cup of tea & Papa's milk at 9. We left here ¼ pt 10 for Ramsgate so had not too much time for breakfast & were dreadfully hungry when we got to Broadstairs at 2. Papa has ordered dinner today at 7 & Mr. & Mrs. Smith are to join us I have no idea what he has ordered & do not mean to ask. it is so jolly not to know any thing about it & we have such a pleasant waiter to attend to us. I shall be almost ready to eat baby when I see her & you may kiss her as much as you like for me till then

    With love
    believe me dear Bess
    Your affectionate Ma

The tremor of anxiety which had sent the governesses packing seems to have stilled, at least through the spring and early summer; but Ada's terse diary jottings open the family door no more than a crack. We know when Daisy cut her first tooth, when she was 'shortened', and the day when Hal had his curls cut off. Tom Fry married a beautiful girl called Emily Dannitt, Tom who was to be such a help in the days ahead. But out of all the domestic incidents of those months only one amused Ada enough to enter in the diary. Eleven-year-old Edith was a great prattler. Her seventeen-year-old cousin, Arthur Fry, promised her half-a-crown if she could go through a whole day without speaking. She won the bet, and spent the money (to Ada's recorded pleasure) on a Bible.

It may have been at the end of June that the atmosphere of the household began to be troubled. Ada had recently come back from almost two months at Springfield, happy there in the company of dear Jessie. On 2 July she was laid up with an attack of neuralgia which lasted for a week. It is guesswork to put it down to anxiety at home, but as time went on her neural graph rose and fell with her father's changing fortunes. When she was better Rowland and Emma decided to take her, with Edith, Lil, and Hal, for a river picnic. Bessie stayed at home to look after Charlie and Daisy, Bertie was away on a long visit to an uncle and aunt in Leicester, and Percy at school, his education soon to be brought to an abrupt end. They went by boat from Kew to

My great-grandparents Hammond

The terrace at Raven Hall, 1870. My great-grandmother Hammond stands holding a basket. Her sister Emma Smith sits on the chair, sewing. The stone table up the steps on the left is where, a few years later, my mother did her lessons on fine days.

Ada Louise

Bessie Mary

Helen Schabner (Lil)

Edwin Bertram (Bert)

Percy Rowland

Edith Clara

Harry Beaumont (Hal)

Charles Edward Bruges (Charlie)

Emma Fry (*née* Spratt),
my great-grandmother

My great-grandfather,
Thomas Homfray Fry

Edwin Rowland Hammond,
my grandfather

Emma, my grandmother;
her last photograph

Richmond. The sun shone, the Thames ran softly, and Papa sang the songs Ada had learnt to play for him. But foreboding must have been lapping at his mind, and Emma's also, as the water lapped against the boat.

On 12 August Ada wrote: 'Had been said the comet would destroy the earth today.' The prediction, as far as the little world of 41 Milner Square was concerned, was only a few weeks out. The two maids, Jane Coney and Ann Webb, left in tears early in September. The nanny and nursemaid had vanished at some unspecified time. Only Mrs. Hart and a servant called Willis stayed at their posts to see the family through to the end of the year. There was a last brave dinner party, for Emma's brothers, their wives, and nine close friends. 'All left about 1 a.m.' Then, with the November fog giving a chill to their spirits, they started to pack. The house was expected to be sold before Christmas. Ada gives no reason for this total collapse of their fortunes. My mother told me it was due to Rowland's reckless playing of the stock-market and trying to recover his losses by backing horses. (His brother, Harry Julius, owned a racehorse called St. Gatien which won the Derby at 100 to 8 in a dead heat, but not, unfortunately, until 1884.) He was not only out of money but also, apparently, out of work.

At the end of November, when the packing-up had been done, he took Emma and Ada to the Philharmonic Theatre, Islington, to see Offenbach's *Geneviève de Brabant*. It was hardly the place that every Victorian father would have chosen for the amusement of a sixteen-year-old daughter. The Phil, as Ada calls it, was also known as the Spittoon. It had made a sensational name for itself by introducing the cancan, by the amenable beautiful ladies in the bar, and by the staging of *opéra bouffe*. Rowland may have felt that the depression in his home needed shock treatment.

Christmas came, the house still unsold. The cupboards and drawers had been emptied, the furniture labelled, everything they wanted to keep already crated. 'Friends very kind in trouble,' Ada wrote. Christmas Day was spent

with the Charles Frys in Ellington Street, near Highbury
Fields.

So 1872 came to an end, and on the 31st Ada made the
final diary entry for December: 'A sad quiet last day of the
year.'

It would seem that Rowland had made no arrangements
for housing his family. Percy went for a fortnight to a Mr.
Lee at Lewisham, Hal to some friends called Bennett, Bertie
was down at Springfield. But it was Ada who, on 2 January
1873, went out and found temporary lodgings for the rest
of them, in Burton Crescent (now called Cartwright Gardens)
off Euston Road. Four days later Emma, Bessie, Edith, Lil,
Charlie, Daisy, and Mrs. Hart (her last day with them) piled
into two cabs and clattered out of Milner Square. Was
Rowland at Burton Crescent to receive them? He isn't mentioned. It will be August before the diary refers to him
again.

Ada had taken refuge at Ellington Street, where the
Charles Frys gave a party on the 9th. 'Dear Jessie slept there,'
Ada says: and the next day they went together to call at
Burton Crescent. The sale was on 15 January. Three days
before, Ada and Bessie had gone with their mother to
wander through the rooms for the last time, lacerating themselves with memories. Then at the end of the month they
moved to a house in South Lambeth Road.

The weather was bitterly cold. Ada woke up in the night
with hands swollen and inflamed and was ill for several days
'from weakness and cold'. Percy, though only thirteen, had
been put to work in his uncle's office in South Square. But
they were still not settled. At the end of March they moved
again, round the corner to 58 Harleyford Road, near the Oval
cricket ground.

Percy had been doing well at school and evidently resented
being taken away to work in an office. By June his Uncle
Charles thought it better to let him leave. On the 21st he was
with the family at the upstairs windows to watch the Shah
of Persia drive twice past the house. The Shah was wearing

a blue military frock coat faced with rows of brilliants and large rubies; his belt, the scabbard of his scimitar and his cap shone with jewels. A week later Percy got another job, at Whitefriars, which lasted for ten days, and then a third, Ada doesn't mention where; but on his mother's birthday in September he gave her 'a marble weight from his place of work'.

Rowland made his reappearance into the diary on 16 August: 'Main pipe burst near Kennington church as Bessie and I were returning [from taking Lil to stay with the Tom Frys]. Parents and I went back to see it. Great excitement and crowds.' He is given two more entries that year: at the end of September, when he accompanied Emma and Ada to the harvest festival at St. Peter's, Eaton Square; and the end of October when he took them back to the Spittoon to see a performance of *La Fille de Madame Angot*. But on Christmas Day 1873, in a separate small exercise book, Ada has one brief sentence: 'Mother & 9 children dined alone.'

It had been a hard year for Emma, more difficult, I suspect, than can be learnt from the diary. Rowland had got through not only his own money but a great part of the £8,000 she had brought to him on marriage. She had been deposited among unfamiliar neighbours, with a houseful of children and the future uncertain. Luckily the Tom Frys were also south of the river, at 281 New Cross Road, and came to see her as often as they could, and her father came up from Somerset to spend an afternoon with her. A great hamper of food weighing 150 lb. had arrived from Springfield on my mother's second birthday, and just before Christmas another weighty hamper came from Rowland's sister Augusta. Aunt Gussie and her husband Willie Bates were to play a decisive part in the pattern of my mother's life. They lived at Leicester in a house called St. Mary's Fields. I remember the house, and Uncle Willie: kindly, jovicular, with dignified white sideburns; and I remember the brightness of a half-crown he gave me.

The prayers the family offered up in the local church (which Ada, Bessie, and Edith helped to decorate at Christmas) seemed to be answered with the coming of 1874.

On 26 January Rowland started work with an auctioneer in Leamington Spa. He rented a pleasant early-Victorian house, 16 Milverton Crescent, with a trim garden on a quiet by-road which had still the air of a country lane when I went there a few years ago. He sent for the family to join him in mid-February. In their eagerness they arrived four days ahead of their furniture and belongings, even (the diary says) before their clothes. They got through the week-end in gipsy fashion, and then quickly began to settle into their new life. Percy went to work 'at G's the builders', and for a month Ada took classes at a boys' school, teaching Edith and Lil when she got home in the evenings. On Good Friday she took Daisy for a walk and got lost in Offchurch Woods, the first of my mother's misadventures in Leamington.

From early June the diary becomes almost lyrical for a while. On fine Saturdays Rowland rows them up the river to Warwick Castle or joins them in expeditions to Stoneleigh Abbey. Emma's sister Ellen comes to stay for ten weeks. They hire a pony-trap and drive through Warwick to Sherborne where they admire a church built by a wealthy spinster in memory of her father. It cost £20,000 to build. They go to the Volunteer Fête in Jephson Gardens and listen to the band of the Grenadier Guards. Emma's brother Charles comes to stay for a fortnight and paints a little water-colour of the house and garden, which I still have. While he was with them Lil scrawled a note to Bessie who was staying with her grandparents at Springfield:

Dear Bessie
On Sunday morning I took little Daisy to church she stoped in all the service & she behaved very well indeed she only began to sing out loud once & when I gave her a sweet she scrunched it instead of *sucking* it. When Uncle Charlie came down he gave me a beautiful green silk scarf but it will not do with any of my dresses as they are all blue. Ada Uncle Charlie & Aunt Ellen

are going out this afternoon in the pony trap we are going to have it all this week Ada has called me to school so goodbye now

I remain
your affectnt sister
Lillie
3 cheers for Bessie

But as the summer faded anxieties began to return. Money – and Rowland, too, no doubt – was still a problem. In September Emma decided to let Ada take the post of companion to a Mrs. Brown in London, and wrote to Bessie at Springfield to tell her of the preparations:

Sun. afternoon [23 September 1874]

Dearest old chick

We are all speculating whether you will return before Ada leaves us on the 3rd & anxiously waiting for your next letter. I hope you will be glad to return home for we all long to have you. Daisy often says 'dear old Neddy coming home, me sleep er Neddy.' I am very busy mending, patching, darning & otherwise repairing all Ada's undergarments & she has a very pretty nightgown case & handkerchief case to match & purposes taking her boot & brush pockets in case Mrs. Brown should be very tidy, she has lined her old plaid dressing jacket with scarlet flannel & doing the best she can with the few dresses she possesses. I was quite in trouble how to procure her a good plain winter dress. We could not get the *plainest* costume here under 2 guineas & I feared by the time we had bought the materials & got a dressmaker it would come to nearly as much & I could not spare so much anyhow for one article & this morning what should arrive but a kind letter from Tom enclosing a post office order saying he intended giving her a dress but not knowing what she would like sent the money instead. Altho' Sunday morning she flew into my room with only her night garment on & no shoes jumped onto the bed and behaved like a maniac with delight I was quietly reading a letter from Pa saying he might be home this evening, he is having such a jolly holiday in town he does not seem inclined to return, his sales did not last two hours on Tuesday & he has had all the rest of the time to himself but he does not say where he has been or who he

has seen . . . We have had a very pleasant week, hard at needlework all day & A & I charring . . . The evening we have passed,
in the kitchen, working & reading aloud with the warm fire &
low gas lamp which I can almost see by without my specs . . . I
am afraid we shall have to leave our washerwoman she is more
tiresome than any we have had & I have a rare blowing up for
her in store tomorrow, the number of things she loses, changes &
keeps back for a fortnight or longer bothers me out of my wits . . .
A train arriving from London at 7 but I do not expect Pa till we
see him. So now dear little chick I shall shut up for the present
hoping I shall fill this up before sending it off tomorrow morn.

Monday 10 o'clock

Dearest child

Your welcome letters arrived this morning & gave us all great
pleasure Papa read his in bed for he returned at $\frac{1}{2}$ pt 8 last evening
so nice & kind & well & seemed more than usually glad to be with
us again . . .

Emma had taken the decision to let Ada go to London
without consulting Rowland. The first he had heard of it was
when he called on Mrs. Charles Fry's parents, the evening
before he came home: 'It quite upsets him to talk of her
going but I really think it will be a change for the better for
her, & Edie is getting old enough to be very useful.'

But the change was for the worse. When Ada came to
recopy her diary she wrote: 'Oct. 3. I went to London for
three months. Hard work and a miserable time.' It was a
foretaste of other lonely, wearying efforts to earn a living,
in a future without even a home to come back to for comfort.

While she was away the diary becomes a case-book of
family illnesses:

Nov. 30. All the children poorly from the damp.
Dec. 9. Bessie had sore throat. Worse on 11th.
Dec. 12. Dr. said the quinsy was added to by diphtheria. A
           bad night. Mother & Percy didn't go to bed.
     13. Mother with B night & day keeping her throat clear.
     14. Crisis passed safely.

18. Children with severe colds & coughs.
22. Bessie out in a rash.
23. Hal's 8th birthday. His cough still very bad.
25. Children better . . . had games & snapdragon in the kitchen.
27. Percy & Bertie both ill in bed. 1st a gathering 2nd Inflammation.
28. Smouldering board discovered under the hearthstone.
31. Hard frost still & bitterly cold. Bessie's rash very bad. Percy & Bertie still in bed. Little ones better.

The next day, the first of 1875, Ada said goodbye to the unsympathetic Mrs. Brown and set off through frost, sleet, and snow to the railway station. She missed the train and stayed the night at Ellington Street. The next morning: 'Walked from E.St. to South Sq. Boots soaked with snow. Travelled to Leamington and arrived in great pain.' She took to her bed for two days, but there was little peace in the house. Bertie, who was sharing her room, was still very ill with inflammation of the lungs, and Bessie only beginning to recover. And the family was into another crisis. They were being forced to move again. It is unlikely to have been simply because the house was unhealthy, though clearly it was, or they would surely have waited until the invalids were better. Were they owing rent? Avoiding creditors? Whatever the cause, three days after she had come home Ada went to look over a house in Rugby Road, and a week later they were packing. Nerves were jangled. Sixteen-year-old Percy turned on his father, rated him, perhaps, for the family misfortunes, and Rowland thrashed him. He limped out of the house, went to lodge in the house of a labourer from his building firm, collapsed into bed for a week, and never went back to live with his family again.

They made the move from Milverton Crescent on 29 January: 'Ada, Bertie & Charlie ill but with Hal went in a fly to the new house. The others walking & Daisy in her pram. Wet day.' Through all these trials, and through the worse that were still to come, Emma remained patient, humorous, and kind, tolerant of Papa, loved by her children, her sisters, her brothers, and her sisters-in-law. 'Rowland's dear Emma', Gussie Bates called her.

Edith was the next one to collapse – 'fear of brain fever', Ada recorded – and Charlie was still giving anxiety; but with April and the better weather the diary begins to cheer up. Ada, Edith, and Lil go for a long walk, gather three big basketsful of primroses and sell them for a shilling a basket. Lil, on Ada's behalf, bids successfully at a sale for some Bible dictionaries. The boys explore the mill at Guy's Cliff. Hal, Charlie, and Daisy decorate Farmer Eales's pet lamb with coloured ribbons; and on Bertie's eleventh birthday, in spite of the four youngest having whooping cough, they play all day long in a hay field.

My mother's first memories belong to this year, or the first that I remember hearing from her. She locked herself into what Ada prudishly calls in the diary 'a small room'; a builder had to be sent for to let her out. (The adventure left her nervous of locks on lavatory doors. In old age she never fastened them.) The very next day she got her head stuck between the banisters; and a few days before Christmas, when she and Charlie were recovering from measles, she fell into the fender, upsetting a kettle of water and was badly scalded. A certain apprehensiveness, a distrust of what the next moment might bring, lingered into my childhood.

In July, to Ada's joy, her dear Jessie came to stay for five weeks. Jessie was now almost exactly the age that Emma had been when she married, and Rowland was enthusiastic in entertaining her. There were three river expeditions to Warwick and a drive to Stoneleigh; and on 14 August Ada wrote: 'Father took Jessie and me a lovely moonlight walk round Emscote & Guy's Cliff from 10 p.m. till nearly 12', a walk repeated, still by moonlight, a few days later.

Whenever Jessie was with her Ada bloomed, the nervous debility and neuralgia attacks vanished. The happy visit came to an end on the last day of August, but Ada was still buoyant when Rowland took her to stay with Gussie and

My Mother Arrives

Willie Bates on 2 September. There were four other young people staying at St. Mary's Fields and Ada had scarcely had time to unpack before they were all off on an expedition. At other times the train journey itself would have taxed her, but the diary entry goes on with a vitality unrecognizable as Ada's: 'Up till pt. 1 a.m. Chatted till 4 a.m. with Flo Balgarnie & ready to get up at 6 a.m. Out at 8.30 a.m. to take father to the station, drove there & back with Effie & again at 11.30 to take Flo.'

Even the set-back of her face giving trouble again ('Face probed and cauterized') left her unsubdued. She was quickly out again and ready to go off with a party of eight and two servants on a picnic to Bradgate. The next day all her brothers and sisters were on the station at Leamington to welcome her home. Rowland was still away – somewhere. It may be that the one-night stay at St. Mary's Fields was spent in anxious talk. Another crisis was impending; and as usual the first sign was that Ada took to her bed, 'believed to be measles', caught from Charlie and Daisy, 'but turned out to be low fever.' When she ventured out again after a fortnight she tried to go on with teaching a class at night school, a group of fourteen and fifteen-year-old boys. She had bravely coped with them for the six weeks before Christmas, but now they were too much for her. Two days after giving up the class a telegram arrived from Willie Bates asking her to go to Leicester at once. She packed and left the same afternoon. It was a remarkably urgent summons, and the only reasons I can give are either that Rowland's affairs demanded immediate discussion, or that Emma had written anxiously about Ada's state of health. If the plan was to give her a rest and change it had failed before she even reached Leicester. She 'had a fright from man in the train', and arrived at St. Mary's Fields in such a state of hysteria that first one, then a second, doctor attended her. The diagnosis this time was Nervous Fever. She was back at home after four days in a far worse condition than when she had left.

The other reason for the telegram seems the likelier. Ada's

43

arrival in a state of collapse would have made any discussion impossible; but a few days after her return Willie Bates travelled to Leamington, bringing a brother-in-law with him, and spent the afternoon in conference with Emma.

It was leap year 1876, and by 29 February Ada was rested enough to enjoy her real twentieth birthday. Emma's present to her was a small oval brooch made of pearls and garnets. Nearly sixty years later, my mother gave it to me to have made into an engagement ring. It went in a burglary a few years ago. Who wears it now?

March and April have only one entry each in the diary. On 26 March Bessie, who had gone as companion to a Mrs. Prince, took her confirmation vows in London. After that the diary is silent – was there nothing or too much to tell? – until 24 April: 'Bessie went to Mrs. Blake's near Oxford', and, huddled in the margin as though almost too painful to tell, 'ERH left for London.' Rowland's demotion from 'papa' or 'father' to his mere initials is Ada's only comment on the situation. He was out of work again, as a letter from Ada's friend Mrs. Carus Wilson will tell us.

The year before, on the day that my mother was rescued from the lavatory, a clergyman had called on Ada to talk to her about being confirmed. He was the Reverend C. Carus Wilson, in some way related to Charlotte Brontë's despot of Cowan Bridge. By the time Rowland left for London the Carus Wilsons were away on a long, ill-fated Continental tour (he died of typhus at Cannes the following spring).

Percy and Ada were confirmed together at St. Mary's Church on 5 May 1876, Percy's seventeenth birthday. Ada was driven to the church by a Mrs. Soulsby, and Percy gave her a bouquet of 'lovely flowers'. For the next forty years the anniversaries of that warm, sunny day were carefully entered into the diary. Ada treasured the memory as though it had been her wedding-day. On 23 May Mrs. Carus Wilson wrote from Lausanne:

... Tho' absent from you we have been thinking very much of you all at this period of Confirmation. We have indeed, & offering

up our constant prayers for you that you may all have strength
given you by the inspiration of God's Holy Spirit . . . I always
think *you* set such an example of cheerful hopeful bearing of trial
& I can't say how I often have admired this in you & thank God
for it. You have had a very trying life & it has often grieved me to
think how much sorrow yr young life has known . . . How glad we
shd be if we cd help in any way! Let me know if this is possible. –
I shall be very sorry if you are compelled to leave Leamington –
& *I* know the trial well of having one's roots continually torn up
& separations from those one loves & cares for continually going
on. But I find all these things make one just feel more & more that
'here we have no abiding city' – & that this is not our rest . . . I
trust yr own affairs are brightening & that there is some prospect
of a post for yr father wh he may like.

Vain hope; on 21 June Ada wrote: 'Mother, I and 3 little
ones left Leamington for New Cross. No house taken.' New
Cross meant Emma's brother Tom Fry, whose second son,
Jack, had been born the month before. The rest of the family
remained one more night with a friend at Leamington and
the next day took train to a homeless London. Again Rowland had made no preparations for them. They took refuge
with the uncles and friends. 'No house in prospect yet,' Ada
writes a week later. But on the last day of the month Tom
found them one not far from his own, in a little cul-de-sac a
mile north of Peckham Rye, where Hatcham becomes New
Cross. The address was 22 Somerville Road. The children,
upset at being uprooted again, missing their Warwickshire
fields, called it Some Vile Road. My mother remembered how
they all crowded into the little dark passage inside the front
door. The strange unlived-in gloom horrified her (she was
five). She sat sobbing on the bottom step of the bare staircase,
Charlie beside her trying to comfort her. 'I won't stay,' she
wailed, 'I won't stay in this hobble house!'

CHAPTER FOUR

The Last of Somerset

As soon as the family had dried my mother's tears, and got over the improbable excitement of the packing cases catching fire, they tried out the local churches. Once they had chosen a church they would have a centre, and their social life would naturally follow. On the first Sunday they attended All Saints'; on the second they divided forces and tried two: St. Mary's and St. James's, Hatcham, where Emma's brother Tom was a sidesman. St. James's was to be the scene of violent demonstrations against ritualism in the coming year, described by Ada as 'a great to do between people in St. James and the crowd outside', which reached a climax with 'Fighting in St. James. Police called in.' Ada took Hal and Daisy there a second time – 'a grand day, procession, band &c not like a service' – before they transferred their allegiance to the lower observances of All Saints' and Ada started to teach in the Sunday-school; though Hal and Bertie sang in the St. James's choir until the affray which brought in the police.

On the day before the grand processional service Emma had her first taste of freedom since the move from Islington. She travelled down to Winscombe with her two brothers, their wives and children, to be at Springfield for her parents' golden wedding day on 1 August 1876. It was the last blaze of light the Frys were to give before their sun sank for ever behind those hills. Already her uncle Peter had died at Compton House, and grandmother Spratt in the cottage across the stream. Sophy Spratt had moved into Springfield, and Emma's unmarried aunts, Mary Anna and Louisa Fry, born in 1791 and 1792, had settled in the cottage.

The local newspaper pulled out all the stops to describe the golden wedding day. After telling how the Frys had lived in the neighbourhood for centuries, highly respected and unusually long-lived, the report heightened its style to match the magnificence of the occasion. The morning had begun with a peal of bells from Winscombe Church, and at intervals they rang out again all the day long. A triumphal arch spanned the approach to the railway station, to leave arriving guests in no doubt about the importance of the day. The village street was hung with flags and streamers, and over the entrance gate of Springfield a banner bore the device WELCOME AYE WELCOME. Luncheon was a family affair, twenty-one Frys round the table, but before the meal was over the Rhine Band from Weston-super-Mare was taking up its position in the grounds, and the stewards, wearing white satin favours edged with gold, were preparing to welcome the guests. At four o'clock all the villagers, old and young, rich and poor, streamed in through the gates and into a huge marquee, where my great-grandfather and great-grandmother presided over a tea-party. A clergyman made a speech, the guests gave prolonged cheers, and the Weston-super-Mare Rhine Band struck up 'an appropriate air'. That done, the company went out into the home field for the sports, which included, the newspaper said, running, sack jumping and blindfold hunting. The report continues: 'The house was "open" during the whole evening to all comers, and many availed themselves of the opportunity of taking part in the somewhat novel entertainment of blowing a fragrant cloud and quaffing the health of their entertainers.'

After dark there was a firework display, a professional affair provided by Marchents of Wells, working up to the grand finale of 'Our Golden Wedding' blazoned under the stars. As the flaming letters trailed away in smoke a bonfire was lighted and everyone danced until the Weston-super-Mare Rhine Band played 'God Save the Queen'. One last paternal gesture came as the villagers were leaving. Every child was given a cake to carry home or munch on the way.

All this should have made enough of a day for my great-grandparents and great-great-aunts, but they now sat down, with sixty guests, to 'a most *recherché* banquet'. A Mrs. Greenway (late Nattriss) of Bristol was responsible for the meal, as well as for the table's centre-piece: an immense wedding cake topped by a golden vase. The wedding presents, the newspaper adds, were both numerous and beautiful; more perhaps than the old couple needed for the short time left to them.

Emma stayed on at Springfield for a week longer, with her sisters Ellen and Jessie for company. Jessie was engaged to marry her first cousin, Herbert Fry, one of the Compton House family, and owner, since his father's death, of a Jamaican estate. Whenever he was in England he found time to visit the Hammonds, wherever they might be, bringing presents for his godson Charlie and the other children. Ada treasured a carved fan he had brought her in 1869 when he was nineteen. Now he was twenty-six, three years younger than Jessie, and in the spring he was coming home to marry her.

When Emma got back to Somerville Road the family depression lifted, and it began to seem as though things might go right again. Rowland was promoted from ERH back to Father for a while. As though determinedly turning over a new leaf he took Emma and Ada on one day, and Bessie and Lil on another, to see Mr. Lee's conservatories and gardens at Lewisham, and the whole family for a river trip to Gravesend. (It was Mr. Lee who had housed Percy when the family left Milner Square.) And early in September Rowland, Emma, and Daisy went to stay with the Arthur Marshalls at Crouch End, an outlying hamlet of Hornsey. Arthur Marshall, who had married Louisa, the eldest of the Hammond daughters, owned a shipping firm in the City, and had seven startlingly beautiful children, with three nursemaids to look after them. The household staff included a butler in tails and a succession of page-boys in buttons. This golden-haired, comely family lived at Asmodée Villa, Mount Pleasant, surrounded by gardens, croquet lawn, and orchard, next to a farm which imported quails.

Rowland's efforts to reinstate himself in the affections of his family were evidently short-lived. After his return from Crouch End, two years go by with hardly a mention of him in the diary. At Christmas, Ada refers to him as 'father' for almost the last time. She says nothing about his being made a freeman of the City of London; but I have the parchment scroll, dated 12 December 1876, on which he appears as 'late apprentice of William Skyring Citizen and Haberdasher'. He is now described as Architect and Surveyor of 3 Adelaide Place, London Bridge. Skyring had also made him a freeman of the Haberdashers' Company which may well have qualified him to receive free education for his children at Haberdashers Aske's. The school was not far from Somerville Road, and Ada went to make enquiries there a week after her parents came back from Crouch End. On the same day she called on her Fry uncles 'about the children'. Four days later she took Bertie and Hal to sit for the entrance exam, and they joined the school on 29 September. Lil would be going to Haberdashers Girls, but the diary says she had 'got a penholder in her thigh when playing', a puzzling accident, which postponed her schooling until January.

Up to this time their education had been erratic, the boys moving from school to school (they had been to two during the year at Leamington) and Lil taking lessons from Ada when Ada was well enough. On the day the two boys started their term Ada began French lessons with a Mademoiselle Noë, no doubt paid for by one of the uncles.

Looking back on those lives I can see how apparently unimportant days had a bearing on the future. One such day was 6 December when their cousin Fred Fry came to see them, now a lieutenant in the navy. The last time they had seen him was four years before, on his sixteenth birthday, when they were dismally packing to leave Milner Square. He was in midshipman's uniform then, and had come to say goodbye before joining his ship. The intervening years had been spent at sea, Ada doesn't mention where, only that he 'amused all with his yarns'. Of all the family I imagine the one most spellbound was Hal. He was now within three weeks of his tenth birthday. Fred's uniform and tales of great horizons dazzled him. Fred became his hero, and the next six years a restless looking-forward to when his own adventures could begin.

25 December: a wet day. Emma and the children spent it together, 'father being away'. The 31st: 'Bessie, Lil, Bert and I to midnight service at All Saints.' And so we come to 1877, the year of Ada's twenty-first birthday, one of those unleaping years when she had to decide between the 28th and 1 March. She kept it on both. On the 28th Emma gave her an emerald and diamond ring, perhaps one of her own; and on the 1st, Mr. Lee of Lewisham sent her two boxes of camelias and azaleas from his conservatories. The flowers crowded the little front sitting-room when dear Jessie came in the afternoon for the birthday tea-party. She had come up to London to prepare for her wedding. If the villagers of Winscombe had looked forward to being *en fête* again they were disappointed; the wedding was to be at St. Mary's, Islington.

Herbert landed in England at the end of the month, and five days later called at Somerville Road, with Jessie on his arm, braving the thunder and lightning and a downpour of rain which was flooding the houses across the road. After the wedding and a honeymoon in Scotland they called again to say goodbye. It was Bertie's thirteenth birthday, 24 June. Ada and Lil walked back with them to Uncle Tom's, reluctant to come to the moment of leave-taking. They set sail for Jamaica on 2 July, and there, on 15 September, Jessie died. The sad story was often told to me when I turned the pages of the photograph album on rainy days, and how Herbert had died as well, three years later, when he, too, was only thirty years old. It was the family tale of tragic lovers.

When the news of Jessie's death was broken to the old people at Springfield it was Herbert they thought of rather than themselves. They had parted from Jessie when she left England, and now, in their late seventies, heaven seemed less remote than Jamaica. My great-grandmother wrote to Tom: 'My heart bleeds for Herbert, but hope that this dreadful blow may be blessed to him & that he may realize in a better world the bliss he has been denied here.'

Ada was shocked into illness and sat in a chair day and night hardly able to breathe. Nearly a month went by before she began to recover. But in between her illnesses (shingles was to come next) she did what she could to earn pocket money, coaching three girls for their school entrance exam, who all passed, and laboriously copying documents for an attorney. She called it law-writing; two months of hard work in which she was sometimes helped by Bertie and Lil. She had little bursts of energy, 'venturing' one day to walk as far as St. Paul's, or performing a piano trio with Bess and Lil at All Saints' schoolroom; but it was Bess who had all the vitality and popularity. In my boyhood I remember Aunt B as stocky, outspoken, strong-featured like a Roman matron, her red hands cracked with chilblains, a trifle eccentric. In her girlhood she was never still and, once childhood was over, almost never ill. It was she who rushed off to Leamington to nurse Percy when he fell off his pennyfarthing bicycle and broke his lame leg, who looked after Uncle Tom's house while he and his family were away, who took Bertie and Hal long walks through London, visiting St. Paul's, the British Museum and the National Gallery, and then trudged all the way home through Kennington, Camberwell, and Peckham. She was off earlier than anyone else to go to Jessie's wedding and stood for hours to see the Lord Mayor's Show. She sang in public, read her essays to the Mutual Aid Society, wall-papered the rooms, did charitable work, and kept up with a growing circle of friends. On her twenty-first birthday, as Ada recorded with perhaps a touch of envy, she had over thirty presents.

Abruptly, on 17 December 1877 comes the diary entry 'Percy married'. He was eighteen, and so was Lizzie, his

bride, the daughter of Joe Powell, labourer, at whose house
he lodged. None of his family went to Leamington for the
wedding, not even Bessie. He may not have let them know
until it was over. The register was signed by the girl's mother
and someone called Thomas Shirley who could do no more
than make his mark. Lizzie seems only once to have visited
her in-laws, though Emma worried about her health. A year
or two later Percy brought his daughter Beatrice to see them;
and after he and Lizzie had moved to Darlaston in Stafford-
shire, Bertie got a job in Percy's firm and lived with them for
four months before coming home. But when Emma and Lizzie
had died, within a year of each other, the family seldom heard
of him. He married again, and in 1904 Ada writes in her diary:
'Heard that Percy has four grandchildren.' For fifty years the
diary remembered him simply as the boy who had given Ada
the lovely flowers on their confirmation day.

Early in 1878 my mother began to wilt. The doctor took
refuge, as so often, in the vague diagnosis 'low fever'. Her
natural good spirits were easily deflated if she felt that anyone was unhappy or cross. She bloomed in light and friendliness and drooped in darkness and displeasure. She had a
horror of black and ran out of the room when a visitor called
wearing mourning. Even her own black shoes distressed her.
Her brothers called her the Impret, her first effort at pro-
nouncing the word 'infant', and Little Brick. She seems to
have been then, as she was all her life, a mixture of toughness
and timidity, game for almost anything but haunted by fears.
She slept at the top of the house with Ada, in an attic room
which had a skylight. Hal had teased her by saying that one
night she would see a pair of legs dangling in from the roof.
Every night after that, before Ada came up to bed, she would
lie staring up at the awful skylight afraid to close her eyes.
A cloud passing over the moon, like the shadow of a man,
would send her running to the head of the stairs, where she
would sit and get comfort from the voices down below. If
Charlie heard her crying he would climb out of bed and go
up to sit beside her, as they had sat side by side at the

bottom of the stairs on the day of the move, in a twin-like sympathy which lasted all their lives. Since leaving Leamington Ada had been giving them regular lessons together, but now, in January 1878, Charlie was sent to a little school, and my mother was left to learn alone. Ada, though loving her dearly, was over-anxious to turn her into a good and clever young woman. As I remember her she was good with children, which makes me wonder if those lessons were quite as painful as my mother, in memories she wrote down in old age, made them out to be: 'I had to stand straight and stiff with my hands behind my back, until I ached and my brain confused all the answers. Then Ada lost patience and said I should never be clever like my sisters. Sometimes she would send me upstairs without any dinner, and Mama, who I think was a little afraid of her, would creep up later with some bread and butter, and comfort me.'

I was to learn the same lessons with Ada, hands behind back, thirty-five years later, but suffered less. Perhaps by then her teaching methods had mellowed, or I was less easily intimidated. I remember her telling me that, when I was restless, my brains went to whatever part of my body was fidgeting, and I amused myself by secretly wiggling first a finger and then a toe, delighted to think of my brains recklessly coursing from one to the other.

Towards the end of March Ada took Daisy to stay at St. Mary's Fields. Gussie and Willie Bates had two children: Altie, now within a month of his eleventh birthday, who looked like an angel, but spoiling had encouraged the demon in him; and four-year-old Katie. The house was on the outskirts of Leicester, in the Narboro Road, now built over but then a place of fields, close to the canal which served Uncle Willie's rubber factory. From the lodge gates a lime avenue curved between paddocks for half a mile to a house which had largely the character of its owner, solid but friendly, prosperous but unassuming, until your eye took in an extension behind the billiard-room where some unruly afterthoughts were barely kept in order by an Italianate tower. In five years' time this was to become my mother's home, where events would conspire to lead her towards my father, and where in 1916 I opened a door and walked into her girlhood.

The earliest of her letters to survive was written from St. Mary's Fields. It bears no date, but I can find no mention of an earlier visit, and if it were written later than this year, when she was six, Ada would have had some reason for thinking she would never be clever:

> dear Charlie
> i went for a ride on pony then alty took me in the goatchaise. alty has got two rabbats. the big black dog is very ill and the little charlie the dog had go to the dogs hospial little time a go love from daisy.

Either she was being very forgiving about Altie's part in the goatchaise ride, or there was another less enjoyable ride to come. She told me how Altie sat her in the chaise, gave the goat a sharp whack, which sent it careering off down the drive; a wheel hit a stone and she was thrown out on to the grass. Ada recorded nothing of the three weeks at Leicester until they got home, when she commented that my mother had been more or less unwell all through the visit; and a few days later, 'Day very poorly again'.

So were the old people at Springfield. After Jessie's death their hold on life had begun to disengage. My great-grand-father wrote his last letter to Emma two days after his seventy-eighth birthday:

> 22 May 78
>
> My dear Emma,
> Convey to the 7 young Elephants my love & thank them for their good wishes on my Birthday – I enclose P.6.o for them & will thank you to divide the same in such proportions as you think fit & according to merit – but I wish *Berty* to have an *extra* shilling for the taste displayed in the letter to me. It was very kind of them to think of poor Granny, who is so ill & weak. Our love to you all –
> Your affec Father
> T H Fry

Seventeen shillings each (omitting Percy, and Edith who was with them at Springfield) and the odd shilling over for Bertie. A week later he might have added an extra tip for eleven-year-old Hal who passed the Cambridge Local Examination with honours, and celebrated a whole day's holiday by falling into a pond at Ladywell. 'Came home soaked.'

Worried about her parents' health, and Daisy's too, Emma decided to take her down to Springfield for the whole of July.

Thurs. morn [11 July 1878]
Before breakfast

This is for the good of all
as I cannot write to each
for want of time.

My dear husband & chicks
I must include all in my letters for I can scarcely find time for writing & must just tell roughly what we are doing. We are very lazy in the morning, breakfast about 9 & there is hardly a sound in the house before we all meet altho' Gpa has been up every morning since we came. Jane goes to Gmas door at 7 & takes Gpa a cup of tea at 8 by which time Daisy has gone up to stir Edie out of bed & I am writing or working & quite ready for breakfast altho' so idle. Day has ham & dry bread & will not be persuaded to take butter to granny's great delight. I have a delicious pan of fryed potatoes all to myself with a little ham & have not had as much butter since we came as in one meal at home . . . Monday morning Edie, Day & I picked fruit for about an hour & were helping granny to stalk them for pies when a servant from the Court House came with a request for Ellen, Day & I to accompany the Miss Folletts to Weston in half an hour, & you may imagine the bustle we were in & only just ready when the handsome carriage & pair, coachman & footman with cockades in their hats etc dashed up to the door.

The Vicar of Winscombe was also called Follett, perhaps younger brother or nephew to the three Miss Folletts who came driving up in such style. Emma knew them as Miss Follett, Miss Mary ('a jolly old lady'), and Miss Helen.

~⦑ 55

Miss Follett insisted on my taking the best place by the side of Miss Mary who cannot ride back to the horses. I had Day on my lap but could still lie back in ease & comfort. Miss Helen had little Dora on her knee as a companion for Day. It was very delicious tooling along at such a rate & the weather was glorious.

While the Miss Folletts were shopping Emma took the children to have a glimpse of the sea at high tide before they went to call on old Mrs. Voules, who had been Bessie's nurse after her birth at Springfield in 1857, now over ninety.

She is as well as ever, nimble on her legs, & sees & hears quite well. She knew me directly & kissed me over & over again & then kept my hands in hers. She wanted to know about her baby Bess & laughed heartily when I said I felt so small among such a tribe of girls.

The Miss Folletts had engaged a table at one o'clock at Carey's the confectioners, in a window overlooking the parade, and while they were eating their cakes and ices ('the little ones shuddered at the ices & had lemonade') the procession of Sanger's Circus passed by. Three of the floats towered above the houses, astonishing them all with their gilded splendour, the queen of the circus perched high 'on the tiptop' surrounded by her courtiers; and there was more excitement to come. '*At ½ past 2 we all went to the circus.*' Miss Follett paid twelve shillings for the best seats.

I suppose you have all seen most of the wonderful things done . . . Day clapped her hands with delight. I think I liked the 6 Elephants the best who went through the most wonderful performances & Ellen was perfectly convulsed with laughter when after they had all *waltzed* round the large arena the tiny one was so giddy that he had to be propped up & led to his washing tub turned topsy turvy . . . It is impossible to tell half the wonders we saw. The children on horseback delighted Day as well as the clowns.

It was early evening when they started back, at the time when the Miss Folletts should have been sitting down to dinner, and they were even later home than they meant to be because of the one misfortune of an otherwise perfect day:

A kind of dogcart with 4 men in it came at a furious rate down Barnwell Hill & altho' old Henry gave them the greater part of the road they struck our hind wheel giving us a tremendous jolt & seriously damaging it. As soon as they could stop, one of the men returned (knowing whose carriage it was) & made most humble & ample apology for the mishap & saying he would pay all expense in having it repaired. It caused some delay & also again when we reached Mabberts who came to examine it & feared it was beyond his ability to repair but we hear he will be able to do it . . . Every day seems to fly past & I have not done as much work as in one day at home & that is not much. Grandpa continues wonderfully well, & quite like his old self. They say he has never been so since his illness began. Tell Uncle Tom what a pleasure it is to have him so bright & cheerful . . .

After breakfast Have been very much pleased with your letters . . . I am glad you get on so well & hope you will hear from Yorkshire before quite out of funds. Daisy is wonderfully improved, she is as brown as a young gypsy & as happy as a bird, really one would suppose there was not such a child in existence. She has not a single fault in anybody's eyes but *all* simply think her a piece of perfection . . . A most distressing thing took place on Wednesday. Henry Mabbert whom no one in the place has ever had a complaint against, a sober, steady gentlemanly young fellow – a great comfort to his parents and a general favourite, married (at Easter) a girl as much beloved in the place as he is, he has not been well for some weeks past & on Wednesday went raving mad attempted to kill his wife & mother & Mr. Wade being sent for ordered his immediate removal to Wells it took 6 men to accompany him in the carriage. We quite believe it is from some temporary cause which he will get over. Ellen waiting for me so must go to Aunt Louisa's. Love to Pa & all chicks from Mother.

Very glad to hear of Bertie's success in laying
eggs & hope his first family will soon fly about.
Very oppressive & a light rain falling.

(The eggs belonged to Bertie's pigeons which were kept in a nesting box hung on the wall in the little back garden.)

On one of the days of this visit my mother was taken to call on the great-aunts Mary Anna and Louisa, now eighty-seven and eighty-six, in the cottage across the stream. They gave her a penny. On the way back across the bridge she stopped to admire the goldfish and the penny slipped out of her hand. As she mournfully watched it sinking to the bed of the stream she said, 'It strikes me very forceable I've lost my penny.' The great-aunts were so delighted that they gave her a sixpence. The story with its happy ending delighted me, too, when I was little, however often I heard it.

But time at Springfield was running out. In August a letter came to Daisy with bad news of the goldfish and of Grandpa:

Raglan Cottage
Augst 20, 78

My dear Daisy
I was much pleased with your nicely written letter, & very glad to hear your Family of *dolls* were well and glad to have you home, I have been out in the chair to-day, George was my coachman, and Ernest my footman, I called on grandpapa and Aunt Louisa and at the Court but could not get out of the chair, your cousins enjoy themselves very much. I am sorry to tell you, many of the Gold Fishes are dead, Mr. Seymour is sorry to lose them. – Mr & Mrs Follett & Miss Mary with all the Children & *two* Servants are gone to the Sea Side for a fortnight near Dawlish, I think they would like to have you with them. Poor Grandpapa is very ill all the rest are well, I hope your Mamma and all of you are in good health with love to everybody and *ten* kisses for yourself. I have sent you six stamps that you may give your doll a treat some day

I remain your
affectionate Great Aunt
Mary Anna Fry

Grandpa died in November, and Emma travelled down to Somerset alone for the funeral. It was an ominous week. Things took an ugly lurch towards the dark days to come. After the funeral, Ada notes, 'Mother had severe pain in the side for the 3rd time during the last 2 years.' And then a sentence in the guarded style which Ada was coming to use whenever she referred to her father: 'Bessie & I had a time of worry during her absence.' From what was to follow there can be little doubt that Rowland had started to drink heavily. I wish I could know what was harrying him. He was still only forty-five, vigorous and well. Emma was fifty-one and iller than she knew. A fortnight after she got back from Springfield the diary says: 'Different arrangements about the rooms, the boys giving up their bedroom to ERH.'

Emma had such resilience and fortitude, for the next four years none of them would believe her illness was incurable. In the new year, 1879, Ada wrote: 'Mother very unwell from what seemed like rheumatism', and on 6 January: 'Mother in bed all day. 1st time since Day was born.' But a week later, on the day when Hal, starting a new term, was made captain of his class, she was judged to be well again. Bess and Edith went off to take jobs, Lil was helping a Miss Jennings in a shop in Putney, Ada was still taking Daisy for lessons every day. 'Mother did nearly all the work this month', she writes in mid-May, 'except when I helped on half holidays & she got quite knocked up & often felt too tired to continue.' At the end of June she had two days of severe pain in the side.

Grandma Fry died in August. Springfield would go, as Compton House had already gone, to strangers; the six centuries of Frys in Somerset had come to an end. Emma travelled down again for the funeral, taking nine-year-old Charlie with her. Mary Anna wrote to my mother on the day they arrived.

August 11th 1879

My dear Daisy

I was very glad to see your dear Mamma & to hear of you, but very sorry you have hurt your hand, it was a pity you would not let them look at it sooner, which caused it to be so much worse. I have sent a sixpence to buy a cake, or anything you like; were you not very sorry at losing both grandpapa & grandmama, I am I assure you, I miss them both very much; how glad you will be to see your dear Mamma home again your little Brother seems to be enjoying himself here how quiet he is, I could not hear a word he said. I hope all the *dolls* are doing well, I hope you do *not* neglect them yet; with my kind love to you I remain your affectionate

great aunt / M A Fry

In old age my mother was most recognizably the child who refused to let them look at her hurt hand. She would prefer any amount of discomfort to the attentions of a doctor; and through all the chances and changes of the next eighty years the little girl was never far away.

CHAPTER FIVE

The Break-up

A few days before Christmas 1879 Emma was taken ill again. When Ada came home from a concert in aid of Christmas dinners for the poor she made her a linseed and mustard poultice to ease the pain. The diary was keeping its long silence about Rowland. Of how he was behaving, or what was troubling him, of whether he was working or at home, Ada has nothing to say. He is simply ignored.

Christmas Day. Fog & frost. Only me to church. Edith, Lil, Bert & Hal to Blackheath to skate. Quiet dinner with Mother, & presents afterwards. All to bed early. Thawed, damp & cheerless.

Dec. 28. Tay bridge broke & a train fell into the river. Mother very unwell from 27th the beginning of her illness.

But the beginning would seem to have been three years before, about the time they left Leamington, and only her indomitable refusal to give way had disguised it. On New Year's Day 1880 she was worse, and on the 4th: 'Mother had a dreadful night. Bessie fetched Dr. Foster before breakfast.' All through the first three months of the year Ada's diary bulletins anxiously charted the days: 'Mother better but still yellow', 'so much better', 'had a good dinner of meat & pudding 1st time since illness began', 'worse again'. At the same time Ada was noting down her own infirmities: 'I had neuralgia badly', 'nearly blinded from cold in my eyes'.

In early March Emma's spirit took charge, and in Holy Week she travelled down to stay with the Marshalls who had moved from Crouch End to St. Leonards-on-Sea. She wrote home to thank the 'chicks' for Easter cards and for a letter from 'Pa', the only glimmer we get of him over these months. She is, as always, ready to enjoy everything, though critical of the quality of the St. Leonards' music and teased by a painful finger. She had put it out of joint when pulling on her boots to go to church on Easter Sunday,

but put it back with a *click* it is now the size of a sausage quite stiff & very painful, cannot work & have great difficulty in cutting my meals, can hold a pen with the middle finger . . . It is the first day without a brilliant sun but it is trying to break through the fog & I believe it will be a glorious afternoon . . . Girls with baskets of lovely flowers are going about amongst the crowds of people on the esplanade while carriages, ladies on horseback & lots of bicycles are in the road. We have very few bands of music & those not very first rate . . .

Her brothers Charles and Tom were keeping anxious eyes on her. She went to stay with Charles for a fortnight in May. Bessie repapered the bedrooms during her absence, and Ada went with some friends to a women's suffrage meeting at the New Cross Hall. She came away unconverted, and afterwards always referred to suffragettes as 'unsatisfied women'. Two days before Emma came home there was a nightmare of anxiety when Tom's three-year-old son Reggie was missing for twelve hours. Nothing is said of how he was traced and found, only three startling words in brackets: '(Tramp took him)'.

Emma's illness was lenient with her that summer, and in June, for one brief moment, Rowland was reinstated as 'father'. Emma spent a day at 1 Highbury Hill with his parents, and 'Father brought mother home'. In some brief notes Emma made that summer, she mentions two visits he made to Margate, and in September for five days to Boulogne. If his affairs had brightened, it was not to be so for long. On 1 August Emma was taken ill in the night; there was more linseed and mustard poultices; Dr. Foster said she had 'jaundice again'. On the 21st Ada writes: 'I took Hal. Charlie

& Day to tea at Greenwich to keep the house quiet. Mother better but worried over ERH's business affairs.'

They were walking a precarious path. September was a good month for Emma; she was taken out for drives by Tom's wife; but in October she was ill again, and the shadowy figure of Rowland and his shadowy affairs were growing more threatening. In less than six months the long tension would snap. Meanwhile the family got on with their day to day lives. Bessie and Ada earned a little by doing needlework, '3 fine linen chemises & Mr. H's fine linen shirts, all to be stitched by hand', and more orders came in to keep them busy. Daisy added up her collection of farthings and found they amounted to 4s. 10½d. Fifteen-year-old Bertie had left school at the end of the summer term, already a promising artist, and had gone to work in an architect's office. With his first earnings he gave Emma on her fifty-third birthday a majolica dolphin milk jug, and took Ada to see *The School for Scandal* at New Cross Hall. In October he exhibited his model railway-carriages. Young Hal was decorating envelopes with comic drawings in Indian ink and selling them for pocket money. When Fred Fry visited them again Hal walked back with him to the station, drinking in everything Fred could tell him about his voyages. He was fourteen on 23 December, two years and five months away from the beginning of his own travels. On his birthday Ada was decorating the church, with Daisy to help her, and on Christmas Eve she and Bessie and Emma (just out of bed from another attack) disguised a tin bath as a basket to hold the presents. 'I was tired out,' Ada adds.

The stresses of that Christmas Day, the last that Rowland would ever share with them, were disguised, like the bath; in a tranquil diary entry Ada says: 'Fine & cold. I, Lil, Bert & Hal to church. Charlie to S. school. Both parents & all the family dined together. Presents afterwards. Bessie & Lil had a long walk in evening.' During that long walk through the dark streets Bessie and Lil had anxieties to talk about which made a younger brother's company unwelcome. A month from now Ada would find even the initials ERH too friendly to represent her father.

January 1881 was a hard month. The water froze in the bedroom jugs. There was snow and a dreadful east wind. On the 19th the snow was so deep, and still falling, only Bert and Hal could go out; and at Haberdashers Aske's Hal found only twelve of the four hundred boys had managed to get there.

On the 31st, when the weather had suddenly turned mild, there comes the diary entry: 'A noisy night from the usual person.' It is possible that Ada meant someone other than her father, a next-door neighbour, perhaps. But in February we are not left in any doubt about who was causing trouble. The night which haunted my mother's memory must have been about this time: the night when, sleeping with Emma, the door locked against Rowland, she heard him stumble up the stairs and hammer at the door, shouting to be let in. She would never, never marry a man who drank too much.

The trouble now gathers momentum through a series of terse diary entries which leave almost everything to the imagination. I try to guess at Rowland's state of mind. Were his business worries due to the drinking, or the drinking due to a combination of business worries and sexual frustration now that Emma was so ill? What had turned the Papa who had given Ada *The Pilgrim's Progress* with his love, who had taken her and dear Jessie on the moonlit walk to Guy's Cliff, into someone dreaded and feared? We can only follow the sequence of events as Ada briefly records them.

Feb. 21. Mother taken ill at 5 a.m. I stayed with her, Bessie did all the work.
Feb. 25. Bessie to Aunt Louie's to sleep. Mother dressed about 10 to 6 p.m. Had a dreadful time with ERH.
Feb. 28. Lil, Charlie & Day not well. ERH went into lodgings.

Emma may have persuaded him to this for the children's sake, but the peace of having him out of the house lasted for little more than a week. On 9 March he was home again. This time it was some of the children who left. Bertie, Edith, and Charlie went to Gussie Bates who was staying with friends at Bournemouth, and a week later Bessie joined them. They were all back at the beginning of April. But where was Rowland? For the rest of March, the whole of April and most of May there is no mention of him. On 21 May the diary has a particularly cryptic entry: 'An unexpected man slept in the house.' The chilling contempt of this if it meant Rowland, as at first I thought, surely goes even beyond Ada's disillusion about him. I can only suppose she meant a broker's man. Whoever it was, events now moved very swiftly.

May 23. Trouble at home. Uncles busy arranging matters.
May 25. Bessie went to various relations for mother. The trouble was ended when Uncle Tom Smith came. Deed about the furniture was sent from lawyers.

Tom Smith was Grandma Hammond's brother, Rowland's uncle. Was the trouble he ended connected with the broker's man, if he existed, and threatened bankruptcy, or with the breaking-up of Rowland's marriage? Rowland was away from the house when his uncle called:

May 28. ERH in first time since 23rd.
Whit Sunday, June 5. Mother & I had a terrible time with ERH & Bt.

Presumably 'Bt' stands for Bertie, though Ada uses the abbreviation nowhere else in the diary, and Bertie, gentle and nervous, was an unlikely person to make a scene. He was not quite seventeen, the age Percy had been when he turned on his father at Leamington and was thrashed for it. Bertie spent the whole of Whit Monday with their friends the Dusseks to be out of Rowland's way; but now there were only two more weeks of upset to be endured.

June 20. ERH left 22 S.Rd.
June 28. The deed signed.

July 4. Heard through Aunt Gussie that ERH intended going abroad this week. 1st intimation on the subject.

July 10. ERH came to say Goodbye before sailing for Adelaide tomorrow in the 'John Rennie'.

There is something very disarming about that farewell visit of Rowland's. There was no need for him to have gone, or for Emma to have received him. It must have been agonizing for both of them. For all his self-centredness and lack of control he had affection for his family. The Legal Separation Act of 1878 had made it possible for Emma to keep the younger ones in her custody, and to get from Rowland, if she could, an allowance for their upbringing. Six of the children were to see him again in his new life at the other side of the world. Arthur Marshall's shipping company, which had a particular concern with the Australian passage, became a kind of family escape-hatch.

My mother remembered vividly that July afternoon of leave-taking. When he stood in the narrow, dark hallway by the front door he picked her up in his arms, kissed her, pressed a sixpence into her hand, and said 'You aren't afraid of Papa, are you, little girl?' But she felt easier, she told me, when he put her down again.

I had always understood it was the Frys who arranged Rowland's dismissal to Australia, until by a strange chance the fragment of a letter was found in New Zealand, a letter written by W. H. Hammond, my great-grandfather, to his eldest son Frank three weeks after Rowland set sail. Frank had emigrated to New Zealand with his family in 1864 and was now highly thought of as an architect in Wellington (he designed the magistrates' court there and other civic buildings). He was also strictly religious, and Rowland may well have preferred, in his fall from grace, not to come face to face with his elder brother. The scrap of letter reads: '*Rowland* has gone to Adelaide for merely a sea trip & shd get back again as soon as he can to try & take to do something for his support or he will get out of business habits – I cant afford to pay his expences to visit you & consider he will be better at . . .' At home, no doubt; but there would be no return.

Emma's mind and spirits now seemed to work a miracle over the cancer in her body. For the next three years, to outward appearances at least, she was almost herself again, and though often very tired, Ada could write of her at the end of 1883: 'Mother in better health this year than had been the case for a long time.' It was Ada who collapsed, almost as soon as the *John Rennie* had set sail, with what she described as 'neuralgia of the brain end nerves'. Was there anything of her old affection for 'dear Papa' still fighting for survival? The doctor said she had narrowly escaped brain fever.

The day after Rowland's visit Hal started work at New Cross Station. He was only fourteen and a half, and had been doing well at Aske's, but Emma's store of money was dwindling fast. Lil was the only one of the girls with a permanent job. Bessie and Edith seem to have taken temporary posts from time to time, or went to stay with friends. When Bessie was at home she was in great demand, singing in the oratorio *Judith* at New Cross Hall, or in Dr. Bradford's concert at the Royal Academy, and reading her essays, on 'Trees' and 'Music', at the Mutual Aid Society meetings. Young Charlie sang, too, in a Service of Song, a piece called 'Bart's Joy'. But Bertie was beginning to give anxiety. 'Very weak & out of health,' the diary says. In September he was brought home from the office in a cab, suffering from a chill and ulcerated tonsils, and from now on until he left England he was plagued with troubles. Emma, too, had a few bad days at Christmas time. She had fallen in her bedroom and hurt her eye, and after the presents were opened on the evening of Christmas Day, Ada wrote, 'Mother & I so tired, glad to go to bed.'

The unhappy year came to an end with Ada, Bessie, Edith, and Bertie attending the midnight service. In the first hour of 1882 Ada walked back alone, 'the others took their friends home'. She was always to be a little separate from the life going on around her, baffled by her lack of vitality, head-aches, and hypochondria, and it was all too easy (as I remember) to accept this and forget to include her in things. Her affection was centred on Emma and Daisy, and neither of them was quite at ease with her. The anxious assessment of my mother's chances of salvation was still going on in my boyhood as it was in the summing up of 1881: 'Great changes in the home life this year. I taught Daisy regularly except when ill or away. Daisy only went to church once or twice, except on the children's Sunday in afternoon.'

My mother was still thought of as the baby of the family, the Impret, and that was how she thought of herself, so that her memory always dates childhood events several years earlier than the time of their happening. At the time of the episode of the rainy day, for instance, as she told it to me, she was six years old, but in fact she was ten and a half. The date was 11 July 1882. Two days later Emma sat down to write to Bessie who had taken a job in Huntingdon looking after children. The letter begins with a description of the flower service at All Saints' on the 9th. Four of them had gone, Emma, Ada, Charlie, and Daisy, carrying a fine fuchsia bought from the nurseryman in Rye Lane, a bouquet of red roses and white sweet peas, and a pink double geranium which Daisy carried up to the communion table. Bert and Hal had been left at home, 'with a small tribe of other boys', to look after the house, 'and amused themselves making toffee & effectually took away Hal's appetite for some meals after'. Then she comes to the day of the Sunday-school treat. It had been a fine week-end:

. . . on Monday even a blanket was almost aired in the hot sun but rain began in the afternoon, poured all night & came down in a deluge on the unlucky Tuesday morning. They were all to meet in the school room ¼ to 10 but soon after 9 Ada decided it would be madness for her or Daisy to go so giving Charlie his satchel full of cake, biscuits & bottle of water packed him off & did not hear anything more of the poor school treat till evening when all the particulars came to hand. The Vicar & teachers were at their wits end to know what to do as about 400 ventured to meet in spite of the dreadful rain, so they telegraphed to Caterham and the answer was 'Pouring old boots' and no signs of a change, so they decided not to go there, but to counter order every thing, tent, dinner, tea & especial train & ordered another train for the Crystal Palace with tea etc there. so after all the brave ones had a jolly day for it cleared up in the evening & they were able to have races on the terrace etc etc & the Lloyds who had given the invitation to Caterham were so disappointed at the change of affairs after all the preparations they had made for their large party, that they ordered all their carriages, packed up hampers of flowers & good things & posted off to the Palace & so added much to the pleasure of all the teachers & school children. Daisy was most bitterly disappointed & smashed her poor little nose against the windows with the tears running down almost as fast as the rain.

Emma had the sudden thought to take Daisy to pay a surprise visit on the Charles Frys, who had moved from Ellington Street to Pemberton Road. Ada was content to stay at home, with plenty of plain and fancy needlework for Grandma Hammond to occupy her. She dressed Daisy in a new frock, a present from Aunt Kitty, and saw them set off under umbrellas and waterproofs to Queen's Road Station. 'Without the least trouble', Emma wrote, 'we soon found ourselves at *No. 6* to Kit's astonishment.' While Daisy played with a doll and romped with a young cousin, Emma and Aunt Kitty 'did a tolerable amount of gossip'. Arthur Marshall had been on a business trip to Australia, and the letter goes on:

. . . No news from Adelaide since the 1st of April & Uncle Arthur did not see *him* as he only touched at Adelaide on a Sunday. I cannot understand it, for I understood he was going there to see the firm he does business with . . . I sent a message to Fred Cox through Lil as he had wished to come on Sunday to take leave but I could not have them on such a busy day, therefore he wrote his *thoughts and wishes*. I am very relieved he is going away for a time & have not the least fear that Lil will break her heart if she can get any one else to spoon with . . . Daisy wants to enclose a letter about her kittens but as it is not yet begun expect you will wait till next time . . . They are the most amusing kittens you can possibly imagine & quite as *sensible as babies*. Daisy dresses Tabby in a long robe & scarlet cloak & it goes to sleep while she carries it about & they both seem to understand every thing said to them . . . Now I think you will be tired of this rigmarole & I must work so with love ever your affectionate Mother.

The only trace of bitterness she showed towards Rowland was that she now always referred to him as 'he', as in a letter to Bess written on 25 September: 'I had an illustrated paper from Adelaide last Monday in which he wrote love & best wishes *to all* & Day had a bunch of flowers picked when he went 400 miles north of Adelaide. I have sent in return the "Pictorial Times" of the War.'

The War was the clash of arms with Arabi Bey in Egypt which culminated in the battle of Tel-el-Kebir.

Yesterday was thanksgiving day for the victory . . . [The Vicar's] sermons on the War have been intensely interesting & has proved how each event has been a prophesy fulfilled. The real battle only lasted about 15 minutes & the odds were 1 to 100. Sir Garnet & the Duke of Connaught accompany the Khedive in state through Cairo to-day. What a glorious triumphal procession it will be.

Thirty years later there was another procession for Sir Garnet Wolseley, Viscount Wolseley by then, on the day when my mother, Ada, my brother and I were making our way across London in a thick fog to begin a new life in a strange town. The bells of St. Paul's were tolling for his funeral.

Emma could even accept with evident pleasure, and perhaps a little irony, a tribute from 'him' which came by way of a letter from his sister Gussie in October:

She enclosed a long letter from Adelaide to herself but which she forwarded as it contained such a flattering paragraph on myself & which I have copied & will send you to read if you like . . . He asked her to procure a book & forward it to me & also enclosed her the inscription or whatever you may call it to paste inside but

which she sent in her letter saying she had ordered the book &
hoped it would arrive safely but it has not come yet . . . The name
is 'Far above Rubies' & Ada says is very interesting.

I wish we had his paragraph in praise of Emma, or the
inscription which she pasted into the book. But the book's
title evidently expressed what he was feeling as he thought
back over their life together. It was a quotation from
Proverbs, chapter 31:

Who can find a virtuous woman? for her price is above rubies.
The heart of her husband doth safely trust in her . . . She will do
him good and not evil all the days of her life . . . Her children arise
up and call her blessed; her husband also, and he praiseth her.

She still had plenty to try her fortitude and her humour
while the cancer lay in wait draining her strength. In March
1882 Bertie had gone to see Dr. Cock with a swelling on his
neck, which increased as the year went on; and in September
Ada was ill again:

. . . a most severe attack of neuralgia in the head & spine & had
not the ice & other remedies relieved the intense pain must have
had on a blister, now she is only dreadfully weak & ready to
faint constantly, & requires no end of little dainties all day long
. . . Cock says she is such a neuralgic subject that she requires
plenty of change of air & very bright society, (both of which we
can't get) & he can only patch her up for a bit without it . . .

On 26 October Emma was writing to Bess again:

You very good dear kind little soul to give me such a nice breakfast this morning, it was pleasant & no mistake coming so entirely
unexpectedly. Your good gift shall be laid out entirely as you
desire & to tell the truth a drop of goody at times these cold nights
will be most acceptable but I could not be so extravagant as to
treat myself to it. Neither A or I have had anything stimulating
for a fortnight & so she says I am to give you her hearty thanks
for the prospect of something more tasty than water & I have not
seen her brighten up so much for a long time as at the thought of
a real little bit of tempting meat for dinner instead of the tin
mutton which we regaled off yesterday & were anticipating again

today. Won't Mr. Frear think we have come in for a fortune to ask for real rump steak; oh my. Daisy is going to write on her own account, as well as do her own marketing . . . I have been sorely troubled about Percy lately & yesterday morning (Lizzie's birthday 25th) had the pleasure of hearing that he was to return to J T's (altho' for a smaller salary than he received before) that very morning. The same day last year he went there for the 1st time. Percy says that after trying for all these weeks J.T. finds he cannot do without a book-keeper & so sent to him to ask him to return which is decidedly better than having nothing to do, especially as he can only get an outdoor letter for the hospital & which I fear will not be of much good to Lizzie if she has to go all weathers. Percy's letter of relief to my mind & your jolly one of this morning has helped me up considerably for really I was very much in the dumps about Bertie who came home Tues Even looking terribly ill & out of spirits; he called on Cock who had told him it (his neck) was beyond his skill, that he would have to be in hospital for weeks have chloroform, cut out etc etc etc The poor boy could not eat any dinner & it kept A & I awake nearly all night thinking. I decided he should go to get first class advice from the Physician in Hanover Sq where Bertie Robins advised him to go some time since & having Mr. Ridges consent he has gone there this morning before going on to business, & I am now longing to see him back & trust it may not be so bad as we anticipate. It is a frightful size & the other side getting large he looks so ill & thoroughly down-hearted about it. Do not say anything to him about it yet, as he is so cross if he hears I mention him to any one. he hates to be talked about or pitied . . . This morning was so foggy we could not see out of the windows & I was quite afraid for Bert to go out in it as he constantly complains of pain in the side & has a short quick cough & says he believes his lungs are bad. Now the sun is brilliant but it is very cold. Have you seen the Comet? which is visible from 4 till sunrise the tail of it is 45 millions of miles . . .

Thurs afternoon
Oh! how A & I have blessed you while partaking of our jolly bit of really prime juicy steak; sent for a whole lb *all at once* because a small piece is never so nicely cut & put by half for tomorrow. Intend getting Leibegs with some of the overfund as A & Bert

have so much to strengthen them up & something towards C's
boots as well . . . the small imp gets on very well, & thanking you
over & over again & sending love & kisses

Ever your affec
Mother

2 kittens 2 rabbits 2 mice
& 2 birds quite well
thank you.

The mice had been bought by Hal earlier that month. The
physician in Hanover Square was a Dr. Cowell, who diagnosed the swelling on Bert's neck as a tumour and, after a
second visit, 'ordered him to leave business & go to the sea-
side'. This advice, and a month's holiday, cost Emma some
ill-afforded guineas. He set off for Margate on my mother's
eleventh birthday. Emma and Bessie gave her an umbrella,
Ada a book called *Grecian Heroes,* and Hal a collar for her
cat. But another year added to her age was hardly enough to
make Ada admit that she was beginning to grow up: 'Nov.
23. Daisy went alone to Uncle Tom's with a message & then
to my District to say I was too ill to go today. A great deal
for the small chick to do by herself.'

When Bertie came back from Margate in December
London sank into a deep pea-soup fog, and Ada deeper into
illness: 'could scarcely speak or move, could not undress till
the next day.' She probably suffered from migraine, though
the word is never used. 'I laid up with a bad headache as
usual,' occurs from time to time in the diary. The London fog
did my mother no good either: 'At 2 a.m. on the 15th Day's
throat was so bad I had to go down to mother for the
needed remedies. No more sleep for mother or me.'

But Day was well enough on Hal's sixteenth birthday to
go out with Charlie taking 'presents to poor people'. It was
Hal's last birthday at home. His job on the railway gave him
the right to free train tickets but he was getting more and
more restless to travel far beyond where they could take him.
The catalytic agent was Fred Fry who came to see them on

13 March 1883 with more tales of life at sea, and four days later he took Hal over his ship in the West India Docks. Hal immediately went the round of his uncles to find out how he could emigrate to Canada. On 19 March Emma mentioned the plan in a letter to Bessie:

He is biding his time now very quietly but still longing to be off. It was very kind of Mr. Sydney to say what he did & we must hope that some opening will be made when he is to start. but I hope not before the confirmation on May 3rd the Vicar has also expressed a wish that he should not leave home before. Suppose you read the account of the boat race. poor Cambridge was nowhere. Also the explosion a nice piece of excitement . . . In todays paper we find Lady Florence Dixie nearly murdered in Windsor Park by 2 men dressed as women. These Fenians are having a pretty game it seems.

But it was not after all Hal who was to be the first of the children to be taken away from her, it was Daisy, the one perhaps nearest to her heart. In April Willie and Gussie Bates invited her to stay at St. Mary's Fields. Emma described the leave-taking to Bessie:

On Thursday morning at 10.15 o'clock Daisy & I started off in rain fog & cold wind to St. Pancras, it was a wretched day, about as dismal & miserable as it could well be. If we had been of the superstitious order I really think I could not have ventured forth with our young treasure, as we *all* had wretched dreams & A, D & I actually had to get up & shake ourselves free of them. I saw the whole funeral of my mother & Ada saw the same of mine while Daisy was scared with the house on fire; but instead of proving ill omens, we did not have the least trouble or annoyance of any kind from the time we left home till I got back again at ¼ pt 1. except in weather. Uncle Willie got to St. Pancras with Alty ¼ to 12 but as he had an appointment before joining Gussie, who was shopping, could only get the children's tickets, & a carriage with one little boy in going to Bedford, press me to have a glass of port wine & biscuit, which I declined, & had to rush away, so I stayed till they started & had a chat with Alty. he is a *sweet looking* gentlemanly boy but does not look 12 altho' *16 today* & is not up to our Hals shoulder. He took Daisy at once under his protecting wing & she seemed perfectly happy to be there. Willie & Gussie were to go by the 5 o'clock train. Next morning I had a nice letter from Nurse to say the children arrived quite safely & that Miss Katie was delighted with the box of dolls we dressed for her. Since beginning this a parcel has come from Guss containing jackets for you, Ada & self (mine is a proper one indeed) yours of black *stockingnet* trimmed with gold braid, A's dark grey, braided . . . No more news from Uncle Arthur. Hal going on very quietly. Charlie been *out fishing* all day & after a good scrub gone to bed. All miss Daisy very much, but just guess she's happy . . .

What had begun as a holiday visit turned into a kind of adoption by persuasion. Letters came 'begging' that her stay be extended. Six months later Ada writes disappointedly in the diary: 'Aunt wrote again about Day though it had been *settled* that she was to return home.' But, except for three brief visits, she never did come back. Once again the object of Ada's affection had deserted her, and for the rest of her life my mother had a feeling of guilt about something she said when the invitation to St. Mary's Fields arrived. In her seventies she wrote down her memory of that morning:

When I woke up Ada called to me to come into bed with her, she had something to tell me. Her voice sounded strange, but I tucked myself in beside her and waited. She said I was going to Leicester on a long visit. I could hardly believe it, it was such joyful news. Ada said 'Won't you mind leaving me?' and I was so excited I said 'No, not a bit. I'd like to live there for ever!' Then I knew by her face how much I had hurt her.

On 3 May Hal was confirmed at All Saints'. His sisters clubbed together to give him a Bible. Now there was nothing to stand in the way of his setting off. He went up to town to ask his uncle Arthur Marshall for any news of a passage, and on his way home called on the Charles Frys and picked up a sea chest they had bought for him. A second visit to Uncle Arthur a few days later encouraged him to have his photograph taken in Lewisham High Road as a farewell gift to the family.

On Tuesday 22 May Emma and Ada were getting the house ready for the house painters who were coming in the morning to start whitewashing the walls. Hal came back from town with the 'startling' news that he was to leave for Canada the next day. Ada rushed out to tell some neighbours and came back to help with the packing of the sea chest which was sent off at eight o'clock that night. The news had quickly spread. 'Hal's boy friends in & out all evening . . . Mother & I went to bed, but scarcely slept at all.' They were up again at 5.30, the workmen came at 6, and Hal set off at 7, one friend accompanying him as far as London Bridge and another seeing him off at Euston. The day's entry ends: 'Mother & I missed Hal very much. Bert's neck and throat worse.'

That afternoon Hal wrote a postcard in the train headed 'Nearly at Liverpool 2.15': 'To family in general All right up to the present time. H.B.H.', and that evening sat down in the Campden Hotel to write at greater length:

I reached here about 2.20 p.m. and having picked up with a decent female with two nippers who are going as far as Quebec, we both put our baggage in the booking office and then guided by a shoe black we resorted to the domicilliary edifice of the Company's agent who was waiting for us all on the platform there. We were all to sleep for the night, but happening to ask what sort of accommodation there was, told 2 in a bed and 4 beds in a room. So I and another young fellow, a little older than myself, but inferior in stature, started off to seek new diggings, not relishing having a dozen kids in the same room. So after traversing the town, which is of the two extremes, the one handsome with large public buildings and broad streets – the other slums, with handsome ladies without boots or stockings, no bonnets and a very limited outfit altogether. These ladies mostly carry large baskets on their backs, which smell nearly as bad as themselves.

Well! we soon sloped clear of these beauties, although they were like the sand on the seashore for multitude, and at last got comfortable lodgings at the above address [Campden Hotel] at 1s. 6d. for bed.

The Break-up

I am writing this before going to bed, and the other chap is doing likewise in the other room, within earshot as there is a door leading from one room to the other. We start at 7.30 a.m. tomorrow to the Alexandra Docks, which is nearly half an hour back on our track, for we passed it in coming here this morning. We had rare fun changing our tickets at the office, a whole mob of us went at once, the son of the agent guiding us through the town, which took us nearly an hour. I am booked through to Winnipeg, there I get out to go to the Dominion Colonisation Land Co.'s office as Uncle Arthur told me, and get my £8 and see about my 160 acres of land and also employment. But I must now retire to slumber to be ready for my sea sickness on the morrow. Harry.

CHAPTER SIX

The Emigrants

When I was old enough to hear about Hal's adventures he almost became one in my mind with the fictional heroes of Ballantyne and Henty, except that we sometimes got a letter from him. The events of the past still coloured the present, and I began to be visited by those confusing moments which increased as I got older, when the present seemed already in the past, my sensations a lingering echo of a life already over. The time of my mother's girlhood seemed as remote as anything in the history books, and yet its reality pressed closely on me, in the family memories, in the old books read to me, survivors of the moves from Islington and Leamington; in the party games, such as Family Coach and Postman's Knock, and in the lessons I learnt from Aunt Ada, unchanged since the daily teaching at 22 Somerville Road. When she came to live with us in 1912 the emotional relationship between Ada and my mother was much as it had been in the 1870s and '80s – inwardly rebellious on my mother's side, lovingly anxious and reproving on Ada's; her concern that Day should be well-educated, ladylike, and a dedicated Christian damped my mother's spirits and left her feeling insufficient. In the pleasant, spacious life at St. Mary's Fields, with easy-going Uncle Willie and Aunt Gussie, with nine-year-old Katie for playmate, gently shepherded and tended by Nurse Emily Kettle, she began to blossom.

Ada missed her dreadfully, and knowing this the grandparents invited her to join Day and Katie for a month's holiday at Raven Hall. On 8 June 1883, two days after Hal's ship had docked at Quebec, Charlie saw her on to the train at

King's Cross. At York she was joined by Day, Katie, and the
maid Sarah. Thirty years later when I was taken to stay at
St. Mary's Fields, Sarah was still there, standing dutifully
against the wall during luncheon, her bones held in position
by the starch of her collar and cuffs and white apron. Thirty-
one years earlier young Rowland had brought Emma, her
engagement ring on her finger, to be bewitched by the wild
beauty of Ravenscar, which in the natural order of things
should one day be their own. Now the Bay of Biscay and nine
thousand miles of ocean lay between them.

'Dreadfully tired,' Ada wrote, 'only fit for bed on reaching
Raven Hall after 11 hours travelling.' It was the eleven miles
in the waggonette from Scarborough railway station to Peak
which took the most endurance. Burrows, the coachman, had
set up a record for the distance. For a bet he had harnessed
two Clydesdales to the carriage and driven to Scarborough
in an hour.

On Sunday 11th Hal reached Ontario. Ada took Sarah and
'the chicks' to the non-denominational chapel half a mile
from the Hall. Another Sarah was buried near the chapel
porch, her tombstone inscribed with words devised by my
great-grandfather:

In Affectionate Remembrance/Sarah Noble/for more than 30
years/an honoured servant at Raven Hall/gentle unselfish &
affectionate/she was beloved by all who knew her/but especially
by those whom she/had faithfully served so long/Humbly trusting
in her Saviour/she died in peace Sept 5th 1875/at the advanced
age of 88 years.

Apart from the newspaper obituaries very little about my
great-grandfather Hammond has come down to me. All I
have are Sarah Noble's epitaph, two tiny fragments from
letters, written in a small, neat, spidery handwriting, less
indicative of the man who had made a small fortune than of
the grandfather my mother remembered, gentle, retiring,
who levelled a part of the Slope Field and built a summer-
house where he could sit and paint water-colours of the view;

who always greeted my mother with 'How's my gal?', and chuckled when she rode the donkey up and down the stone-flagged hallway on wet days.

There were plenty of wet days that June and July. When Mrs. Meade, the housekeeper, took them to find winkles at Robin Hood's Bay they got soaked on the way home. That night, the 14th, Hal slept on the floor of the immigrants' hut at Winnipeg; and on the night of 29–30 June, when he was lying ill in a tent on the prairie, a mighty thunderstorm broke over Raven Hall and raged for hours. My mother never forgot it, or how the family and the servants crowded into one room to keep each other company. Two days later the rain and thunder cleared just in time for an invasion of the Hall by a clergyman and thirty-eight of his parishioners. They all perched themselves on the rocks below the terrace for a group photograph, the Reverend R. Balgarnie cloaked, romantic, with a head like Longfellow's, my mother in a tam-o'-shanter, her hair cut in a fringe, Ada in a self-millinered hat and a kind of ham-frill round her neck. On that day, Tuesday, 3 July, another clergyman was writing from Canada to Somerville Road, breaking the news to Emma that Hal's illness might be fatal. Almost a month was to go by before the letter reached her. Meanwhile Hal's description of his voyage, posted at Quebec, was waiting for Ada to copy and send round to the aunts and uncles and cousins. The bad weather had whipped the Atlantic before it came sweeping over England:

It blew hard ever since we left land, and the ship rolled something fearful, but I kept to my bunk, so it did not effect me much. But on Saturday afternoon a gust of wind caught the ship, and she heeled over, right on her side. Nearly everyone was in his bunk, and I think I told you that only two boards about 3 inches high divided you from your neighbour, and being 5 in a row, we all rolled on top of one another, and I being the last but one came nearly on top of all, and all being muffled in rugs could not get out. Then came the shouts of men, the smashing of glasses and clatter of tins, the rushing of feet and calls for the life boat. And then the ship keels over to the other side, and back they all rolled on top of me, but I had disengaged myself from my rug, and kicked and pushed them all back again. But the ship soon righted and we went on our way.

Sunday brought no change except for the worse, the wind screaming in the rigging sounding like another steamer in the distance, and at about 10 a.m. we heard a fearful hammering on the deck, then a loud report. We thought the pirates were boarding us, for we heard the boatswains whistle, with shouts and tramping of feet. We were nearly all in our bunks because the ship rolled so much. One of us (but not me) went on deck to see what was up, but instead of that he saw something down, for the foresail had shot its bolt ropes and come down with a run, hammering the deck with a large block pulley as the wind blew it about, and the gale was so fierce that in the afternoon when they put it up, it burst and came down again. The sun was shining all day, but that didn't stop the wind from blowing . . . Monday passed in like manner. Tuesday was fine, wind abated a bit and the sun shone warmer. Got up at 4.30 a.m., quite light, and had the first wash since I had been aboard, salt water in a tank. The soap would not lather and it was as much as you could do to get clean. Then read on deck and felt awfully hungry about 7 a.m. so eat a dry loaf, but was not satisfied, so my mates and I got round the baker to make us a pie. He wanted 1/6d at first, but we beat him down to a tanner each. My mate fetched it at 12.30, and we got in our bunks which are side by side and eat it. It was rhubarb, but it all went down and we felt a thirst, but the water is so vile. Hardly anyone can drink it, it is filtered since it is sea water, and it tastes like drains. So we got around the steward for a bottle of ginger ale for which he charged us another tanner . . . and we mixed it with two bottles of water and had one each. That took off the taste of the vile water.

There had been some excitement with the discovery of five stowaways, four men and a boy, 'miserable creatures . . . like bags of bones, and filthy'; he never knew what became of them. There was a day of fog on Friday, 'it was like steam of a most filthy taste' and 'Once we thought we were aground and there was rare excitement caused by casting the lead.' On Sunday there was 'Church' in the saloon –

everything was crimson velvet and gold, one of the ladies played the grand piano for an organ, and having three clergymen on board we did pretty well. There was an open air meeting in the afternoon, and in the evening another service which I did not go to, not beginning until 8.o when I was asleep, ready dressed for the morning, even to my boots which were too much trouble to take off.

Monday morning was up at 5.o with Mate on the forecastle. At 6.o we first sighted American shores. We gave the hail to those below, who also being in a state of semi-dress soon tumbled up and there was rare excitement as we drew near. I was right up in the bows, and thought I saw steam coming out of the sea. I showed it to some others, and it turned out to be two whales spouting. You may imagine the excitement of everybody. They spouted every few yards, keeping on the surface until we were quite close . . .

We are now close inshore, and houses are just discernible . . . Kept a bright look-out for more whales and to our, or my, delight, instead of whales we passed close by six seals, all swimming about together . . .

Captain says we shall reach Quebec some time tonight, now that the Pilot is aboard, and shall land tomorrow (Wednesday morning). Shall not write again until I can send my address, so goodbye till then. Harry.

Ada had been back from Yorkshire for ten days before the next letter came, taking up the story from the landing at Quebec. A two days' train journey took him, he says, to 'Ontario'. (Did he mean Owen Sound?) He was in great spirits.

Coal is very scarce, so that the engine had to burn wood, and all along the line there are vast piles of chopped wood and the train had to stop at these to take in a supply, so out I got and marched about. Sure enough, it was a treat, and then the engine whistles twice to give notice to those who have got out that she is about to start, whereat there was a rush to get in, but I waited and got on while it was going, sometimes having a near shave of being left behind. Then I sat on the steps, which resemble those of our tramcars, and enjoyed my ride exceedingly. The thing rattled along like everything, and I guess I had to cling tight for fear of being precipitated without much ceremony onto the rails and thus ending my career . . .

My mother (on the left) and Katie with Willie Bates

St. Mary's Fields, Leicester. Willie Bates and who?
The billiard room is on the right.

The day nursery turned into the girls' sitting-room,
St. Mary's Fields

At 'Ontario' they had breakfast at the Queen's Hotel (three exclamation marks): 'Sounds grand, but it was only a long, low log house, very prettily put together, and was very neat inside . . . Had breakfast for 25 c., consisted of rump steak, new bread, butter, various kinds of biscuits, tea, etc.'

To fill in the day he walked with three other boys along a cart-track through the woods to Lake Huron and bathed. Back at 'Ontario' they bought a stock of food at the General Stores to last them on the next stage of the journey, watched men fishing on the quay ('The fish must be numerous, the way they got hauled out') and boarded the lake boat at 9.30 p.m. 'It is the funniest ship I have ever seen. It is almost square, and is a tremendous way out of the water. The bunks are double, we had eight in our cabin, where two would have been almost too many.'

It was a long letter, but by the time he got to this last week of the journey the descriptions became uncharacteristically brief and spiritless. Someone had stolen his watch while he was asleep. At Duluth he got on to a train for Winnipeg. Two men with revolvers robbed one of the passengers of £50. He wandered about the evening streets of Winnipeg feeling out of sorts, and spent the night on the floor of the immigrants' shed. The next morning he bought some biscuits and a stick of maple sugar but felt too giddy to eat and gave them away to a shoeblack. He found the company office, only to be told that the man he wanted to see, a Mr. Gillespie, was at Toronto, not expected back for three weeks. He was advised to go on by train to Qu'Appelle and see the head man there. 'So I returned to the shed. The sun was fearfully hot. I got to the place about 10.0 and could do nothing the rest of the day. My head throbbed dreadfully.'

When he got to Qu'Appelle he found that the office was eighteen miles away up at the fort; a stage coach would be arriving soon for passengers.

The fare $2.50, and 50 c. for box sent afterwards. Began to feel funny, for I had expected to receive the £8 forwarded over, but now everything has to come out of my allowance to Winnipeg. Well, I got up behind on the stage, being the only place left. Had a clergyman beside me (only holds 3 beside the drivers) he asked me several questions about my prospects which I answered and told him that I had only 2 or 3 dollars left, and at present no prospect of getting work. Reached the Fort at noon, when Rev. Mackay took me around to everyone, but no-one had any work till the very last of all. Mr. Wright, a carpenter, was going to begin a house on Monday, and he would take me on for my board and lodging. Mr. Mackay invited me to his camp over the hill . . .

He begins to describe the arrival at the camp, and then half-way through a sentence the letter breaks off. With it was a second letter, in a different handwriting, dated 3 July 1883:

Dear Mrs. Hammond,
I enclose you an unfinished letter written by your son, Harry. I am sorry to tell you he has been unwell, and since his arrival in this place he has contracted a fever, evidently in the emigrant shed in Winnipeg as the doctor thinks. I met him in the stage on the way here from the Qu'Appelle railway station for the first time, and saw at once that he was not very well. There is no hospital here, and very poor accommodation in the way of houses. We have, however, got him into a little room where he has plenty of fresh air. The doctor sees him every day. We have also hired the services of a young man, son of Dr. Balfour, Edinburgh, Scotland, who has had two years medical training, to nurse him.
We do not suppose him in danger, but he is very weak and may not be able to go about for weeks, and may not be able to work for a much longer period.
Please write as soon as possible,
Yours faithfully,
R. Mackay

P.S. Dear Mrs. Hammond, the first part of this was written in Harry's room and read to him. But now I add a few lines in my own tent. Harry is suffering from typhoid fever and is, as I said, very weak. I have appointed a small committee of gentlemen who along with myself take the responsibility of seeing everything done that can be done for him. You know how lingering typhoid is, and with what little confidence one can speak with reference to those suffering under it. Still we have no fear in regard to this. I have only been here a couple of months, and will be leaving for the coast in a few weeks. Any letter addressed to me will be forwarded to me. I do hope you will write to Harry by return of post. Yours, R.M.

P.S. Should he be much worse, I will let you know.

They wrote off at once, Ada writing to Mr. Mackay while Emma wrote to Hal. It was five weeks before they heard again. At last on 27 August Emma came in at tea-time to find the letter she had been anxiously waiting for, and a second letter came in the evening. The first was short, to say he was convalescent. Three of the four boys who had travelled with him had also contracted typhoid, though not so badly. It was put down to the foul water on board ship. Mr. Mackay had raised a fund to pay for his nursing expenses:

I am now at Smith's Hotel to get strengthened, costs 7 dollars a week, and I have 3 left, not having received the £8 from Uncle Arthur yet . . . I have not received a mangy [letter] or a sound one either from anyone up till now – 5 p.m. on Monday the 6th August 1883 . . . So I guess and calculate that niver another letter you will get till I have received one, now that I have let you know that I have recovered, and only want coin to cover expenses . . .

But he received two with delight the next morning, from his mother and Charlie, and sat down to write at length to all the family about his arrival in Winnipeg and all that had happened afterwards. 'Dears . . .' he began. He asked for photographs of Bessie, Percy, Edith, 'as I have everyone else, and calculate I want all the family'. He described the immigrants' shed at Winnipeg, and went on:

I did not feel at all well, but went out about the town. It is very large, every place built of wood, dreadful roads, single horse trams running along the main street of very funny shape, with rails like the trains. The vehicles are all light spring buggies, owing to the state of the roads, and planks are laid down for passengers to cross over, and there is sometimes a drop of over 6 inches from the road, over which the light carriages or buggies jump, and they are built so light and springy that the occupants get nearly chucked out . . .

The train to Qu'Appelle

was *swaggers*, crimson velvet and polished brass, like gold, a grand ice-water can in one corner, a large stove in a perforated sort of cupboard in another, w.c. in another and in the other another stove. Brass lamps hung from the ceiling, and the walls and ceilings were decorated with Chinese pictures. Axes, saws, and large hammers were arranged at intervals along the walls. I suppose in case of accident to hew a way out . . .

We reached Qu'Appelle exactly at 10 to 12 midnight after having been running over endless prairie with seldom a tree or a shanty in sight. I still felt giddy, and not seeing my box put out I asked the conductor if he had seen it. I told him what it was like, and then he said jump in and see if this is it, before the train starts. The car was high and had no steps, but I got on the pile of luggage with which the platform was strewn and somehow found myself in the luggage car. My box was marked 'Regina' a large town further down. I compared checks, and just then the train started slowly. I scrambled out on the top of the boxes. Anyhow I got my box shoved out by the conductor, all confusion, for there was no room on the platform and it was grated against the steps of the carriages as they passed, while I used frantic but vain efforts to put it further on, but was detained by the other luggage behind . . .

Then he tells again the story of his providential meeting with Mr. Mackay, of the long walk to the tent and his first meeting with a Red Indian. Mr. Mackay had gone off to fetch fresh water when a wild-looking Indian galloped up, dismounted, and lay down by the stove. Hal thought it advisable to pick up a hatchet and chop wood for the fire. But the Indian, Mr. Mackay said when he came back with the drinking water, was 'quiet enough'. He tried to sell them his pony, but after drinking three large bowls of tea he rode off, contented with a present of biscuits, a packet of tea, and a can of tongue.

The next week was a nightmare for Hal. He started to work for Mr. Wright the carpenter, but on two of the days he felt so ill he had to give up.

Saturday 23rd June I worked but could eat nothing. Sunday I remember, or portion of it, too ill to eat anything, but after that I remember nothing . . . One night the doctor has told me since I have got well, he thought he should have had the burial service read over me; he said he never left me for five hours, but after that I have mended wonderfully quickly . . . I am now convalescent and expecting many letters, I remain, xxxx Harry.

Ten days later he could walk three miles a day and was thinking of getting work. Five hundred Indians of the Assimboia, Bear, or Blackfoot tribes, had taken up winter quarters about a mile down the valley. He watched a 'Buffalo Dance' and sent home a drawing he made of it. It arrived for Emma's fifty-sixth birthday and gave her, Ada says, great pleasure, though the letter which came with it disturbed her night's rest.

The Chief's name is 'Pegriod', and it is reported that he has said that he will slay every white man in the valley if they can't get enough food. For they live entirely on what their chances get them. They never have more than one meal a day, then they 'gorge' and sleep over it. So every one has his gun and pistols handy. We have two hanging up ready in case required.

He got work at first in the Post Office and Stores, and then on a farm, 'as head cook and bottle washer for myself and Boss, or as the English say "Guv'nor", for we two are the only humans on the farm'.

27th September, 1883

The Boss has gone to the Fort to attend to business and I am left alone . . . Far as the eye can reach, which is over 5 or 6 miles, you can only see one shanty, in which dwells another solitary human by himself, and who is now backturning and ploughing, so seeing a speck moving on his ground, I determined to go over to him, if only for company's sake . . . Just as I was crossing the ploughfield, a large retriever dog jumped up at my throat. I put my hand in front to knock him off, and he seized the two middle fingers of my right hand, biting through one nail, and tearing a piece of flesh nearly an inch long from the other. Mr. Fraser (that's the solitary human's name) came in time to rescue me from further maltreatment. It was not his dog, but he said it had been about there for two or three days. The place bled profusely, and Mr. F. bound it up for me.

Charlie, now fourteen, was finding Hal's adventures as absorbing as I was to find them, at the same age, forty-five years later. He wrote asking whether carpentry would be a useful preparation for life in the North-West Territory. He was good with his hands. He had made a photographic camera in the school laboratory, and on prize-giving day at the Technical and Commercial Schools he was awarded the South Kensington certificate for freehand and model drawing, and a prize for 'magnetism and electricity'. Hal, addressing him by one of his two curious nicknames (Skybobbles and Chobblemiss), answered the question in the middle of a letter he was writing to his mother:

. . . respecting Chobblemiss, or Master Charles Edward Bruges Hammond. I think you have picked on the very trade most useful, a carpenter, for all the shanties are of wood, never a brick anywhere, not even in the large towns . . . But he mustn't think that fortunes are made here very easy. For the first year it is seldom anyone makes more than their board. After that they are more used to the ways of living and can get on better. But still the life makes up for the lack of coin, riding, shooting, rowing or skating, there's no end of, and no policemen to stop sliding on the pavement, or game laws, or licences for canoes. Oh no, 'tis free! What more do you want? Nearly everything is done by trading, if you want to borrow a pony, instead of paying some large sum you plough for an hour, or dig up spuds, or something of the kind in return . . .

Bess, Edith, and Lil were at home for a week-end in mid-

October and went with Ada to the harvest festival at All Saints'. The preacher was the Reverend Herman Flecker of Lewisham, whose first child, a boy, was born three weeks later and called James Elroy. When, a long time in the future, I was learning by heart a poem beginning 'I have seen old ships sail like swans asleep', Aunt Ada told me how she had sat with the poet's grandmother on the shore at South-bourne watching the ten-year-old boy build a sand-castle. It was a new thought to me that poets were once children.

When Bess, Edith, and Lil had gone back to their jobs a letter came from Hal which gets a special entry in the diary: 'Oct. 22. Hal's exciting letter about prairie fire arrived. I copied it at once to send to the others.' He and another young man called Jack Cameron, who couldn't get back to his own shanty because of the dense smoke, had fought the fire from noon until an hour before sundown when the wind changed.

Towards night the glare was dreadful. The whole horizon was one red flare. I heard shouts and yells as the fellows at the next shanty about 2 miles north were calling each other, for sound travels a long way and can be heard distinctly for miles. I patrolled round and round till very late, to see that no sparks had caught the stacks or stable, and after I thought the danger was past I went to help Cameron who had now got to his shanty, a new one he is just building. Two minutes later would have been fatal, the chips around were in a blaze, but the fire had past so our united efforts soon put this out.

I then came back, black and scorched from head to foot, all my moustache singed off as clean as a monk's crown. My shirt and pants, all I had got on, were singed and blackened, I was indeed a spectre to look upon; and as yet the Boss is in blissful ignorance of the late danger to his shanty and all he possessed. Guess he ought to say 'Thank'ee' when he comes home . . .

It was just at this time that letters came from Gussie Bates every week or so asking to keep Daisy with them, and by the end of the month my grandmother had capitulated. From now on it was accepted that my mother's home was St.

Mary's Fields. On her twelfth birthday one of her presents was a pair of moccasins from Hal. Charlie still plied him with questions, such as whether arithmetic was used much in Canada. Not much, Hal said; he had done only one small multiplication sum in the six months he had been there, but nevertheless a carpenter needed to have a small idea of figures for measuring timber. What would he have to do when he came out? 'The answer is very simple indeed, WORK, although the work is rather hard, the play is grand to make up for it . . . and I think anyone, even the "Baboon" himself could get on here if he went the right way to work.'

'Baboon' was his nickname for Bert, now nineteen. Hal, seventeen that Christmas, had a faintly affectionate but caustic scorn for his ailing, highly-strung and, according to him, lazy elder brother. He was heavily sarcastic in a letter to his mother in February 1884:

Now respecting this miserable, superannuated, long-faced, bump-necked, crossgrained, lazy Baboon. Send him out by all means. The work will kill him? Twaddle, kill his bumptious grumptious-ness if you like, but nothing worse. Wait till he finds himself in a strange place, with everyone and everything new . . . with no home to go to and no work to step into, no one to advise him and night coming on, very few cents in his pocket and very little sense in his head. You may bet your boots he'd turn over, both his cents and sense pretty sharp or else be left, which he would deserve to be. 'Them's my sentiments' as the old woman said.

He relents a little towards the end, when he says:

And now I enclose an epistle received from the Baboon, to show he ain't so awful bad as he seems. I sent him a stunner back, and if it doesn't knock him down I'm surprised . . . P.S. Please return enclosed valuable letter.

But by the time this letter reached England Bert had already made his own decision about what to do with his future. For the past four months he had been working with Percy at Darlaston. He came home at the beginning of November, and a week later went up to Raven Hall for a long stay, looked after by Mrs. Meade the housekeeper while his grandparents and aunts were at Highbury. Emma hoped the rigorous winter air of the Yorkshire coast would do him good; and although when he came home in the middle of February his neck was no better, he had done some thinking and planning. He went to see his uncle Arthur Marshall about going to Australia, and a week later the passage had been arranged. When Hal wrote on 30 March he knew only that Bert meant to emigrate, not his destination.

I heard from Percy that E.B.H. is going to skip the country, which immediately solved a problem which is this: Uncle Arthur told me, when old enough to take up land (which I am now) to write to him and let him know, and if I would promise to pay him off in the course of say 5 or 6 years, that he would lend me the £100 to start on. I wrote and received no answer, waited and wrote again, thinking maybe that the first had got lost, but I have not yet had time to get the second answer, and don't expect to now, as I am afraid that you are overdoing it, and he sees the more he does the more he may do. Why not have tried some of the others – but there, never mind.

He was beginning to worry about his prospects. His first farm job had come to an end when the boss wanted someone more experienced. He was now with a man called McDonnell.

Mac simply lives on what he can earn out, and keeps me on it too, so if there is no work, such as digging wells, putting up shanties and stables, etc., to get, we have to starve, because the Farm of course is just Prairie; a little is broken but there being such a short time the first year you come up, the summer passes before anything is done, and as there was not an erection here a year and a half ago, you may imagine the state of things. Bread, beans, bacon, day after day, but we don't seem to get tired of it somehow, no vegetables, no milk, no eggs . . . Mac is away as much as possible working out, for that is the only way to earn coin unless you have some small amount to begin with, which he has not. He told me that when the grub played out I must 'git' . . . as he hadn't another cent. We set snares for foxes and wolves, I caught 2 and Mac 1. These we traded at the Fort for food . . . Better days dawned, however. Mac got a well to dig, which set us up for another week or so, and now we are just scratching along barely making both ends meet with enough to tie . . . I wrote to some Land Co. at Winnipeg, offering my services on a surveying party to the Rocky Mountains . . . but as you have to sign articles for 18 months, and as it is a matter of being on foot and travelling every day for that time, and having no coin to buy the clothes necessary for such an expedition, I gave it up and accepted a place from Bill Hayes, close to here, 'one of the Boys' (Boys are the young fellows just starting in business) who said he would take me for my board etc. and 5 dollars a month. Barely enough to supply my clothes, but accepted it as the best I could do under the circumstances.

The winter had subdued his excitement in the adventure. The cold of a chain had stuck to his ungloved hand and torn off the skin; his right foot had been frostbitten; the oxen had bolted, dragging him into a snowdrift:

I saw the oxen trotting on ahead, and myself in a snow-drift nearly to my shoulders. My agony was great, how to get out I knew not, so after vainly endeavouring to wade I pitched or dived. This made it worse. I tried to feel ground with my hands but could not, and at last getting frantic I ripped and tore away until by some little freak of nature I got out. I set off as fast as the deep snow would let me after the oxen, falling down innumerable . . . badgers holes. At last the oxen were blown, so stood still and I caught them.

But one thing that jaunted up his spirits was the clothes he was wearing. The teenager's delight in costume had opportunities which England lacked until the King's Road, Chelsea, provided them in the 1960s.

I now go flaming in buckskin clothes. I have a jacket of moose skin which cost 15 dollars – over £4 English. This I got by working for two or three days on another farm . . . Besides that I got my grub and a splendid half bred's cap of blue and scarlet cloth, awfully thick and very warm. But the jacket's the very dandy . . . It is all made of moose leather with thin stripes inserted like a fringe, this bobs about when you walk, but really looks quite gay . . . Can you imagine this child, clad in leather with bobbing fringe and with bowie knife and gun, likewise with axe, etc.

But he begged for more letters from home and photographs of the family. In acknowledging a picture of my mother he adds: 'I want that photo of our Dear Dad that you promised me before sailing, as I have only an apology for one where he looks a little over half asleep. Likewise one of Charlie, I have none whatsoever of his important self.'

In his letter of 30 March, after mentioning his great feat of killing two rabbits with one shot, he is cheered to have seen a large crane flying north, 'a sign of approaching summer', but a postscript has a hint of disillusion: 'Tell the Baboon not to come out here, to go to Australia.'

Two days before this was written Bert had gone to High-bury Hill to say goodbye to his Hammond grandparents, and the next day Lil went with him to look over the ship. The emigration fever was spreading through the family. It was already in Charlie's mind, as we have seen, and on 8 April Ada writes in her diary: 'Edith home & almost immediately commenced the startling news that she & Lil wished to go to New Zealand.'

On the day that Bert left home – it was Easter Sunday – Hal was sitting down to a letter in rather more cheerful spirits:

Summer is approaching, bare spaces are to be seen in the vast sheet of snow which reaches farther than the eyes can see. And in proportion to the length of days such is my work, so that I have not half the time now that I used to have. The latest news is as follows. More fun with the Indians. There is a store situated about 6 miles west of the Fort, where the Indians and settlers trade. Well, you must know that the Indians have reserves granted them, where they live during the winter, and the Government gives them rations of one meal per day to each man with a small sum of money. This is dealt out once a month, but it happened that these supplies were some days behindhand, and the Indians thinking they were not coming at all, thought that they would take them. So they gathered together 300 warriors and encamped on a hill above this store, where there is a small settlement and a few mounted police. And then the Indians without any warning sent a small party down to sack the place. 'Twas done, and they returned before the settlers could do anything at all, but the officer in charge of the police got all his men together, in all about 40, and went to the Indian camp to get an explanation. But the Chief came out of his Tepee and stuck a bowie knife in the ground, which meant that anyone crossing it would not return alive. So the poor whites had to return, because the Indians were far too numerous for them . . .

But civilisation is fast coming on. We, or rather the folks at the Fort, have now got a resident clergyman, and instead of the old wooden building with casks and planks for seats, as the church is now, an order has been sent to England for the materials for a church and parsonage. Only fancy, and also an Indian industrial school is to be erected, likewise a large mill for which all the boys up here contributed either in wheat or corn . . .

I wish somebody would present me with £100 that I might start. If I had a Pa, or my Ma was worth any money, I would request that portion which falleth unto me. But suppose I must jog on in the hopes of keeping body and soul together till a better time comes.

Bert left England in the three-master *Homesdale* on 12 April 1884. He wrote from Adelaide at the end of June:

Dear Mater
I send off a few words in haste to catch mail to tell of my safe arrival here. Ship arrived here on the 27th inst after only seventy four days' passage, coming from the Cape in twenty days under continuous gales & being under water all the way. A terrific gale was experienced off the Cape which carried away several sails with a lot of the gearing including new iron chains also part of the bulwarks & palisading round the poop. A leak was sprung too low to be got at & the pumps had to be constantly worked. For 48 hours no one tasted of sleep & several bunks were washed away & the water in the cabin was up to our waists as the doors were carried off their hinges & the windows smashed & some of the older sailors of thirty years experience said they had never witnessed a heavier sea . . . I am delighted with the City here the cleanliness of which is extremely pleasing after filthy black

London. I attended the Cathedral twice on Sunday with the Pater & took a stroll in the Botanic gardens which licks anything of the sort in England all to fits as oranges grow wild, as large as your head, & grapes can be bought at *one penny per lb* . . . Shd be pleased to hear of Lil as I parted with her at Queens Rd. Station in such unsettled exuberant agony.

The Pater was the nearest on the quay to meet me & seemed overjoyed at the meeting . . .

He was a lazy letter-writer. It was November before he wrote again, and then all but two pages of the letter was taken up with seven stanzas of doggerel about the voyage. Here are two of them:

> And I lay in my bunk at midnight when
> I was, as I tried to turn,
> In a semi condition of nudity flung
> Into sudden & wild concern
> For my boots & my tin-ware all took wings
> The water can broke from its tethering strings
> And my clothes flew about like fierce wild things
> As I frantically followed astern.
>
> But long since this has the raging flood
> Been at peace as well as my can
> And the salted pork with molasses & cheese
> Have wearied the heart of man
> And there's nothing to do but to sit & to muse
> Over sky blue & sea blue of different hues
> For I've suffered from nothing so much as the blues
> Since the blooming voyage began.

He had gained nearly a stone in weight since he landed. 'I am delighted with the liberty of the Colonies & have no desire for England again yet. . . Wages are two & three times higher than in England with every chance of rising to a sober man.'

When he was writing his first letter, and asking for news of Lil, she and Edith were already at sea on the *Chimborazo*. By the time he came to write his second letter Lil had been married for two months to Robert Staveley, known as Jack, a young man she had met on the boat. 'Our home breaks up,' Charlie wrote in his diary. 'We scatter over the face of the globe.' He was fifteen on 15 February 1885. Six weeks later he, too, was on his way to New Zealand.

CHAPTER SEVEN

Hal

Between May 1883 and June 1884 when Emma said goodbye on the doorstep of her home or at Queen's Road Station, first to Hal, then to Bert and Edith and Lil, she knew what little chance there was of her ever seeing them again. She saw my mother occasionally, two or three times in the year, only to lose her again to Willie and Gussie Bates. Day had come up from Leicester in January 1884 bringing Katie with her and two white Persian kittens in a basket. Bessie was at home to help entertain the children; she and Emma took them to see *Cinderella* at Drury Lane, and with Charlie to a children's party at the Tom Frys'. 'I at home as usual,' Ada wrote in the diary, in the plaintive way she had of feeling out of things, even when she chose to be. Her part in amusing the 'chicks' had been less festive. She had taken them to pay calls, to the tea given for her Bible class girls and to a service at St. Paul's Cathedral. When they had gone she relapsed into illness. As soon as Bessie had seen them off on the train to Leicester she took to lying on a board all day with what she described as neuralgia in the spine.

My mother returned with joy to the life at St. Mary's Fields. I can know how she felt from the memory of my own two visits there during the Great War, the distances of the garden, the amplitude of the rooms and staircase after the pinched quarters at home; one visit shadowed by the shame of breaking a croquet mallet. I went back in the 1930s to look at it again. By then the town had eaten into the surrounding fields. The house was an institution for retarded children and the croquet lawn an asphalt playground. But, like something left behind by the ebb-tide or like Firs at the curtain fall of *The Cherry Orchard*, Stedman was still there. He had been gardener's boy at first; under-gardener in my mother's childhood; head gardener, and married to the cook, in mine; and now seemed to be there by the unbroken habit of sixty years. He pointed out the window of the room where Uncle Willie had died, as gravely as a guide might point to where on the deck of the *Victory* Nelson had fallen. He led me to see the old apple-tree which my mother climbed and hid in while Nurse Kettle searched and called for her in the fading light of the garden. At milking time Day and Katie would go to the home farm and dip their mugs into the pail for a drink of cow-warm milk. There was the old pony, Paul Pry, for my mother to ride on, until he lay down under her and was put out to grass; there were dogs of all sizes and a tortoise called Tommy Dodd; and at the centre of her memories the kind, ebullient Uncle Willie. When I knew him his activity was limited to walking to the end of the drive and back every evening after 'late dinner', but my mother remembered him as a great romper. He organized ghost hunts in the garden after dark, hiding himself in the shrubbery, draped in a sheet. Day and Katie, with visiting cousins, set out to search for him, 'their hearts in their mouths', knowing that suddenly the apparition was going to leap out of the bushes with a blood-curdling shriek. Or, after they had gone to bed, a pillow would come hurtling through the door, a challenge for a pillow-fight which left feathers all over the house for the maids to sweep up in the morning. Aunt Gussie sat at the open door of the drawing-room enjoying the fun.

His lively good nature made for friendly relations with his workmen. When industrial strikes hit Leicester his rubber factory was unaffected. My mother remembered strikers clearing a way for the dogcart when she and Katie were being driven home from school and giving a cheer as they passed. But he was less successful in bringing up his own children, particularly the spoilt and beautiful Altie, 'his lordship' as my mother called him. In February 1884, the week after she and Katie got back from the London visit, he and two other boys vanished from home for eight days; and at the end of the year he was expelled from his school, my mother never knew why.

Long and frequent letters had been arriving from Hal. One came at the end of May. He was working with a yoke of bullocks at harrowing and ploughing from five o'clock in the morning until half past seven at night, for which he was paid five dollars a month, the equivalent then of one pound in English money. There were twenty-five acres of open prairie to be ploughed and forty acres to be fenced. His clothes were now sewn together with string. When a new family arrived in the neighbourhood, bringing the female population up to four, 'two spouses and two spinsters', he got his boss to give him a shave, the first of his life, and spent his first month's wages on a pair of pants. On Easter Sunday (it was Bert's first day at sea) he attended a service at which half the congregation of fourteen were using *Hymns Ancient and Modern* while the other half sang from the *Hymnal Companion*.

The Hymn began all right, but oh, towards the end two would be singing one thing and two another, and each trying to drown the other, until both sets stopped at once, when rather a loud smile took place... Seemed funny church to have fowls come walking in the door and dogs of high and low degree walking about, with ponies and buckboards, saddle horses, ox carts, in which the congregation had arrived, standing around, and to have sundry Indians and cows peering in at the windows . . .

The letter reached Somerville Road in time to be part of a family gathering at Whitsun. Bessie was at home, Percy had come from Darlaston and Day came up from Leicester to say goodbye to Edith and Lil who were getting ready to sail. They all went to church on Whit Sunday, and on Monday Emma took Day to watch the bank holiday crowds go by. In Canada that week-end Hal took up his pen to debate his future.

1st June 1884

My dear Mamma,

I am kind of awakening to the state of affairs I am in, and begin or rather have been thinking for some time past that this rolling stone business is not very profitable, and never will be, for I have no home of my own, no coin, for as soon as I can earn the exceeding small amount I am now getting it goes on absolute necessities. When I tell you I go about without socks, sometimes without boots having only one pair of the latter and none of the first, you may judge I am well off; still I don't want you to trouble, I ask for none, but I can see only three inevitables, and they are these.

The first is for you to decide whether or not you are able to do it, it is to lend me for the space of say 4 years the sum of £100 (this by consulting Uncle). You might get out of your capital, thereby losing the interest thereon for the above-named number of years, and which I should hope to refund to you with the rest, thereby losing nothing but the interest for the 4 years, or as long as you could spare it, say not less than 3 years. For at the end of 3 years the land etc. becomes my own, and if no other way of paying it occurred I could sell out and be no worse off than I am now, but I think that by cattle rearing I could make up both, sum and interest. Pig breeding pays enormously too, being the only meat here used.

I could then take Charlie off your hands, and in due course perhaps offer you and A.L.H. a home. I think this is worth consideration, and I think it possible, but of course it remains with you, or rather perhaps I should say in the *possibility* that you can do it.

The second course open to me is to join the 'Mounted Police'. I should then have a home, food and clothing provided with 25 dollars a month, and at the end of 3 years for which you have to join, you can leave and settle on the police reserves . . . The uniform is red coat with gold buttons, blue riding pants with yellow stripes, large jack boots and spurs, polo cap with gold lace, horse and accoutrements.

The only objection to this is the length of time to join, I think I should feel rather tied but don't know, their business is to keep order amongst the Indians with whom they have constant small rows. I should then receive 900 dollars or £180 and get spliced and live happily ever after. I could also sign myself H. B.

Hammond, M.P. and be thought a member of Parliament . . .

The third course is to pay an Indian half a dollar to accidentally on purpose shoot me.

These are the three inevitables. Read, mark, learn and inwardly digest them, and let's hear your sentiments . . .

Emma sent what little money she could afford out of her rapidly dwindling capital from time to time, which he briefly acknowledged in his next letter: 'Received yours containing the coin, with the usual exuberance, like a drowning rat catching a straw.'

On 24 July, the day that Edith and Lil stopped off at Adelaide on their way to New Zealand, my mother was taken seriously ill at Leicester from swallowing cherry-stones. Ada received an urgent summons to go to her, and travelled down on Bank Holiday, 4 August – a date of dark meaning thirty years later. She found Day 'painfully thin & looking worn out', with a trained nurse at her bedside; but by the middle of the month she could wheel her along the terrace in a Bath chair, and a week later she returned to London. No one met her at the station. Bessie was hardly ever at home, her days crammed with activity. Charlie was at school. My grandmother walked as far as Queen's Road Station, but the day was hot; she was too tired and ill to wait until the train arrived. No one had yet understood how ill she was. She was fretting about Hal. He had written unfailingly, at least once a fortnight, but two months had gone by since his last worried letter, and for the first time he forgot his mother's birthday in September. October was almost over before they heard from him. Ada took the letter with her to read to a tea-party of cousins. The reason for his silence seems to have been that he had found, temporarily, another family. He addresses the letter from Hayward's Post Office, Fort Qu'Appelle:

I was hunting cattle one day, and had ridden far and wide, was wet through and likewise terribly hungry, when I struck this place. The Boss's wife came out, fetched me in, dried me, etc., felt my shirt to see if it was wet, and otherwise was a mother to me. I stayed to supper, and while talking with the Boss agreed to take on with him for the winter as soon as my time was up at the present place. The women seemed very delighted at the prospect of the change, as they are not near any place where they can see new faces.

My time being up I came, and have been here two months tomorrow. There are only two girls on the settlement, Agnes the Boss's niece, and Amy [his sister] . . .

These two sweet nymphs, *this child* had the distinguished honour, not to mention pleasure, of taking to the Fort last Wednesday shopping. And as they had not shopped before in Canada of course I did the honours. We drove down in the buckboard, and then went for a walk all round the Echo Lake. We came to an arm of water about one foot deep, which we had to ford, and I had the pleasure of carrying these damsels over one by one, as I had top boots on . . . We got caught in a snowstorm in returning, and I shared the sweet Amy's shawl, and can boast of being the only boy in the settlement who has been allowed to take the girls out alone, showing what confidence the elders place in me.

Mrs. Nelson, the Boss's wife, is going to make me some flannel shirts in payment for the game I shoot. I keep the family pretty well in prairie fowls and ducks. Rabbits are not much out yet till the winter comes on, then I expect to get plenty as I did last winter . . .

But the idyll came to an abrupt end two weeks later.

I've been and gone and done it, I've fixed myself this trip. I have rushed headlong upon my destiny and joined the M.P.'s.

I told you of the place I had got for the winter where there were women, and how well I got on with them, especially the young one. But with the old man it was different. He was mean and this caused several petty rows, but last Friday we had a bad one outside Hayward's House. He told me he was going to kick my 'West End' without any provocation, and of course he did not say so in such decent terms. I told him he couldn't, that I didn't count him Man enough, that I should leave him next day. Fact was I was kind of mad, I had been chafing at some unfairness for some time, and that finished it. The women knew nothing about

it, and were surprised when I said goodbye. I don't think the
old man thought I should leave for a minute, knowing that I had
nowhere to go, and had no time to make any arrangements. But
he little knew this child. When once I say a thing, I stick to it.
As soon as breakfast was over I took my hat, swung my jacket
over my shoulder, and leaving all my worldly goods in the house
just as they were, I started.

Then commenced the hardest time I have ever spent in my
life, I counted on being able to borrow a pony and thus be able
to look round sharp, but in that I was disappointed. I went to
everyone I knew who had horses, but they were all working, and
at last after having been walking all day and not got any work
or food, I stayed with a man for the night for which I put in 2 or
3 hours work. Next day was Sunday, I started again, walked mile
after mile, struck one or two shanties but with the same result,
until I struck another man who put me up for the night, although
I had to work despite it being Sunday. Then came the thought,
where shall I go next, what shall I do, where am I going, where
are my goods? Why, in the hands of the Philistines, and I an
outcast and a wanderer.

Next day I started again and struck a man who wanted a feller,
he was a Roman Catholic, he had plenty of work but little coin,
he said he would take me on for my board but could only pay me
by the Grace of God. I told him that I had heard of people living
on hope, but that I had found it not very nourishing . . . Well, he
said, I want to send two men off trading with the Indians on the
Peter Trail. I was to have a team of horses and wagon loaded with
flour, bacca, etc. and was to have one out of three dollars I made
in furs. Well things were shaky, they might pay and they might
not, so I decided to see first if I could join the M.P., if not I would
accept that.

He trudged all day back to the fort, stayed the night at the
barracks, and the next morning caught the mail coach to
Troy, twenty miles away. There he caught a midnight train
bound for Regina. The temperature was twenty degrees
below freezing and he was wearing only a shirt and a jacket
with no buttons to it.

I reached Regina at 4.30 a.m. and not thinking it worth paying a dollar for two hours rest, I ran over the line to some Indian tepees camped on the Plain. I entered one with a fire, found an old man, his Squaw, three good looking young squaws and three youngsters. Well, I sat down without saying anything. They all lay just as I found them. I spent the rest of the night, or rather morning, with them, and then got breakfast in the town, as the few wooden buildings are called. I then struck for the Barracks about a mile and a half on the Plain. Well, after fiddling about a bit I was ushered in to the Adjutant, who asked a few questions such as 'How many mothers have you?' and then said that the Doctor was out, but I should have to pass a medical inspection tomorrow and then I should be sworn in . . .

There are only 60 M.P. here now, for 200 have just been sent to Battleford to quell an Indian row. There are 16 prisoners here and they are dressed like harlequins, half black and half yellow. They work in pairs, guarded by an M.P. armed to the teeth. These prisoners are Indians and Halfbreeds, horse stealers and so on.

Well I will write again soon, and tell you of the rest of the swearing in, that is if I pass the Doctor tomorrow, which I don't doubt.

He passed, as he said in his next letter, with flying colours, though he was two months younger than the age for enlistment and half an inch shorter than the requisite height of five feet seven inches. However, the doctor said he would make a special report in his favour, and later that day he was sworn in – 'a very solemn proceeding, before all the big bugs, after which I was called Constable Hammond.' He was very cock-a-hoop about the uniforms, particularly the dress breeches, 'skin tight for *cutting the swell* down town', and painstakingly listed every item of his kit down to the blacking brushes and a steel burnisher. A letter had come from Lil and her husband offering him a job on their sheep farm. 'But that's all up a tree now, for I am booked for five years, that being the shortest time of service now.'

His first spell of duty landed him in trouble.

Owing to the large number of prisoners and the small amount of men, I was ordered on prisoners' escort as soon as my arms were issued to me. I had three prisoners, one of whom was shackled, the other two being only for short sentence were only dressed in prison clothes, half black and half yellow.

These prisoners were under sentence for hard labour, and as there was a large bungalow or barrack room to be painted, I was ordered to keep them hard at work. I was sitting on the stove . . . as cool as possible, with loaded carbine revolver, and issuing orders to these three men, all white and old enough to be my father.

Of course, it was pretty cold, the snow in places being 4 or 5 feet deep already, and away from the stove, although in a room, the prisoners soon got very near freezing. At last one of them asked me if he might come and warm his hands for a minute. Well of course I didn't want to be hard on the poor cuss, so I said yes and let him come. He had hardly reached the stove and started to warm his hands, when the door opened and in walked Captain Fraser. I saluted and ordered the man to go on with his work, which he did. Time passed away and the bugle went to return with the prisoners. I put them in line and soon reached the Guard Room, here I handed over my prisoners and the Corporal of the Guard came up to me and said: 'Constable Hammond, consider yourself under arrest, be in the orderly room at 11 o'clock to-morrow, right about turn, dismiss.'

'Jerusalem,' thinks I when I got outside, 'what's in the wind now?' Well before a quarter of an hour had passed the whole Barracks knew I was under arrest, the fellows in the Guard Room having spread it. The advice I got from all quarters, the pity and the chaff at being put under arrest the first time I had been prisoners' escort, would have filled a large room.

Next day I put on full dress, the shining of boots and buttons, pipe claying, gauntlets, etc. was quite a business, and in due time put in an appearance before the Adjutant. Captain Fraser then came forward and stated that while visiting the escorts yesterday he had caught me with a prisoner close to me as if talking. I was asked what I had to say, and I stated that it was perfectly true. They looked at me as much as to say 'that's pretty cool for a recruit' and then gave me a small warning about desperate prisoners, and dismissed me without further reprimand. The amount of questions as to how much imprisonment, what fine was it and such like from the boys, clearly showed they had thought me in a very critical condition, just for letting a poor cuss warm his hands for something less than a minute.

Regina, the coming capital of the N.W.T. consists of two streets of wooden erections and that's all. I went down town to Church last Sunday in full dress, spurs clanking, gauntlets flashing, buttons gleaming, 'all there'. It was a pretty cool service, and very good singing considering. I shall try and go again next Sunday if I am off duty . . .

In all I am getting on all right. It is the softest job I have struck since I struck the country, and have fully reconciled myself for the 5 years. When Skybobblums, alias Charlie, gets old enough, if nothing else turns up, enlist him and he's off your hands.

Goodbye, I am, Hal.

But it was almost certain now that Charlie would be joining Lil and Jack Staveley on their sheep farm in Auckland. This was his last term at the Technical and Commercial Schools, though he was not yet fifteen. My grandmother and Bessie went with him to the Victoria Baths, Peckham, on prize-giving day, to see Lord Mayor Nottage present him with prizes for drawing and science.

Bessie was as full of energy as Ada was empty of it. The diary can hardly keep up with her activity: Bess singing in the Sankey and Moody choir, reading her essays at the Literary, serving on the Robin Committee, which as far as I can make out provided meals for the poor; 'Bessie off at 6 a.m. walked to the Embankment for 2 services & walked home again, then to Sunday School & to church with Mother in the evening'; Bess to Robin dinner at Deptford, Bess helped at a cabmen's tea at Clapham; a Robin breakfast, a Robin dinner at Southwark; 'after helping at home, Bessie to District Mothers' Meeting, and to the Dinner concert with Charlie in the evening. I was not well enough to go.' Any effort Ada made, such as helping to decorate the church for Christmas, would end with the comment 'Very tired' or 'So tired could scarcely stand'.

It was Emma's last Christmas. Her brother Tom provided coal, wine, and money. There were so many presents that most of 20 December was spent unpacking hampers and boxes, and on Christmas Eve there were eight deliveries by Carter Paterson. Emma was making a brave effort not to give way. Ada only notes that she had a wakeful night and was too unwell on Christmas morning to cook the turkey. Bessie had gone off at eight o'clock in the morning, Ada was at church, and Charlie at Sunday-school. So they dined on cold pork and cold Christmas pudding, and the next morning, while Ada was making shirts for Grandpa Hammond, Bessie cooked the turkey before setting off to a Robin dinner at Greenwich.

On the third day of the new year, 1885, Emma was busy in the house when she had a shivering fit and severe pain in the side. Ada put on a poultice and she recovered a little, though the side was very painful for several days. As soon as she was about again Ada took to her bed with 'neuralgia'. The diary conveys, in the oblique way Ada had, that she felt Bessie should have stayed at home: 'Mother alone most of the day. Bessie at Mrs. Summerfield's. Mother felt very tired & lonely, did all the work.' They were cheered by a letter from Hal, written on 28 December:

Dear Mother, You may perchance have been marvelling exceedingly at not hearing from me at Xmas, but really I forgot all about it until the day before, and as I have had a very stirring time lately this is the first opportunity I have had to write. After all is said and done, here I am at Fort Carlton, fifty miles from Prince Albert . . .

It was a long, hard journey, and every man, he said, had his nose frozen. He describes crossing the Great Salt Plains, passing through Chief Great Bear's reserve, the Indians crowding to see them pass. They reached Fort Carlton, an old Hudson Bay post, on 23 December, his eighteenth birthday. The fort, like Fort Qu'Appelle, was built in a valley. A high palisade surrounded it, flanked at each corner by a tower built of logs. On one side of the single entrance-gate was the guard room, on the other the prison.

The tower and pallisade are covered with bullet holes, for it has stood many a siege by Indians in days gone by. There is a small burial ground just outside, where large stones mark the graves of the old Hudson Bay men who died here . . .

I found when I got here I had been transferred from B to D division and was to stop here until further orders. It was now close to Christmas, so we all put in a little extra and had an enormous BLOW out. In the evening we had fruit and cigars, invited all the officers in and singing and so on until midnight when we turned in after spending a very different Xmas to my last one.

Next night there was to be a dance. Everyone was invited who could come, of course there was no town here and no building outside the Fort, but a few breeds and one or two white men live a few miles in every direction, so they came, especially the breeds who are always found where there is grub. I was on picket this night, and got a glimpse of the goings on. There were about a dozen girls, all breeds save one, but they are as a rule daisies to dance. I and another fellow were on picket 6 hours each. I took last beat so was round from 1 till 7 a.m. and owing to the noise and dancing got no sleep that night. And only got a few hours the night before, so was pretty well worn out, as for three days and two nights I only had about 5 hours sleep, and that added to walking around in the night in a snow storm doing sentry, threw me into a slight fever, which lasted 3 days. But soon got all square again.

The party who followed us from Qu'Appelle were four days late, owing to two men being frozen. One when found in his sleigh was insensible, the other nearly so. Ten minutes more and they would have been frozen to death; this was across the Salt Plains. The barometer at the Mail Station was 65 below zero . . . The two men were left behind to follow two days later in the mail; they spent their Christmas on the prairie with hardtack, pork and snow water. Oh my!

He wrote a fortnight later to say that his Christmas mail had just reached him at Fort Carlton: a letter and a book from his mother, texts from Bessie, a Testament from Ada, letters from Edith and Percy and an almanac from Charlie.

We have organised a 'Kangaroo Court' in our room for the purpose of punishing the evil doers. Everyone in our room is in it, and we vie with the other rooms who can keep the cleanest. Some of the rules are: no spitting on the floor, no gambling, no swearing, everyone to keep his own kit clean, etc. We held a meeting to appoint the officers. After some were chosen the Corporal, who was Chairman, got up and proposed me for the Constable of the Court, and was immediately seconded. He said he thought I was as fitted as anyone for the office, for since he had known me he had seen I would as soon knock a man down as look at him. I then rose, and thanked him exceedingly for the great praise he had given me, and stated that if he used such exceeding rare expressions in Court, I should, on the strength of my new appointment, try my powers on him. There were loud cheers and great laughter, and I passed into office. The punishments are fines, rope-ending, hanging by the wrist for so many seconds to the beams, etc.

Two days before Charlie's fifteenth birthday Bessie went to see Arthur Marshall about getting him to New Zealand, and on Ash Wednesday arrangements were finally made for him to leave on 26 March. Willie and Gussie Bates sent him 'an outfit' from Leicester, and Tom Fry called to inspect it. Bessie went scurrying off to the East India Docks to arrange with a Mr. Grey about a berth on the *Arawa* before going on to the Literary. Emma was busy doing up parcels for Charlie to take to Lil and Jack Staveley. On 17 March: 'Mother collected Charlie's things, then in great pain, and went to bed.' The doctor came the next day and diagnosed the illness as jaundice, as he had two years before. Bessie finished Charlie's packing and a man called Jackson soldered down the case. There was deep snow on the ground, and my grandmother was sad not to go with Charlie to church on his last Sunday. He had just had a letter from Hal, sent belatedly for his birthday, ending with a paragraph which, together with the thought of Charlie's departure, kept her awake at night:

I think this is about all the news except rumours of a war with the halfbreeds next Spring, who are contending for reserves like the Indians have got granted to them, and which the Government

do not seem willing to grant. There has been talk of this for a long
time past and nothing has occurred yet to contradict it. They are
only waiting for the snow to go away. Certainly there is a riding
school and drill twice every day now, which is unusual during the
winter, but still it is only a rumour at present.

On 26 March, the morning Charlie set off, Emma got up
after breakfast to say goodbye. Bessie went with him to
Tilbury to see him aboard the *Arawa*. When they had gone
Emma opened the newspaper and read a report of a rising of
the half-breeds at Fort Carlton.

There had been an earlier rising, fifteen years before, led,
as now, by Louis Riel, in protest against the sale by the
Hudson's Bay Company of the Red River Settlement to
Canada. Colonel Garnet Wolseley (who was to ride in triumph
through Cairo in Emma's letter of 1882 and whose funeral
bell I would hear in 1912) had swiftly suppressed the rebellion
without loss of life. Louis Riel disappeared across the American border. Now he was back. The Indians and the French
half-breeds had been roused by the dominion's immigration
policy and its repeated surveys of the North-West Territory.
They saw the tide of immigrants flowing into the Red River
country, their land passing into the hands of strangers. When
the Hudson's Bay Company had been their master that great
trading association had favoured and protected them because
of their skill as hunters and trappers; but they were of little
concern to a government that raised its revenue by the sale
of state lands to European emigrants. A newspaper cutting
of the time, preserved among Hal's papers, had this to
say:

The Indian in Canada is now probably in a worse plight than in
the States. There he is quietly but promptly killed off. In Canada
. . . he is allowed to live, but by way of getting rid of him, the
buffalo and game on which he subsists are exterminated, and he
is expected to exist on the exhortations of missionaries, eked out
by the sheaves of tracts, with which he is supplied by good
people who are more concerned about the welfare of his soul than
the sustenance of his body . . .

On 28 March the papers reported that ten of the Military Police had been killed and eleven wounded. Two more days of suspense passed for Emma, Ada, and Bessie before they read that it was thought no Englishman had been killed. Emma was also worrying about not hearing from Charlie. Bessie went round to see a Mr. Boddy, to ask if he had heard from his son who was also travelling on the *Arawa*. A letter had just reached him, and in it the son explained that Charlie was too seasick to write.

Easter came and went, and a letter arrived from Hal written before the rising, on 17 March:

. . . a Roman Catholic halfbreed Priest, from the Duck Lake Mission 15 miles South of here, came tearing in on a bare-backed pony, in fearful excitement, and was taken over to the Officers' quarters by the Sergeant Major. We knew something was going to happen, so rumours circulated in consequence. Presently the Priest came back into the Square and kept walking round in terrible anxiety, saying 'God forbid that it should happen' over and over again. So one of the fellows who sometimes goes to the Mission and knew the Priest, asked him what was wrong. And it was then all round the Barracks that the Breeds were only waiting reinforcements from Frog Lake to break out, and he had come to give us warning, and to try and stop it before it went any further.

After evening stables a Council of War was held in the Mess Room. Everybody, staff men, Officers and all attended, and each man was told where to fall in, in case of alarm . . . After having told us our places, they doubled the Guard, and warned every man to sleep in his clothes, ready to turn out at a moment's notice . . . [Three days later] a reinforcement of 20 men . . . and one commissioned officer Captain Howe arrived in answer of the telegram sent from Duck Lake to Battleford. Then there was more excitement for the Fort could hardly hold them all, the pinching and screwing to find quarters took up all the rest of the day. They brought a piece of artillery with them, and gun drill has been the order of the day ever since.

I am now doing my Guard, and writing this in the Guard-room . . . During the day we do sentry go *inside* the Fort, at night *outside* the Palisades, walking about around the Fort in the cold through deep snow, and in pitch dark with the knowledge that the Breeds are in arms, and a turn out expected every minute, makes you look twice at a corner before turning it, and shooting into every bush before passing it, but my Guard will soon be over now, and I am still alive. My turn will come in less than a week though. I have just received your letter, including Daisy's to whom I will write.

On 15 April Bessie travelled up to Cornhill to try to get news of Hal, without success. It was the day when the *Arawa* came in sight of Cape Town; Charlie, recovered from his seasickness, sat on deck drawing a picture of the coastline. The Charles Frys had invited Emma to stay with them for a week to keep her from worrying. While she was there she went to see Grandpa Hammond who was ill at Highbury, had tea with the Marshalls, attended a choral concert which her two nieces were singing in, and on St. George's Day helped to get the children ready for a 'Living Waxworks', followed by a big supper party. She had done too much, and returned home the next day more fragile than when she had left. The anxiety about Hal continued. There was a rumour that Fort Carlton had been destroyed and Battleford surrounded by half-breeds.

On 16 May 1885, when news reached London that Louis Riel had been captured by three scouts and taken to General Middleton's camp, Charlie was being met at Wellington by Lil. The *Arawa* had made a record run of thirty-eight days to reach Hobart, but three days out from Plymouth the ship's cook was found to have smallpox. This meant there could be no going ashore at Cape Town or Hobart, and before sailing on to Wellington the passengers and crew spent ten days on the quarantine island off Port Chalmers. It was no hardship. To Charlie the island was as near to paradise as anywhere he had been; scarcely visited, luxuriant with strange foliage, bright with unfamiliar birds, as though the world had been newly created for him. It surpassed, he said, his wildest expectations. He wandered buoyantly through the forest, fished from the rocks and searched for oysters, and at night sat by a wood fire under the stars, listening to the crew telling their travellers' tales. When the quarantine time was at an end they were taken into a long room filled with sulphur fumes before going ashore at Port Chalmers. 'There was one sad note in the glorious harmony,' Charlie adds. 'It was a solitary grave in the little cemetery. I thought long afterwards of the poor fellow, who had travelled thousands of miles from his home, and had reached the promised land, only to die on this lonely island.'

The land seemed promising to Charlie for only a few more hours. He had been looking forward all through the voyage to life on Lil's sheep-run, dreaming, he said, of green hills, flocks of fat sheep, wild fruit, and ponies to ride. When Lil met him on the wharf at Wellington she told him that the sheep-run had been given up; she and Jack Staveley were living in a house at Pollhill Gully, Micheltown. He drew a picture in his illustrated diary of his gesture of consternation as he heard the news, with the caption: 'It was the greatest disappointment I had ever had.' By the end of June he was working as office-boy for Heaton and Miller, shipping agents in Wellington.

In London, while Charlie was recovering from the set-back to his hopes, Day and Katie came to Somerville Road on a visit which also ended unhappily. It began pleasantly enough. On the day they arrived, 22 May, Ada was taken quite out of herself by a present from Grandma Hammond (Bessie was also given one) of a white dress; but that night she was kept awake by a woman screaming in one of the nearby houses, filling the darkness with terror. Then followed a week of peace, the last comparatively untroubled days for a long time to come; seven days of paying calls, shopping with Emma, church-goings, a children's tea-party which was spoiled for Ada by a severe headache. Whitsun Bank Holiday was pouring wet. Day and Katie amused themselves by dressing-up in shawls and scarves and bits and pieces from the dressing-up box. On other days, while they did their needlework, Ada read to them from a book called *The*

Old-fashioned Girl. On the 29th Bessie took them to Highbury Hill to call on the grandparents. Grandpa Hammond was failing, but alert as ever to the progress of the Scarborough–Whitby railway, now only six weeks away from the official opening. But he knew that all his loving improvements to the Ravenscar estate would be in the hands of strangers after he died. Two years before he had written to his son Frank in New Zealand: 'Your idea of the Hall becoming an Hotel I expect will be carried out some day as many say it wd pay well.'

One more day passed calmly at Somerville Road. Ada took the children to a Scripture Union meeting in the choir vestry. And then at four o'clock in the morning of the last day of the month, sleeping in her mother's room during the children's stay, she was awakened by Emma crying out in great pain. It was the beginning of the last difficult round of her fight of endurance.

Bessie had taken the children to St. Paul's when the doctor came, and the next day she went with them to the Crystal Palace. Emma, between bouts of pain and sickness, was worrying about Hal, and Ada scribbled a note to the Commissioner of Canada, hoping for news. On 3 June she wrote in her diary: 'I was up nearly all night. Dr. came twice . . . Two injections. Bessie did shopping. The children very good in the garden. Heard that Hal's name had not been mentioned among accidents.'

Hal in the prairie dress of the North-West Mounted Police;
a photograph taken in 1893

My uncle Charlie Hammond in his studio, Australia

CHAPTER EIGHT

Duck Lake to Jubilee

On the day the welcome news came from the Canadian Commissioner, Hal was sitting down to write his second letter since the battle at Duck Lake. The first, describing the battle, arrived at last on 8 June, when Tom Fry was visiting Emma, and they read the letter together. On 25 March 1885, a party of teamsters with a small escort had been sent to bring in some stores belonging to a man who had come to the fort for protection. When they were three or four miles short of Duck Lake, where the stores were housed, they were attacked by Indians. Outnumbered, they withdrew to the fort, where Major Crozier, commander of the northern division, ordered every man to stand to his arms:

I had just been taken off Guard and put on the sick list with chafed legs, but was told that if there was any fighting I must do it. So when fall-in sounded I seized my arms and jumped into the first sleigh . . . There were 96 men all told, 39 volunteers and the rest M.P.'s . . . Well, we had got within about 2 miles of Duck Lake when the advance guard came galloping back, with the Indians and Breeds in close pursuit. We had scarcely time to draw the sleighs up in line when the enemy came within 100 yards. An Indian Chief came forward waving a medicine bag and the Major and interpreter went out for a parley, but this was only a ruse to gain time for his followers to find cover, for which he paid with his life. Joe McKay, the interpreter, shot him with his revolver before retiring on us.

The volunteers extended to some bush on the right. We got behind the sleighs. I was standing between two sleighs when the word to fire was given, the enemy having already started . . . I heard the Major, as it were in a dream, yell to me to seek cover, but did not do so, until a young friendly half-breed who was speaking to me and loading up fell dead at my feet shot through the mouth, and another bullet tore up both sides of the sleigh not a foot from me. This brought me to my senses, and as there was no one near me I threw myself in the snow and crawled to where some of the other fellows were. Men were dropping round me, both killed and wounded, for we were all in a heap in a regular ambush . . . Not an Indian or a breed could be seen but their bullets could be felt as many a poor fellow can testify. I did not get the least rattled, it seemed quite natural to see these men lying around me, and I cracked away whenever I saw a head. I numbered two killed, one mounted Indian fell as I shot at him and another Breed whom I spied about 200 yards crawling round a bush during a pause in the firing fell to my shot, as I was the only one firing at that moment. Instead of being sorry and sick at the ghastly spectacles that surrounded me, at this last shot I was so delighted to think that I had got my work in on two at least of the Red Deer men that I could not care a cent whether I got shot then or not, and popped away without thought any more to cover. During a pause in the firing . . . the order was given to hitch up, for of course the teams were taken to the rear before the firing commenced. Then there was a rush to get the wounded on the sleighs, but the volunteers who had gone into the brush on the right had suffered fearfully . . . Two of the men died of their wounds during the night and they and the one dead M.P. we brought in were buried with Regimental Honours near the Hay Kraal next day. There were 13 killed, and 7 or 8 wounded, and when you read of the Army in the Sudan only losing 11 out of 6,000, you can see what a fearful loss ours was out of so few men.

Carlton . . . is situated all by itself with no settlement near it, so now that the war has reached such a serious climax, the officers held a Council of War, and it was decided to evacuate Fort Carlton and fall back on Prince Albert, quite a large settlement containing both women and children. This was situated about 50 miles across country, and on the banks of the Saskatchewan like Fort Carlton. So two days after the battle, or rather in the middle of the night, the order was given to pack up 50 lbs of our kit, what we wanted most, and be ready to travel by 2 o'clock in the morning. The racket that then ensued is past description, the Hudson Bay folks packed all their furs and valuables, and then gave away everything else.

Talk about an Indian raid, that's nothing to what the scene was; all the officers were behind the counter and the fellows crowded round asking for anything that took their fancy, and it was thrown to them. I got a splendid shirt, a pipe, a large box of cigars, a fur cap, some woollen underclothes, socks, topboots, candies and so on, and the other fellows got things more or less, such as whips, guns, spurs, etc. I could not help thinking of the frailty of human nature. Here were all these men in imminent danger of their lives, getting the most useless things because they don't have to pay for them, and probably might not keep them 5 minutes.

When the sleighs were all loaded, the wounded men carried out and put in the Bobsleighs, the Fort was then set on fire and the march started for Prince Albert . . .

Since writing the above some weeks have passed by, occupied in digging trenches and otherwise fortifying our position in Prince Albert . . . I am now one of the party of men sent to the Hudson Bay crossing, south of Saskatchewan, an escort to some wounded and also the mail. Will try and send this to General Middleton's camp by a scout . . . I sent Daisy a letter at Leicester, with a sketch of my first battle, which I hope she will answer.

When he was writing his second letter, on 3 June, he was still glowing with the excitement of the fight, of seeing the Indians 'tumble off their Kinses' in mid war-cry: 'The first time I heard that yell, at Duck Lake, I wondered what the deuce was up, but as the British cheer came from behind it kind of set me on my base again.' He had been paid five dollars by the editor of the *Prince Albert Times* for a sketch of the battle, though his gift for drawing fell short of the talent his brothers Bert and Charlie were showing.

On 6 June Bessie saw Daisy and Katie on to the train at St. Pancras. On the 11th Dr. Cock, though still insisting that there were no dangerous symptoms, called in a second opinion, a Dr. Carrington, and together they decided that the worst of the danger was over. Indeed, towards the end of July there were slight signs of improvement, enough to encourage thoughts of a holiday. Emma 'ventured', to use one of Ada's favourite words, across the road to sit in a friend's garden, and rooms were taken in a farmhouse at Forest Hill. Day came up from Leicester again to share the holiday and the hoped-for convalescent time. Emma wrote to her sister-in-law Gussie Bates on 30 July:

My very darling Gussie

What can I say in even attempted thanks for your magnificent contribution towards our country change, indeed dearest you are a great deal too good & loving & it makes me feel more cold blooded than ever, not to be able to express all I would fane say to thank my precious sister for so many useful & luxurious articles. We cannot get our room till next week I am sorry to say, so the perishable things that will not possibly keep, we shall have to enjoy during the next few days at home but the money that I should have needed for our daily dinner etc will replace those we use, so it will come to nearly the same thing dearest in the end. I long to thank you separately for everything so lovingly & thoughtfully put together but writing is still difficult to me, as I cannot look long at anything either reading, writing or working, but I shall hope to give you a longer scrawl while at Vine Farm. Daisy looks in splendid condition, but am glad for her sake that we are going a trifle out into the country, as no doubt she would soon lose her good looks here altho' I am thankful to say the weather is much cooler & looking like rain at present. On Sunday the glass in the sun was *161.* & was enough to roast a niggar. I am so pleased to have the little hands & feet to help me a bit, for we have much to do. You have allowed her a nice collection of clothes. Tiny has sorted every thing this morning, so that she should not use anything she will take to the Farm. I do so hope to hear that you are quite strong, do dearest take every possible care of yourself & *rest*. Katie also I hope will much benefit by the sea breezes, this unusually hot weather must have tryed every ones strength. & now with very dearest love & whole heap of thanks, hoping you will have a very pleasant holiday Ever believe me dearest

your loving sis
Emma

They were driven over to Vine Farm on a dull, thundery day in early August. That evening, while Emma and Day did their needlework, Ada read aloud from a book called *Nellie's Memories*; and the next morning Emma got up for breakfast for the first time since the end of May and walked a little in the garden. It was the last day of the brief improvement. From then on the diary is an increasingly despairing account of the progress of the disease. By 25 August even Dr. Cock was gravely saying that nothing further could be done. Day amused herself as best she could, and one evening, when a little friend had come to tea, someone called Mr. Gilsley played the fiddle for the two children to dance to in the farmhouse kitchen. Ada went down for a short time to see them, but Emma was too ill to be left for long. It was three days before her fifty-eighth birthday; she longed to be at home; and on the birthday, 10 September, after five weeks' stay, 'Mother, Daisy and I left Vine Farm and drove very slowly' back to Somerville Road. She went into the little front room for a few moments and then painfully climbed the stairs for the last time.

A letter had come from Hal while they were at the farm, addressed from Woodmountain, North-West Territory:

This is an old M.P. Post abandoned since 1882, but owing to the unsettled state of the country, and the fearful extent of horse thieving, it has been decided to post men all along the Border to stop all armed parties and suspicious persons . . . from crossing from the States. There is not a living white man within a circuit of 100 miles, and the nearest Halfbreeds are at Willow Branch 50 miles distant. There are two Tepees of Indians close to the Fort, with three young squaws and the old folks. The old man is a wonderful hunter and keeps us in antelope when we can't hunt ourselves. One young squaw named Kickuawawa, whom the boys call 'Mrs. Chunky' ('Chunky' being my nickname) does all my washing and mending in great style, beads my moccasins, and has made me two bead rings which of course I wear. These are the only people we ever see, it is just like being buried. We get no money, no mail, and can only send any off when a scout goes into Moose Jaw . . . I was over at the Tepee all the morning for want of better to do, watching the progress of a pair of buckskin pants she is working for me . . .

On the 13th, a Sunday, another letter came from him. Emma had spent a quiet night and enjoyed some bacon for breakfast. In the evening she was better and brighter, reading over Hal's description of a trip to the Cyprus Hills after some Indians, who heard them coming, mounted their cayuses and 'skinned' across the border.

On the return trip the grub played out, and for three days we lived solely on Hard Tack and sleugh water, riding night and day almost. What a Huckleberry picnic . . . My sorrow was great indeed to hear of your illness, don't take such pranks into your head again . . . I might mention in passing that my collection of Bead work is progressing, owing to the exceeding loving attentions of Mrs. Chunky, whose delight it is to paint her face yellow, with red lines and blotches. She made me a splendid knife sheath . . . besides a small pouch for the belt to keep matches in, etc. I would like to send some, for the work is both beautiful and marvellous, but being so far from any Post Office, I am scared to trust them to a scout or others.

The doctor told them Emma's improvement was only temporary, and that night was disturbed, not only by Emma in pain but also by Day whose night-light had gone out. She still feared the dark, as much as when Charlie used to go and sit beside her at the head of the stairs to comfort her. Hal had mentioned his two emigrant brothers in his letter. (Bert was working for an interior decorator in Melbourne.) 'Am pleased to hear that my affectionate brother the Baboon is making use of his talent, instead of burying it in his stomach, like the chap in the fairy tale; and that my junior brother "Skybobbles" alias "Milky" has fallen on his feet likewise.'

But Charlie was still unreconciled to life in New Zealand. In August he had left Wellington and gone to lodge with Edith and her husband (her first cousin) in Auckland. On 1 September he started work in an accountant's office in Queen

Street. But of all the girls Edith was the most difficult to get on with. Charlie drew a picture of her taking him to task and wrote below it: 'Always in trouble. If I'm not doing something I'm doing something else (as paddy would say). Forgot to open bedroom window; left a collar on the bed; did not bath enough; came into house with boots on, etc . . . Taking one thing with another my life is not a happy one (with Edith).' His one thought now was to save enough money to get back to England. He seems not to have known about his mother's illness.

Dr. Cock was still saying on 16 September that he thought Emma a little stronger. She asked Ada to wear the white dress which Grandma Hammond had given her, instead of the grey woollen dress she was wearing; it would have the look of summer on this dark September day. One of the aunts brought a great basket heaped with flowers, and Emma's sister Ellen came to see her, the sister she had taken with her when she paid her first call on the Hammond children on the June day in 1849.

That afternoon she was taken suddenly worse. She begged Ada not to let anyone see her, and prayed constantly for release. Ada broke down, and at night was violently sick, which the doctor told her may have saved her a serious illness. The next day she wrote:

I went down as soon as I could stand at 2 p.m. Mother greeted me with a smile, and said I looked like a little ghost . . . Mother was beautifully calm and quiet, and looked very pretty. I lay on a small bed by her side and she talked constantly of her early days. Also of her wish that I should bring Daisy up that she might become a useful Christian woman.

The last two days, as reported by Ada, are so in the style of one of the books she was so fond of reading aloud, I am tempted to wonder how close her recollection came to the truth.

Sept. 18. Day not up till 10, being very tired. I in Mother's room all day, feeling very tired and weak. Dr. came, said Mother was just the same . . . Mr. Caley [a clergyman friend] came to read and pray. Nettie Hammond & Flo Fry saw Mother. Heard that Grandpa Hammond was weaker. About 6 p.m. Mother was taken worse again . . . got gradually weaker, but she was quite conscious, and her memory was bright and clear. During the night she pointed upward and said distinctly, 'Look! I see Jesus.' And later on she murmured her last words, 'Perfect Peace'.

19. (Saturday).   A strange night. Mrs. Bristow, Bessie and I sat up and watched Mother slowly going Home. Daisy slept upstairs with Lizzie Peake, it being thought better for her not to be present in case there should be any painful scene at the end. But the struggle with death evidently took place on the 16th for after that time Mother had a lovely light on her face and was calm and serene to the end. At 7.15 a.m. Mother breathed her last . . . Daisy spent the day at the Worseldines as she looked ill . . . Dr. came expecting to see Mother still alive. Bessie and I had a fire to take off some of the loneliness.

Day was thirteen, a very young thirteen, and still haunted by her childhood horror of black, when even her own black shoes distressed her. Now, surrounded by the rustling black of relations and friends, the house dark with drawn blinds, and answering letters of sympathy in the little white space allowed between the broad black edges of the writing-paper, she wilted. On the morning after the funeral Tom Fry's wife, Em, sent one of her sons at nine o'clock in the morning to collect Day and take her to the Crystal Palace – 'to cheer her up, *as Em thought*', added Ada disapprovingly. It hurt her, this disrespect for a time of sorrow. On the evening of the funeral day, when Emma's 'little ornaments' were divided according to her written wishes, she felt it was impossible to go on living.

She had put up a fight to keep Day with her, but it was not to be. 'Sept. 30. Bessie finished Day's packing and at 10.30 took her to St. Pancras to return to Leicester. Mother's wish that she should live with me not able to be fulfilled owing to lack of means . . . I felt still more lonely without Day.'

The lack of means was made clear in Emma's last will and testament: '£10 to each of my children and all the remainder of my property to my daughters Ada Louise, Bessie Mary and Emma Marguerite (Day) Hammond in equal parts share and share alike. I appoint Ada sole guardian of my daughter Emma Marguerite Hammond.' Making Ada Daisy's guardian showed Emma's determination to keep her away from Rowland; a precaution soon justified, when he wrote asking for Daisy to be sent out to him in Australia.

Emma's personal estate, apart from the little ornaments and furniture of the house, amounted to £156. 10s. 9d., all that was left of the £8,000 of her wedding dowry. The house itself was a rented one and was given up less than a fortnight after the funeral. On the last evening at Somerville Road Ada and Bessie 'sat over the fire very lonely and forlorn', and the next day found a temporary home with the Tom Frys. Two weeks went by and it was time for another funeral. Grandpa Hammond died, leaving £100 each to Ada and Bessie, and as an afterthought £300 to the disinherited Rowland in Australia.

By the end of November Bessie was working in Hatton Gardens, and on 1 December Ada travelled to Manchester to nurse in a hospital, though she had no nursing qualifications except a few lessons with the St. John's Ambulance. A week of it completely prostrated her. The superintendent told her that she was a good nurse but not strong enough. A lady on the hospital committee, hearing she was 'homeless, nearly penniless, and too ill to work', looked after her for two weeks, until, three days before Christmas, she went into a 'home for ladies'. The diary for 1885 ends with two entries:

Christmas day.   I did not even have a card or letter though some came later in the week. A quiet day, most of it spent lying down.

Dec. 31st.   Out on business and then spent the rest of the day lying down. A sad lonely ending to a sad year. Alone among strangers.

Letters took about fifty days to reach Auckland, so it

would have been a day in early November which Charlie describes under a drawing of himself sitting sorrowfully at his office desk:

One day as I sat alone in the office with a fearful headache from worrying over books, my thoughts drifted back to England and Mother. I wondered how long it would be before I saved enough to return home and make her happy for the rest of her days. How different things had turned out to what I had expected. I was aroused by the postman's knock. A letter for me with a deep black border. It was news of Mother's death. All I seemed to have been living for had gone.

He was no longer living with Edith and Frank Hammond junior. Edith was expecting her first child, and he had gone to lodge with a family called Davis at Mount Eden, free from Edith's mothering and scolding. His uncle, Frank Hammond senior, Rowland's elder brother, also an architect, had a large enough range of children for some of them to be near to Charlie in age. Four of them, Arthur, Bob, Rollie, and Horace, helped him to regain his spirits. 'It took Uncle all his time to keep us boys in order,' he wrote.

Every chance we got we slipped off through the bush down to the bay, where we spent the time swimming, gathering oysters and shell fish, Neakau, Maori potatoes, etc. & cooking them on a log fire, making rafts and having all sorts of fun . . . On Sundays I wandered through the forest . . . It seemed to take me nearer to Heaven than sitting in a stuffy weatherboard structure listening to the same prayers & hymns that I had heard hundreds of times before . . . But my Uncle, who was the local preacher, did not agree with me and I was set down as a very bad boy.

Uncle Frank was well established as a leading member of the community, the architect of many important public buildings in Auckland; some of them still stand. To young Charlie's eyes he was a psalm-singing slave-driver. On Charlie's sixteenth birthday he kept the boys working from early morning until late at night cutting roads through the bush, and when Charlie and Arthur pitched a tent to spend the night under canvas he stood over them and made them clear the scrub round the camp site, though by then they were dead tired. They were even more tired by the morning, as Charlie describes:

We were just comfortably asleep & warm when a sudden and terrific thunderstorm struck the tent & carried it sky high & we were left out in the wide, wide world, so scrambling into our clothes we made tracks for the house through the blinding rain & wind, falling over logs, bumping into trees & groping in the darkness. We arrived at last wet, cold & hungry . . . So ended my 16th birthday.

There were storms of a different kind going on in England. Ada notes in the diary on 8 February: 'Riot in London by Socialists', not an accurate description. Following a meeting in Trafalgar Square a mob of unemployed had smashed windows in Pall Mall and looted shops in Piccadilly and South Audley Street. On Charlie's birthday, the 15th, the industrial unrest had reached Leicester; it may well have been the day when Day and Katie were cheered by the strikers on their way home from school.

Now Charlie struck his own blow for freedom. He left no record of what precisely happened, only a sequence of drawings with the barest captions, which simply tells us that, soon after his birthday, he threw up his job and with a kitbag under his arm and no prospects set off to make his own way. One drawing shows him sitting on Queen Street wharf at midnight, staring into the water 'feeling very sorry for myself'. In another he is sleeping in a forest at two o'clock in the morning. 'Commencing life at the bottom of the tree with the softest stone for a pillow,' he calls it. The following morning he was given some bananas by Darky Joe, the fruit vendor on the wharf, who thought he looked hungry. The next stage of his wanderings is lost to us. I only know that he took a mysterious midnight sail alone in an open boat to Mototapu. By the end of April he was at Helensville (where, twenty years later, his cousin Rollie would be manager of the Kaipara Steamship Company; both he and his brother Horace married Miss Masefields, relatives of the poet). He signed on as cabin boy on the S.S. *Minnie Casey*, and swiftly worked his way up to being purser. One unexplained drawing shows him being tossed on a stormy sea alone in an open boat for four days and three nights; in another he is rowing with a girl called Louie in search of a missing cutter. And there is a drawing which later on he must have considered too naughty, an innocent enough picture, but he hid it from view, sticking across it an ink-sketch by someone else of a week-end shanty. The drawing he decided to censor was of his first visit to the theatre at Kaipara. He shows himself sitting in the front row of a little fit-up theatre with his fingers spread before his face, peeping at a buxom young woman in tights playing the Fairy Queen. Underneath it he had written: 'I didn't like to look (except through my fingers). I thought she had forgotten to finish dressing.'

That summer of 1886 Willie and Gussie Bates took my mother to Llandudno for a month, as they did almost every year. She used to tell me about those holidays when I was little, how they sat on the hillside of Happy Valley listening to the Nigger Minstrels. Their favourite minstrel was called Alan. She and Katie would take him presents of chocolates and flowers for his buttonhole. On Sundays they climbed Great Orme and attended the service at St. Tudno's, or went to the special mission held on the beach by a Mr. Arrowsmith. There was sometimes a lantern service, when the children carried Chinese lanterns up the dark, winding path to St. Tudno's churchyard and sang 'Praise God from whom all blessings flow'.

Blessings were not flowing very freely for Ada. After leaving Manchester she moved restlessly from place to place, looking after two children at Gunnersbury, nursing a bronchitis case at Dulwich, keeping house in Wickham Road while Uncle Tom and his wife were away. The happiest day of her year was a Sunday-school treat at Epsom. By a tragic coincidence Percy's ailing wife, twenty-seven years old, died the day after the anniversary of Emma's death and was buried on the anniversary of her funeral.

On 15 February 1887, Charlie's seventeenth birthday, he joined the crew of the brigantine *Parnell* and sailed to Melbourne with a cargo of timber. On his first evening ashore he went to the Bijou Theatre (burned down in 1934) to see Minnie Palmer in a musical play called *My Sweetheart*. It was an evening he never forgot, no performance ever held for him quite such magic again. Fifty years later he was still playing and singing the songs which the hero and heroine, Tony and Tina, sang that night. When he got back to England in the autumn he taught them to Day, and for the rest of their lives they called each other Tony and Tina.

Next morning he went to find his brother Bert who was working for a man called Mouncey, described on his letterheading as 'Artistic Decorator (late of London and New York)'. Bert called him the Old Duke. There was no one at the studio when Charlie got there except a young man called Reg Robbins. When Bert came in through the door Robbins introduced Charlie as 'Mr. Johnson' and Bert had already started to raise his bowler hat politely before he recognized his brother.

Charlie stayed on in Melbourne for nearly a month, walking with Bert in the Botanic Gardens, visiting the art gallery where Bert studied painting with a Mr. Folingsby, and nearly getting trampled to death in a stampede for seats when he went to the New Princess Theatre to see *Harbour Lights*.

Towards the end of April he was loitering about the quayside when a man came up to him and asked him what ship he was on.

When I told him I was looking for one he seemed pleased and said he had a good one for me. Crews were very hard to find for any ships at that time, American ships in particular having a bad name . . . Captains were paying boarding-masters good prices to find men for their ships, drugging and shanghai-ing being resorted to when men were unwilling to ship of their own free will . . . The man who addressed me was a 'runner' for the notorious lodging house called the All Nations, known to every sailor as The Chausan, though I didn't know it. He lied to me that he was 'going mate of her' – the Boston ship The Great Admiral, bound for Hong Kong – 'a good living ship' and he would look after me. I needed no persuasion. We hired a cab, drove to the city for my sea-chest and on to the lodging-house where the man was employed. I shall never forget the three days I spent there. Here was a mixture of all nations, smoking vile tobacco, drinking and gambling. The next day I was taken aboard the Great Admiral to sign on. She was a full-rigged ship and looked huge to me, although she was only 1,500 tons, but with no ballast in her holds her black wooden walls towered high above the wharf. Some gentlemen sat at the cabin table, and one of them rapidly read the articles; but for all I could hear he might have been reading prayers or our death sentence. I was then handed an advance-note of £1, which the boarding-master took for my three days' board and lodging. On the third day (Saturday) we were taken aboard in boats, some of the drugged men brought to them in wheelbarrows. The ship was now lying at anchor, so no man could escape once he was placed aboard. The boarding-master said he would fetch our kits, but I never saw him again. There was I, bound for a foreign country, with no money, no oilskins, and very little else but what I stood up in . . . At times the bos'n would throw his cap on the deck, jump on it, curse the ship and every man aboard . . . then, a few minutes later, he would be smoking his pipe and cracking jokes with the men.

He might easily have killed me on one occasion, through no fault of mine. We were chipping rust off the bolt heads, 'tween decks with iron hooks. The bos'n called down through the open hatch, 'Port fore brace!' Immediately we jumped up and ran to carry out the order. I happened to be the farthest away from the ladder and was the last to go up. The second mate stopped me, saying it did not want all hands for that, and to go back to work, which I did. The bos'n came to the open hatch a minute later, saw me at work as before, and thought I had disregarded his order. He instantly flew into a rage, wanted to know if I belonged to this something ship, and heaved an iron hook at me to remind me that I did. It sent my cap flying and grazed my scalp. The last

I saw of him was in Hong Kong after a night out. He had knife marks near his heart, and his shirt had a long cut in it. But he was joking . . .

The mate was a typical Yankee slave-driver, and had them all scared for a while. There was no walking when he gave an order, we had to run. But one day we were going 'about ship', and after the yards had been braced some of the men were going to haul over the headsheets. A big German sailor was the last to climb the ladder to the fo'cs'le head. He was walking instead of running, so the mate gave him a kick to hurry him on. The mate followed the sailor up, and when they reached the top the German swung round and hit the mate between the eyes, knocking him down to the deck below, then followed him down and jumped on his chest. The second mate, bos'n and Bosn's mate ran to the mate's assistance, while the men went to help the sailor. Things looked very serious for a while. It was mutiny. But when the captain came up with his rifle the men quietened down again. There was no one badly hurt, and the German, instead of being put in irons, was treated with more respect by the mate for the rest of the voyage. I did not see this little incident, for I was lying badly injured in my bunk a few feet away. I had fallen down the hold in the dark on the previous night, on to the stone ballast below. I had been brought up unconscious, and was suffering great pain in my back and head, and felt as though all the bones in my body had been broken. But I had to turn out with the watch as usual, and although unable to walk or stand, I managed to get about by holding on to everything for support. I did light work for a few days until I could go aloft again.

Through having no oilskins, I probably suffered more than I otherwise might have done. In bad weather I had to go aloft in blinding rain and howling wind in wet clothes. One night I went up with nothing on above the waist and very little below it. A wet and cold singlet clinging to my body was worse than none at all. So I took it off. Old hands, clad in oilskins, sou'-wester and seaboots, asked if I wanted to die; yet I felt no ill-effects. We ordinary seamen had a far harder time than the a.b.'s, because the lighter sails on top, royals and sky-sail, were more often furled or set than the lower ones, and it was always the boys who had to go up to loose or stow them. It seemed a long way from home on that skys'l yard, but I was told that some American ships carried several sails higher than that, called 'star-rakers', 'moon-grazers' and 'heaven-disturbers'.

He reached Hong Kong in time for Queen Victoria's Jubilee on 21 June. In England, Ada, after 'working for some German ladies at Forest Hill', had gone to stay for a few days at Uncle Tom's and went with him and his son Jack to see the bonfires on Hilly Fields. Day and Katie were in Scotland, with Uncle Willie and Aunt Gussie, exploring the Kyles of Bute.

Charlie was now looking out for a ship that was bound for England, and found one in the S.S. *Propontis*. It was a slow voyage. They were held up for six weeks at Manila, unable to load because of the monsoons. It was Sunday, 5 October before they sighted the cliffs of Dover. Charlie made straight for Uncle Tom's, 86 Wickham Road, and broke in on the family at dinner. On the wall of the dining-room hung the portraits of his great-grandparents, Peter and Joanna Fry of Axbridge. Bessie was there, recently engaged to be married, and in the afternoon she took him to Nunhead cemetery to see Emma's grave. The *Propontis* went on to Liverpool where he got his Certificate of Discharge, and where, he writes under a picture of the docks, 'I spent the most miserable time of my life.' After the excitement of reaching England, as he stood among those forbidding warehouses which I came to know so well during the Hitler war, he was suddenly shaken by the knowledge that there was no mother, or family life or home to receive him. But there was St. Mary's Fields. On 19 November, a week after my mother's sixteenth birthday, she was running along the platform of the railway station at Leicester to welcome him. It was the beginning of eighteen months of loving companionship, the Tony and Tina days, remembered all through their lives, and told to me, as a golden legend of youth and happiness.

CHAPTER NINE

Tina and Tony

Mr. and Mrs. Willie Bates of St. Mary's Fields owned two conveyances. There was the stylish carriage drawn by a pair of horses, Moro and Bruce, driven by the coachman West in top hat and buff greatcoat, an irascible man who had been known to lash out with his whip at the driver of any other vehicle which got in his way. In his photograph he looks amiable enough, his broad face framed in a fringe of whiskers. Up beside him, on formal occasions, sat the young under-coachman, ready to nip down to open gates or the carriage door when required; and when West was otherwise occupied he drove Day and Katie to school in the dogcart, a neat, springy affair, in which my mother had come to meet Charlie at the station. Four years had gone by since they were last together. Charlie's sketch-book still glows with the delight of that November day: the drive back through the country-side of the Narborough Road, their heads close in eager talk, in through the lodge gate and up the curving drive to the portico of the house. That evening they sat round the fire in the old day nursery with Katie and Altie, and Charlie distributed the curios collected on his voyages. The room had been turned into the young people's private sitting-room, and because it was a real room, a grown-up room where grown-ups never or seldom came, it was also a magic room, at least I thought so when I inherited it for a day or two nearly thirty years later. In 1915 nothing had changed, only that it was rarely visited except by the servants with their dusters. It was neither too large nor too small. On rainy days it was intimate and comforting, with its carpeted floor and armchairs at the fireside, one a rocking chair. On fine days there was the glass door leading on to a little balcony to give light and air. I remember a small round table with a flowered plush tablecloth reaching to the floor, and on it a wooden musical box. I set it going. It played a tinkling echo of those winter evenings at the end of the Golden Jubilee year. I opened the lid of the upright piano and fingered out a tune. The sketch-book has a picture of Katie at the keyboard, Day playing her violin – she told me that Charlie could play it after a few days better than she could, for all her lessons and practising – and Charlie in the rocking-chair smoking his pipe and dreaming of his travels. On one such evening he taught Day the songs Tony and Tina had sung in *My Sweetheart*, picking them out on the ivory notes, turned yellow and out of tune by the time I reawakened them.

Although my mother was sixteen that November, and Charlie would be eighteen in February, there was none of the confusion or chafing of growing up, or none they remembered, only delight, high spirits and well-being. New Year's Day 1888 came like the sun rising over Eden.

But for Hal, in Canada, the day was anything but cheerful. For the past six months he had been in camp near Wild Horse Creek, British Columbia. He had been posted there with a body of Mounted Police to quell a rising among the Indians. The trouble had started after the arrest of two Indians for the murder of two white miners at Dead Man's Gulch. But, since the posting, there had been almost no activity, only mountain fever raging in the camp and a succession of military funerals. Hal had been keeping a diary since October.

Sunday, Jan. 1st, 1888. Dull day – no work going on outside – snow a foot and a half deep – everything quiet as the grave – not a soul moving about or a dog barking – one of the most depressing days I have known – Smythe came over in afternoon – I spent the morning in looking over old letters – both felt the melancholy effect of 'dead nature' – sat by stove and smoked, could not summon up any conversation.

For the past two years he had been looking forward to the end of his enlistment time. In his letters to Emma just before she died he wrote:

I have had enough of 8 month winters, and intend to skin into a warmer climate as soon as I am free and have the means.

There is talk of the Government giving the men who were in action a half section of land, but I would rather have a medal, if only of tin. I am sure I shall never settle entirely in this country, and the land is not worth much, even supposing you are able to sell it.

He got his medal that spring, almost three years after the Battle of Duck Lake; and when he left the Police he got his grant of land, too. At the end of 1889 he exchanged it for a wad of tobacco and took off to join his brothers in Australia. Before very long it was worth a small fortune.

The new year came in as dismally for Ada as for Hal. She had returned to London from 'a most trying time' in Tunbridge Wells, nursing a mental case, a week before Charlie's unexpected return from China; and on 19 November she and Bessie had taken him to visit the Greenwich Museum before seeing him on to the train to Leicester. She was still struggling to be active and useful in spite of nerves, headaches, and sleepless nights. She had taken lessons from Dr. Cock in bandaging, continued classes with the St. John's Ambulance, and in between nursing jobs had built up a boys' Bible class from six to nineteen attenders. But of New Year's Day 1888 she writes: 'Feeling almost too weak and ill to do anything, but kept about till Jan. 22nd when I broke down from physical exhaustion.'

Early in January she wrote anxiously to Tom Fry about her father's efforts to get Day sent out to him in Australia, efforts which had begun soon after Emma's death. On the 15th Tom had answered from his place of business (listed as Antimony Refiner), Norway Wharf, 202 Rotherhithe:

Dear Ada, I am sorry to hear that your father has again written to suggest that Daisy should go to Australia but I should hope that her own good sense would make her see the undesirability of so doing, but, if it did not, of course *he* could in no way compel her to go & *you* could restrain her from so doing even if he or any of her friends chose to find the money for the passage which I imagine would be most unlikely. You say 'the choice has been left to Daisy'. I scarcely think you can mean by the Bates but presume it has only been put so by your father but even this he has no power to do. By the Deed of Separation dated 28th June 1881 (to which your uncle Charles & I are both parties & should certainly see that it was not broken) your father amongst other things agreed that he would not 'compel your mother to live with him or in anyway interfere with her or her children in her or their way of living or otherwise', and further agreed to respect any Will which she might make & he lay claim to nothing she might leave, consequently he entirely debars himself from in anyway interfering with Daisy's affairs & even if *she* wished to join him *you* by your Mother's Will (which your father agreed to recognize) could prevent her doing so. I suppose you have written to Daisy & shall be glad to hear what she thinks about the matter.

Is Charlie still at Leicester? If so I think it a great mistake. I am quite sure the Bates do not *really* wish him to stop there & I much fear his remaining will spoil Daisy's prospects. He had to trust to his own resource when in New Zealand & he had much better do so here, every day of idle life doubtless makes him feel less inclined for drudgery & the sooner he buckles to the better.

I am very sorry to hear you are feeling so unwell but hope to hear better news – your affectionate uncle Thos H Fry.

He couldn't be expected to know that while Charlie was still at Leicester there would be no thought in Daisy's head of leaving it, though that was hardly likely anyway; life was far too agreeable for her to wish to change it. She had her own horse to ride and rode well, almost as well as Altie and with more daring than Katie. At the first cub hunt of the season there was no mount for Charlie. He had to follow in the saddle of Altie's old tricycle, which, he remarked, had never been schooled over fences. But a horse was soon found for him, and before long he was as adept up on its back as he had been sure-footed aloft in the rigging, and was riding beside Day, Altie, and Katie with the Cunnard, Quorn, and Pytchley. He was quick to master anything he turned his hand to. After a visit to Buffalo Bill's Wild West Show he decided that 'what man has done man can do'. He practised trick-shooting with revolver, shot-gun, and a rifle he had won by beating Altie at billiards, and enthusiastically lassoed the hunters and ponies from his uncle's stables, which was not applauded, except by the young under-gardener Stedman. The sketch-book for 1888 and into the first half of 1889 effervesces with unflagging energy and delight in a nostalgic wonderland: snowfall at Christmas, full moon at harvest, but never a day of rain or boredom. The tough life at sea brought him, on that first night at St. Mary's Fields, to stand in awe beside the width and soft luxury of his bed. There was a kindly, spacious reliability about the place, as I was to sense on my brief visits; even the subtle smell of the carpets and polished furniture was reassuring, and time seemed as calming and deliberate as the clunk of the great clock at the foot of the staircase. Charlie must have felt so too, to judge by the detailed affection of the drawings: the day beginning with family prayers when the domestic staff filed in to take their places against the wall, and God, it was pleasantly assumed, paid due attention; breakfast in the sunny breakfast room, with a grey parrot conversing from its cage, and a penny-farthing bicycle (unexplained) propped against a bookcase. He had Mowbray pork pie and fresh eggs on that first morning, remembered for their superiority over salt horse and 'forty-niners', and after breakfast Day and Katie were driven off to school in the dogcart. The school was kept by a Miss Harrison and her sister Rose. By way of one of the pupils, Ada Garner, they became part of the sequence of events which led to my mother marrying my father.

The Garners were evidently well-to-do. Charlie made a drawing of a grand fancy dress ball given in their house, my mother in the costume of a contadina, Charlie as a sailor. A companion drawing shows a more formal, but equally splendid, evening dress dance at St. Mary's Fields, 23 January

1889, by which time Charlie had been rigged out in tails and white tie. The Garners would certainly have been there. Ada was a great friend of my mother's, about the same age, attractive, lively, impatient of parental control, and her brother Bert Garner was a friend of Altie's. It was evidence of the go-ahead spirit of the young Garners that Bert possessed a safety bicycle, a Starley Rover, introduced only two or three years before this time, even perhaps with up-to-the-minute pneumatic tyres which Dunlop's brought out in 1888, soon to be produced by Uncle Willie's factory. We talked possessively about Bates's Tyres in my youth.

Bert Garner challenged Charlie and Altie, who rode the now outmoded ordinaries or pennyfarthings, to a five-mile bicycle race on the Leicester Track. Bert Garner set a cracking pace at the start; by the time they came to the last lap Altie had begun to leave the rest of the field behind, but then, Charlie recorded, 'I lay my ears back, set my teeth and put on a mighty spurt, overhaul Alt at the home turn and win the principal event of the day.'

There was no English reticence about his enjoyment of his own prowess; winning was simply part of his praise of life, but win or lose the life was good. He played lawn tennis with Day as partner, bowled to her in the cricket-nets put up beside the house, and defeated Altie at billiards. After a heavy fall of snow he sculpted a life-sized snow effigy of Uncle Willie and the Newfoundland dog called Barry. He was misguided enough to join Altie, who seems to have had a cruel streak in him, in setting the dogs after stray cats, to the blowing of horns and shouts of yoicks, tally-ho, and, curiously, for a professed animal-lover, recorded the chase unashamedly in the sketch-book, as he also recorded the practical joke of lodging a bowl of water over the partly open door of the day nursery. Fortunately it was not the poor chambermaid, Louie Denman, who got drenched as planned, but tolerant Uncle Willie.

Besides the Miss Harrisons and Ada Garner I would add to the list of those indirectly responsible for my existence (at least in the form it took) two brothers, Sam and Will Farmer, sons of the Congregational minister. How it was they became friendly with the young people at St. Mary's Fields was never told me. It may have been through Altie – they were about his age or a little older – but it was with Katie and my mother that the friendship ripened. Will Farmer owned a little boat called *Ida* and took them sailing on the canal. Will steered, Charlie played the concertina, and the girls sang; innocent pleasures which not very far in the future helped to change the course of my mother's life.

Early in 1888 Uncle Willie had apprenticed Charlie to a farmer called William Warren, of Westfield House, Arnesby, who taught him the buying and selling of cattle and horses. Warren was a stout, dark-bearded widower, soon to make his children's governess his second wife. Charlie got on well with him, and Warren delighted in Charlie's Buffalo Bill performance, introducing him to friends as 'Professor Hammond' and getting him to give an exhibition of knife-throwing, roping, and trick-shooting. His most spectacular feat, calling for the greatest precision of eye and exquisite co-ordination of hand, was to hang a bottle or glass net-float from the branch of a tree, set it swinging, and then with his back turned to it, the gun rested across his shoulder, barrel rearmost, he would hold up a pocket mirror and fire at the swinging object, splintering it to fragments.

On Primrose Day, one of those minor festivals (Oak-Apple Day is another) which we no longer celebrate, a fête was held in the grounds of Westfield House. When it was dark the young people danced on the lawns to the music of a Leicester band, by the light of a full moon, or wandered, each Jack with his Jill, where the shadows cast by the trees had edges as sharp as an axe. It may be that one of the dancers there was the son of a neighbouring farmer, a young man called Will Payne; at any rate, a day or two later he rode over on a fiery Irish pony to invite Charlie to go rook shooting with him the next evening. They struck up a friendship and before long Charlie had joined him at Hall Farm, Foston, three miles from Arnesby. There he learned dairy farming, and Amos the ploughman taught him to plough a straight furrow with the three horses, Punch and Blossom and Flower.

Charlie and Will Payne were kindred spirits. They hunted together, broke in young horses together, had a 'fearsome' gallop both sitting together on a half-broken mare. 'If I didn't become a nervous wreck,' Charlie wrote, 'it was no fault of my chum Will Payne.' Payne challenged him to lasso him round the neck and pull him off a horse in three tries. 'He beat me in the first two by lying along the pony's neck at the moment of throwing,' but not the third time.

Although, between these exploits, he worked with zest, sheep-shearing, sheep-dipping, harvesting, his adventurous temperament was unlikely to settle to a life of farming. At the moment it was all good fun, and as Uncle Willie was paying for his apprenticeship he had a greater freedom than the farm workers. One morning, when he was chaff-cutting, the Cunnard hounds passed through Hall Farm on their way to Peatling Covert to draw. The chaff-cutting had to wait; he was off to the stables and on to a horse, Blue Roan, and joined the hunt in a great run from Foston to Arnesby. To the sketch he painted of that morning he added a verse by Adam Lindsay Gordon, a poet he was to illustrate in later years, illustrations still on display at Adam Lindsay Gordon's cottage at Ballarat:

> And some for their country and their Queen
> Would fight if the chance they had.
> Good sooth, there's a sorry world, I ween,
> If we all went galloping mad;
> Yet if once we efface the joys of the chase
> From our land and out-root the stud,
> Goodbye to the Anglo-Saxon race;
> Farewell to the Norman blood.

Then as a footnote to this he writes: 'I was told that I was going galloping mad and following in the footsteps of my father.' It could surely only have been Aunt Gussie who said this to him, thinking of her brother Rowland and the trials he brought to dear Emma. But by now Rowland's passion for gambling was on a winning streak; married again, he was buying and selling property in Victoria on the crest of the great land boom.

Things were rather more cheerful, too, for Hal in Canada. At the beginning of August 1888, after a year of the boredom of Wild Horse Creek, his company was moved back to Fort McLeod, where he found enough female companionship to complicate life very pleasantly:

Went to a dance at Bertrand's Ranch, had a glorious time with Charlotte and Marianne (at different times). Got a gold ring from both (at different times). Danced half the evening with Charlotte, had a spoon on ladder in the corner boxed in for stairs . . . Supper table full, got Charlotte and Marianne on the side and rustled for all three of us, started to walk home with them about 4 a.m. . . . dropped Marianne and went on with Charlotte. Had a great time, felt awfully mashed.

A dance at the Spanish Ladies about a week later . . . Mary L. put me on to a cache of whisky in a cord wood pile, got there with both feet, failed to dance. Left early. Went to see Charlotte a few nights later, showed me some smoking caps she was making, gave me a crimson velvet with golden tassel. Still have the ring – all serene. Saw May next night, gave me a silver brooch with rubies to wear in my shirt – this up at Bertrand's Ranch. Had a chew the rag in a dark corner for a lark.

Went several evenings to the McLeod Hotel to see the fair trio – Janine, Sarah and Lizzie. Asked me to take banjo down some evening – I did. Taylor and I arrived after supper, went upstairs to living room, played and sung all evening – window open, could be heard outside. All McLeod turned out as if to a concert, and kept encoring under the window . . .

Met the trio out walking next day, went with them, kept them smiling loudly all the time, went in and stayed an hour or two afterwards. Went to funeral of Vick's baby, rode with Charlotte – saw Janine and Lizzie in a buggie – gave me an awful look – felt beastly, but no getting out of it. Saw Janine and Lizzie in the evening, told them I was making sketches of a halfbreed funeral for paper – swallowed it – all serene again.

Charlie's sketch-book portrays the year as bathed in continual sunshine and moonlight; Ada's diary for 1888 gives a different picture. The middle of June was as cold as winter; snow fell in London in the second week of July, and by the end of the month there had been six weeks of dark, cold, and wet weather. For the first half of the year at least, always tired and ill, she had nothing cheerful to record, except that Day had been confirmed at St. Peter's, Leicester, and Hal had received his medal. She notes, on 9 March, that the ninety-four-year-old German Emperor had died, and in mid-June that his successor, the Emperor Frederick, on whom so many liberal hopes had depended, was also dead. The dark and cold of those weeks was an apt meteorological response to the accession of William II, the Kaiser Bill of my boyhood, if we make of him, as we then did, the scapegoat for the idiocies of Europe. Ten days into his reign, Lil gave birth to a son, my cousin Bob Staveley who, as I shall tell, brightened a day in my life in 1916 before going off to his death in a German prison camp.

In May, Emma's younger sister, Ellen Fry, had dropped dead in Pemberton Road on her way back to Uncle Tom's after having tea with friends. She left Ada a legacy of 'less than £60', which with the money Emma and Grandpa Hammond had left her and a small annuity (£24) from Uncle Tom, increased her income to a little under £35 a year. Tom had suggested to her, eighteen months earlier, that as Daisy was being well taken care of at St. Mary's Fields, she should use at least some of the interest from Daisy's money to help her pay her way; it could bring her in an extra £15 a year. At the time he wrote she was paying 13s. a week for her rooms and he comments: '13/- a week for board only is I think quite enough unless it includes washing and beer.' Some years afterwards Ada wrote firmly across the bottom of the letter: 'I never used any of Daisy's money at any time, it was invested for her until the whole amount was paid over to her when she came of age. ALH.' When that time came Daisy had good reason to be grateful for it. But for the present, as she said when describing these last years at Leicester, she 'went gaily on, never dreaming that all our lovely times were coming to an end'.

Soon after Ellen Fry's death and just before the June weather turned wintry Ada decided to go to Easebourne, near Midhurst, as companion to an elderly lady, Mrs. Arthur H. Marriott, whose husband was a Professor of Music. The move turned out well; she soon became very fond of Mrs. Marriott, referring to her constantly as 'my dear friend', 'my dear old friend', even though she had not, Ada thought, fully understood the need for redemption. However, Ada soon set about curing this deficiency, and by the following March she could triumphantly write in her diary: 'My dear old friend understood the way of salvation.'

For the first time since leaving Somerville Road she had something like a settled home, and as Mrs. Marriott was well thought of in the district Ada found herself privileged to take tea in Lady Egremont's tent at the August Flower Show in Cowdray Park. I remember, during my school-days, how she enjoyed the interchanges of polite society, the calling and receiving calls, the at-homes and tea-parties, which my mother always avoided if she could or approached with trepidation. The new interests at Easebourne and Midhurst, and the companionship of her new friend, evidently quietened her nerves for a while. There was no mention of her health until December, when she was 'far from well' all the month, and on Christmas Day she felt so weak she had to sit through the morning service. It must have puzzled her, if she noticed it, that her body so often stood up to secular pleasures better than to the enjoyment of religious observances. New Year's Eve was cold and foggy but she managed to visit a few poor old people, and by 20 January, in default of any ailment to record, she reminded herself that she had broken down 'this day last year from nervous exhaustion'. It was Bessie, the indomitable one, who was now going through an unhappy time. Charlie Sanders, the man she had been going to marry, suddenly died, and as 1889 came in she travelled up to Nottingham to stay with his mother and clergyman father.

Christmas at St. Mary's Fields, the last English Christmas Charlie was to know, stayed in his memory as the yuletide indefectible. Maybe the weather records for 1888 have no mention of snow (there was none at Midhurst) but for Charlie it lay deep and crisp and even; they drove through it in the carriage to morning service; it lay sparkling on the windowsills when the pudding was carried in, flaming and sprigged with holly; and when the curtains had been drawn, the candles lit and the presents distributed, it surrounded the house with the absolute silence that memories have.

Not long after Charlie's nineteenth birthday in February he got a letter from his brother Bertie, written on the office paper of S. R. Mouncey, Artistic Decorator (late of London and New York). It suggests that Charlie's peculiar nicknames had been given him because he stammered, or had at one time stammered, on the letter B.

Melbourne, 29 Jany 1889

Dear Old Sky bobbles – Chob-b-b-bles

> I stood on my head on the office floor
> And joy was the cause of my act
> I felt as I'd never felt before
> Insanely glad in fact –

& you bet your old boots I was jolly glad to get news of you again after your Chow-chow trip & to hear of your good luck at Leicester. It cost a bob extra postage but never mind old man. It was worth more than, as we used to say, 'forty b-looming bobs' (don't burst in spluttering the B-looming).

Thanks for the photo. Wish it had been yourself in person but I say why the d.v.l. (diving bell) did you think that I left the Old Duke & was *outer work*. Why I have been making my fortune since you left. Look sharp & come out here again & save up all your sugar. I have bought a good block of land for abt £100 right above the sea beach just beyond where us two tracked that day at Brighton beach. It is the best spot round the bay for either good sands for bathing, smooth water for yachting or natural beauty. Come & help me build my shanty & act captain of the yacht & we can do the Robinson Crusoe & Friday tip-top.

He enclosed a water-colour drawing of the shore and Port Phillip Bay at Sandringham, with his plot of land coloured red, and a pencil drawing of the house he would one day build there. The adventurer in Charlie sprang to attention. He decided to make his way to Australia as soon as ever he could. In May he went to London, played a farewell game of lawn tennis with Uncle Tom at The Elms, Blackheath, and took himself off to a sailors' home near the docks. There was evidently a chance of his getting a passage on a sailing-ship called the *Collingwood*, perhaps arranged by his uncle Arthur Marshall, but another opportunity turned up two weeks before the *Collingwood* was due to sail, as he described to my mother:

My dear little Tina,
I darsay you will be pleased to hear how your Tony is getting on so I will tell you. Was not it a caution how I cleared out all in an hours notice. I was in the Sailors' home on Saty Morng & the 2nd Steward of the 'Riverina' came to me & told me he wanted a steward for the Steerage passengers & asked me if I would go. You can bet your life I didn't say 'no thanks' for I knew she were a steamer & the 'Collingwood' were but a blooming old 'wind bag' so I went down to the South West India Docks where she was laying & saw the Chief Steward. I didn't see him till noon & then he engaged me. I am only working my passage I am not getting any wages, well! I went back to the Home packed up settled up & bought a few necessary articles for the voyage & got down to the ship again by tea time. pretty quick work. I went to see Uncle Arthur & he thought me very lucky & has promised to send me a little 'something' out to Melbourne. so I shall be all right. we sailed from London at Midnight. I have 53 passengers to look after. we are now rolling about in the Bay of Biscay. we have a great many Women & Kids aboard & they are 'sh shaving' & 'swimming' & 'heaving up' all day. such a treat & the Kids youping & bellowing all the time. I should like to chuck a few of them overboard & put the women down the forehold for the rest

of the voyage. we could have some peace then. The ship will put in to the Canary Isles for coal so I shall post this from there. How did Alt do about the revolver. I hope you didn't send it before you got my p.c. you must ask him to take it back again as it will come too expensive to send it to me now. but I shall consider it a present all the same as if I had it. I wish you had been able to send it to me at the Home it would have been useful to me if I go farming. but I guess you thought as I was not going for nearly a fortnight there was plenty of time . . . Has Will Payne been down yet to see about the pony . . . Does Will [Will Farmer] come up to play tennis with you often. Remember me kindly to him & Annie & thank Will [Will Payne] again for his testimonial it was a great help to me in getting this ship. I don't think I could have got the ship without it . . .

He reached Melbourne on 6 August and was reunited not only with his brother Bertie but also with the father he last saw when he was thirteen years old, a now quite prosperous Rowland, and met his stepmother, and his half-brother, Page, born only a week or two before Charlie landed. Rowland's property development schemes were centred on Sandringham and Fairfield, now suburbs of Melbourne, and as one of the Fairfield houses was still empty he let Charlie use it for a month while he decided how to employ himself. From there Charlie sent off a letter to his Tina, and on 17 September 1889 my mother wrote him a long letter in reply which, fifty years later, he returned to her with his own comments added in brackets:

My own dear Tony,
It does seem such an age since you went away leaving little Tina all alone with no big brother to come & cheer her up & play to.

I was so pleased to hear about your arrival & Father & Bert meeting you because you won't have felt so lonely as if no one had met you. So Bert is getting on fine is he not? I wish he would paint Tina something very small & send it for Xmas. Will you ask him Tony dear?

Fancy having a little brother I should like to see him, I wonder whether he will be like Father.

Last Saturday was Katie's birthday & we went for a ride in the afternoon. My lord being at Huddersfield (as usual) Katie rode Snowes pony & I had Tommy & a nastier more bad tempered horse you could not have found.

Uncle wanted me to get into the dog-cart but I said I would rather ride as I did not want to give in. But I suffered the consequences as I had strained ribs sore knee (with sticking on) & general stiffness. But I enjoyed it nevertheless as I did not feel afraid. [*My brave little sweetheart that used to stand up to my fast bowling at the nets like a man! Tony.*]

Altie is probably going away the beginning of next month to America & we shall all sing 'Oh won't it be joyful', but we must not count our chickens before they are hatched must we? . . .

You know that young fellow you met in Will's boat Mr. Adams well he thought that you were going to Australia & then coming back to marry me. Was it not an idea to get into his pate? He heard you say to me 'Well I would rather marry you Tina than anybody' & he was surprised when I told him you were my brother. He spent three days at Llandudno with us where we enjoyed ourselves very much although we had wet weather part of the time. We went on two steamers & both times it was rough & only once in a small boat as there were so many accidents & such rough seas the boats were not let out.

I saw Bess the other day for she was staying at the Sanders because Mr. Sanders died suddenly & I went over to her. She was very nice & kind & says she will do all in her power for me to stay here. And Uncle says he will never let me go except by my own wish. Is he not jolly?

I ought really to be at school instead of writing this as it is reopening day but we thought somehow it was nicer at home!

I should dearly love to be with you all fancy having two big brothers to look after & love I expect our new mama takes care of Father & baby so I should not have any chance that way . . .

I will send Papa the next photo I get but so many are wanting one & I have not got *one* farthing left. Poor stumped up Tina. Uncle has got a long bill to pay so penniless Tina will soon be rich again.

We leave the school at Xmas & then I don't know where we are going but when I do know I shall write & tell you as I expect it will be right away somewhere to finish us & where we shall jabber French from morning to night . . .

I am going to put a few lines in to Father but I wish you would tell him why I don't write it is not because I don't want to because I *do* but I may not & even these few lines will have to come unknown to Ada & the others. [*He was never any good to any of us. Selfish to the end.*] ... Teacups [Emily Kettle] is writing so you will have quite a budget. Visher cat [Katie] sends her love & says that as we are both writing she will do so next time ... I do hope you will get on all right & mind you write as often as you can & with lots of love & kisses I am your own loving

Tina
All the servants wish to be kindly remembered.

On the day she wrote this letter Bert and Charlie were balanced on scaffolding painting, in delicate colours and gold leaf, the elaborately plastered ceiling of a mansion in Studley Park Road, Kew, Victoria. Charlie's plan had been to get hold of a parcel of land in Queensland and farm it, but after three weeks in the company of his brother, during which they inspected Bert's plot at Sandringham and thought of one day living happily there together, painting pictures, boating, bathing, fishing, he decided 'to follow art', and as a first step joined Bert at Mouncey's studio.

In early December Hal turned up in Melbourne from Canada, his five years with the Mounties over, and by chance on that same week-end Edith, with her little daughter Jessie, was there too. Edith and her husband had left New Zealand after the Rotorua earthquake, and had just come to live a hundred miles west of Melbourne. This family reunion was celebrated by a trip to the Bay View Hotel at Ferntree Gully, Bert driving Edith and Jessie in a pony and trap, Charlie and Hal on horseback. The old joke was played of introducing Hal to Edith as 'Mr. Johnson'. According to Charlie Hal's identity remained a secret until they were all sitting in the Bay View Hotel, when Edith ventured to remark that Mr. Johnson had something of the look of her brother in Canada. Before they parted she invited them all to spend Christmas at her home in Hamilton.

My parents at the time of
their engagement

The Harris brothers. From left to right,
Herbert, Charley, Walter.

Tina and Tony

My mother wrote Charlie a Christmas letter, full of prattle about washing her hair, breaking a fan, the school dance and how Miss Harrison, the headmistress, said that Charlie was *too* bad to go away and leave them in the lurch. She was beginning to attract the young men in the neighbourhood, but took no serious notice of it:

I wonder how the painting is progressing. I can paint fairly well in sepia now & soon am going to colours. Will [Farmer] painted me such a lovely little picture for my birthday & framed it especially so that when I am a little 'Mrs' I may remember my old friends. As if I should ever forget them. I don't think it very likely do you? I had a gold ring with a single diamond in it, such a pretty one & I had numerous other things, among them a splendid gold brooch from Green that young fellow that was in the boat with us that day. Uncle teazed me like anything because I could not at first find out who it was . . . I daresay by the time this reaches you Hal will have joined you & you will be a right merry trio, don't I wish I could make up the quartette thats all . . . I am going to try & squeeze in time to write to Hal but I really feel as if I could go on writing nonsense for ever, you are such a nice Tony. I never have any one to sing 'Now Tina my darling don't you get cross', it is awfully dry to lose ones sweetheart. Nobody nurses me (because I won't let them) now & says I have got cast-iron legs. Well mind you all have a happy Xmas, give my best wishes to all & wish everyone a very merry Xmas from the baby far away in England . . . Ever your own loving little Tina.

It is hard to believe, reading these letters, that she was now a young woman of eighteen.

CHAPTER TEN

The Other Charlie

1890 is the first year in my mother's life, the only year in her girlhood, to have passed without leaving a trace of what was happening to her. She had left school after passing the College of Preceptors examination, so much we know; but nothing, apparently, was done about 'finishing' her education as she expected in her letter to Charlie. It remains a mystery year, a hiatus before the commotion of what was to follow. In other years certainly, and in this year presumably, there had been evenings in London to hear concerts at the Queen's Hall, to see the Christy Minstrels, or Maskeleyne and Cook, the conjurors, though none of the playgoing she best remembered falls within 1890: Henry Irving and Ellen Terry in *Faust*, for instance, or Charles Wyndham in *David Garrick*, or her particular idol, the handsome young Hayden Coffin singing 'Queen of my Heart' in *Dorothy*. She would often sing it to me when I was small, very quietly, as though it were more memory than song, drawn up, it seemed to me, from such a legendary distance that when in 1929 I opened a theatre programme and found Hayden Coffin's name in the cast list, playing Bumper in *The School for Scandal*, I felt that time was falling apart.

This was by far the happiest year for Ada since Emma's last illness. It came in with weather so warm that she enjoyed using cold water, and before the end of January the spring flowers were all in bloom. In April Bessie came to stay with her for a fortnight, and in May she went to watch the sports at Midhurst Grammar School when her old friend Mrs. Marriott presented the prizes. She welcomed in June with

the cheerful diary entry: 'Heard that one of my dear girls
L.T.J. knew the blessedness of sins forgiven', and during
July friends took her for pleasant country drives, to Fern-
hurst, Haslemere, Heyshott, and Selham. It was in this
month, and the weeks following, that an event took place in
Argentina, then the centre of world speculation, which later
on affected the lives of Bert and Charlie and fairly capsized
my mother and father: a financial crash that sent shockwaves
round the world (Barings of London failed in November) and
within two years was to reach Australia where the rush to
invest in real estate, which Rowland was busily exploiting,
had forced up prices far beyond any real value. But this was
not an item of news likely to reach Ada's diary. Instead, she
tells us that Uncle Tom's wife had borne a sixth boy, that
Edie's baby son Norman was dangerously ill with diphtheria,
and that Altie had married. Here at last we can know what
my mother was doing on one day of the year. She was certainly at the wedding, and in after years described the bride
to me, a little, pretty rosebud called Cissie, who wilted under
Altie's egotism, separated from him, and died young.

The rest of the year went by as equably for Ada as the
earlier months. On 10 September she noted Emma's birthday and wrote: '5 years ago Day & I took her home from
the farm at Forest Hill.' On 3 October a letter came from
Bess telling of her engagement to Sidney Bridger, a good-
looking widower with a trim reddish beard and three
small children. In November, after recording that Day was
nineteen, Ada writes: 'Servant ill. Had no less than 4 helpers
in 24 hours, as only the last could stay.' And on 22 December:
'Ice so thick people could skate in the road.' 'The year ended
in the greatest cold & frost I ever remember.'

This is all I can glean of 1890 in England, but of Bert,
Charlie, and Hal in Australia there is information in plenty.
In January Hal had found work with a land agent called J. R.
Morton, one of the many agencies which had mushroomed
during the land boom, in a small, wooden office beside
Tooronga Station, Malvern Vale. Bert and Charlie decided to

move out of Melbourne, and all three settled into a house in Tooronga, with two acres of rough orchard and a view to the distant Dandenong Ranges. They called it Bachelors' Hall, a timber bungalow standing on stilts, hardly more than one large room, in which they slept, and ate, and made music, Bert and Charlie on violins, Hal on a banjo. Except in the recess to the right of the fireplace where a life-sized, full-length picture of a woman hung, painted by Bert, the walls were covered with trophies and weapons, bear skins, the skull of a Rocky Mountains sheep, an Indian's scalp, beaded buckskins and moccasins made by 'Mrs. Chunky', and the hide of a buffalo covered one of the improvised beds.

Bert and Charlie were still working for Mouncey, helping to decorate Government House for Lord Hopetoun, and the mansion of Sir Simon Fraser, grandfather of Malcolm Fraser, the present (1978) Prime Minister of Australia. They were also branching out on their own. Charlie constructed a front-sliding shutter, before focal plane shutters were invented, and, together with Bert, took the first instantaneous photographs of horse-races ever made in Melbourne, of the Victorian Racing Clubs Derby in 1890, the Caulfield Cup, and the Melbourne Stakes. Bert had already made something of a reputation for himself as a horse painter. According to Charlie, two years earlier, at the time Bert bought his plot of land at Sandringham, he had been promised £100 by a Mr. Craig, a racehorse owner, for a picture of his horse if it won the Melbourne Cup. It won; but Mr. Craig promptly dropped dead in the paddock and Bert's hopes with him.

They had two horses of their own at Bachelors' Hall, Baron and Sunshine, on which Bert and Charlie had decorous trotting races. Bert's temperament was cautious, even apprehensive. It was Charlie and Hal who went for wild gallops, dressed in Canadian buckskins, playing what Charlie called 'Indian and Possum', trying to lasso each other, and who sat at the breakfast table shooting with their revolvers at the fearsome spiders which crawled up the walls, to improve their marksmanship. But Bert did take part in one astonishing episode. The girls of Tooronga, curious to know more of the three eccentric characters who had come to live among them, decided to invade Bachelors' Hall and give them a surprise party. The brothers got wind of the visit, lay on their stomachs underneath the house, shot-guns at the ready, and when the girls arrived peppered the ground in front of their feet. The girls turned and ran for their lives, 'a much surprised party', as Charlie said.

Two days after Ada had described in her diary how the people of Midhurst were skating on the ice of the roads, Hal's twenty-fourth birthday on 23 December was celebrated during a camping holiday with his brothers. They had hired a wagon, loaded it with provisions, cameras, guns, and hammocks, and with Baron between the shafts and Charlie riding Sunshine, set off towards the mountains. Their destination was Fernshaw, which was as much as to say they were making for paradise, a place of steep hills, fern gullies, cascading water, and a forest of gums, blackwood, mountain ash, myrtle, sassafras, and wattle. The Mathinna Falls watered the roots of blanket bush, Christmas bush, corranderrk, coral, shutter, star, fisherman's net, fairy and maiden hair, and treeferns uncountable, their trunks covered in mosses and lichens, cryptogamia and staghorn, their branches webbed with clematis and sarsaparilla. Hal shattered the peace a little by shooting at parrots, and he and Charlie amused themselves by shaking Bert's vulnerable nerves with practical jokes; as when Hal, having found a dead snake, pretended it was alive and attacked it with a stick. Bert was greatly alarmed, even when Hal announced that it was killed, standing astride it like David over the fallen Goliath. 'Do be careful,' Bert said anxiously. 'It won't die until sundown!' He got wrought up, too, begging them to take care, when Charlie harnessed Sunshine to drag a tree-trunk out of the way. The horse bucked and reared and plunged, hurling Hal and Charlie to the ground, and galloped wildly away with the tree-trunk, while Bert, appalled, stood at a safe distance shouting 'But I *told* you to be careful!'

When they set back home, the holiday over, Charlie found
that Sunshine had a fistula on the withers. Bert and Hal were
already ahead in the wagon. Charlie had to ride the thirty-
five miles back to Melbourne, bareback and at a walking pace,
in a cold wind and driving rain, with nothing to eat or drink
from eleven in the morning until nine at night. With wandering steps and slow, the paradise of Fernshaw behind him,
he took his solitary way. It was the end of 1890, and in the
year about to be born my mother was going to find her own
expulsion from her childhood garden, and an unfamiliar
world all before her.

On New Year's Day 1891 Bessie married Sidney Bridger.
They spent a four days' honeymoon at Easebourne before
setting up house at Sidcup. During their stay Ada was
finishing her first venture at authorship, a booklet called
What is Eternal Life? Five hundred copies were printed, but
none has survived to give us her answer to the question.

On 28 January she wrote in her diary: 'Dr. H. called,
having dreamt I wanted him', and then had scratched out
'wanted' and blotchily written 'needed' instead. 'Another
Dr.', she adds, 'did the same years afterwards.' The renewal
of ill-health could possibly have been due to anxiety about
news from Leicester, though there was no hint of trouble
until, on 4 April, she went to stay with Bess and Sidney
Bridger at Sidcup. My mother joined her there three days
later. Together they went to see Emma's grave in New Cross
Cemetery, and to tea with the Tom Frys. On 14 May they
chose, for some reason, to visit the Naval Exhibition. These
weeks in Daisy's company would have seemed delightful to
Ada except for the vague atmosphere of trouble that surrounded them. On 15 May she wrote: 'I took Day to Margaret
St. to join Uncle & Aunt. I slept there. An unpleasant visit.
Felt very worried & anxious.' A week later she went back to
Easebourne, leaving Day with the Bridgers.

The Uncle and Aunt must have been Willie and Gussie
Bates. The crisis, though I have only my mother's side of it,
was a storm in a teacup, or perhaps in Gussie's brandy or

whisky glass, for she had taken, like her brother Rowland ten years before, to a love of the bottle. It was her opinion that my mother was leading Katie astray. She had taken fright at the friendship of the two girls with Will and Sam Farmer, and my mother, in her scribbled memories, makes particular mention of the boating parties when Will taught her to handle the sail and Katie 'flirted quietly in the stern' with Sam. 'Emily Kettle always knew when we went sailing, and sometimes she came too. She really was a brick and no spoil-sport, and she knew we should come to no harm with these friends.'

I was never told what brought matters to a head, if anything did. It may merely have been that Aunt Gussie woke up to the fact that my mother was two years older than Katie, even though young for her age, and held her responsible for Katie's spooning. 'And yet,' my mother wrote, 'I suppose I was the one who had least to say about what we should do or where we should go, for Katie was very self-willed and ruled me with a firm hand.'

The shock of being considered an unsuitable companion for Katie was great. She had thought no more of a quiet flirtation in the stern of the boat than of sitting on Charlie's knee and being told she had cast-iron legs. But, from what she also told me, the Farmer brothers took things more seriously. She was quite sure that Will would have proposed to her. 'If I had married Will Farmer,' she used to say to me when things had got too much for her, 'my life would have been very different.' It set me wondering where, then, should I have been, or not here at all? And as time went on and I began to have some notion of procreation I wondered even more. Would the consciousness of being alive be mine (though a different me) if she had married someone else? Was it only because she had married my father that I was aware of being alive, or would that part of my consciousness which came from her still be, at the moment I was thinking, myself, but a self which was partly Will Farmer? The mystery, even improbability, of selfhood baffled me.

What chiefly worried Ada was that Day now had no real home. She was in exile with the Bridgers, but it was hardly to be expected that she could stay there indefinitely. Bessie would presently be starting her own family to add to the three stepchildren. What was to happen to Day?

Uncle Willie, without the urging of his wife, would never have let things come to this pass. He was anxious to do what he could to ease the dilemma, and the Miss Harrisons provided him with a solution. They had given up the school at Leicester, which they had run, my mother said, with no great success, and had opened a boarding-house for students in Trebovir Road, just round the corner from Earls Court Station. Day's schoolfriend Ada Garner was there, attending the Royal College of Music. It was decided that Day should join her; pocket-money, board, lodging, and college fees to be paid by Uncle Willie; and on 4 August 1891 she presented herself at the pillared front door in Trebovir Road and started, with some fear and trembling, on her new life. She was still adjusting to the turn of events when she wrote to Charlie three months later:

> 20 Trebovir Road
> Earl's Court
> October 26th 1891

My dear Tony,

Are you still in the land of the living? If so have you forgotten the little girl named Tina? You are a bad, bad boy because I am for everlasting thinking of you & yet you are too lazy to spare so much as a thought for me. Heaps have happened since you went, in fact I feel almost dazed life seems so strange. You will see by the above address that I am living at London where I am studying music & painting. I have been here three months so have got another 9 to get through to the best of my ability. I dont have a bad time of it on the whole especially as Ada Garner is in the same house. Then there are two other jolly girls & at present four Germans & an Englishman. Taking the life altogether it might be a great deal worse. I ride with Ada once a week & fine times we have too, then whenever we can we go to a theatre.

Just before I came here Altie's dear little son died only three months old. He was a lovely little chap & we were all passionately fond of him as he was not one of your screaming kids. I dont think Alt minded much though he was very proud of his boy, but poor little Ciss has not recovered yet from the blow.

How are you progressing? I can get no news of you anyhow & I am always being besieged with questions. I heard from Will Farmer this morning & he says 'Do you ever hear from Charlie now? I hope he is doing well – please let me know all about him in your next letter . . .' He said some more but I dont wish to make you vain. Now you see if you dont write how can I let him know, therefore when you get this, dont put it straight in your pocket & think no more about it but get some paper & ink & sit straight down & write to me for the sake of the old 'Tina & Tony days' . . .

Much more had happened in those three months than she let her brother know.

When Charlie answered the letter he, too, had changing circumstances to write about. One June night, while my mother was still lodging, unhappy and bewildered, with the Bridgers at Sidcup, Bert and Charlie walked out of Bachelors' Hall with a hurricane lantern to light their way to a distant corner of the garden, where they could discuss their future out of Hal's hearing. A new moon lay on its side over the fruit trees. They sat close together in the yellow circle cast by the lantern and plotted what they should do, like a pair of conspirators. When they went back to the house they had decided to leave Hal at Bachelors' Hall and rent a studio in Melbourne, to take themselves seriously as artists. It may well be that they found Hal incompatible. If his old vein of sarcasm towards the Baboon still lingered, Bert probably resented it from a younger brother, whereas Charlie had a deep affection for him and after his death dedicated the sketch-books to his memory.

They managed to find a big studio in Melbourne, splendid for their purpose, though all their savings must have been spent on acquiring it; at any rate Charlie suggests as much in his story of the shilling dropped in Sturt Street, Ballarat. He and Bert, with other of Mr. Mouncey's assistants, had been decorating the interior of Ballarat Cathedral. That finished, they were all put to painting the railings outside. 'My mind', Charlie writes, 'was on a water-colour painting of a racehorse which I had started but was completely stuck for want of a shilling cake of cobalt, and not a penny with which to buy it. While worrying as to how I could get one, a coin was dropped behind me by a passer-by. Two minutes later I was prompted to turn and look and there lay a shilling. Why was it dropped behind me?'

He had been inclined to believe in guardian angels ever since his lonely wanderings in New Zealand after his sixteenth birthday. While exploring the upper reaches of the Kaihu River in an old rowing boat he had climbed out on to a floating tree-trunk. The boat was carried away by the current and he was left standing on the Kauri log in mid-stream. Swimming was something he had never learned to do, and by now the boat was some distance away. But as though the spirit of the river had taken pity on his quandary it swung round, strangely piloted, and returned upstream, nudging beside the log while Charlie clambered thankfully back.

The shilling dropped in Sturt Street was the beginning of quite prosperous days until what they earned by their painting and photography was enough to keep them in simple comfort without having to work for Mouncey. Charlie, after a few lessons from a German sculptor called Kretchmar, began to model horses and portraits in clay, and became so obsessed that if he woke in the night he had to get up and go back to his modelling. Life was full of hope, and music, and vigorous exercise, as he described to my mother when he sent her a photograph of the studio long after it had become a place of memory:

On the left is a Singer safety bicycle on which we did our trick riding (the first imported into Australia). The bust on the pedestal is the one I knocked over in the dark and scared Bert (one of my own casting). The photos on the left wall are the first instantaneous ones of jumping horses in Melbn. At the end of the studio on the left was our bedroom and on the right the dining-room.

The dark-room was behind the figure in the foreground (the wall of which I crashed through on the bicycle). The swing and trapeze is shown in the centre, also the hammock and cross bar for high jumping & hurdling (these were all detachable). I regret the bucking horse is not shown here. The horns over dining-room are the same as shown in the view of Bachelors' Hall. My violin, zither, concertina & accordion are seen on the right. Our saddles, guns &c are at the end of left wall. The picture of a white horse on end wall is Bert on his horse 'Baron'. The floor space was 60 ft x 30 ft. The decanter on table is the one the burglars drank our health from after plundering the studio.

Bert made four pencil drawings of life in the studio, one showing Charlie crashing through the wall into the dark-room during a bicycle tent-pegging contest; and in another Charlie and a pretty girl are standing swinging together on the trapeze while a second girl careers round the studio on roller-skates. It was the carefree life Bert had promised for them when he wrote enticing Charlie away from Leicester, and lasted until the catastrophic year 1893, a year which also saw the climax of the events which Tina had omitted from her letter to Tony.

She had been astonished when she found that four young men were staying at the boarding-house. It added a twinge of anxiety to her sense of already being in disgrace, being sure, as she was, that Uncle Willie and Aunt Gussie knew nothing of it.

The four Germans were over for the German Exhibition at Earls Court which after a mismanaged opening ceremony in May drew huge crowds until it closed in October. Two other girls, Pat and Mabel, were students, with Ada Garner, at the Royal College of Music. At dinner on the first evening my mother's place at table was beside one of the Germans, a fat young man called Rohleder who made up for his lack of English by a generous amount of ogling. She took an instant dislike to him, all the more because he had clearly taken a fancy to her. When dinner was over, and the men had gone off to the Exhibition, the girls told her to be sure to lock her door when she went to bed because Rohleder was not to be trusted. The bedroom she had been given was not on the third floor with the other girls but on the second, where the men slept. Rohleder let no grass grow under his feet. That night my mother woke to hear the door handle being turned, the door being gently shaken, and the creak of floorboards as he tiptoed away. It was as though she had been pushed across a border into an alien land and she cried herself to sleep.

Next morning, prompted by the other girls, she asked to be allowed to sleep on the third floor, without saying why, and she was put to share a double bed with Ada Garner. It was a sizeable room; Pat and Mabel used to join them there for midnight feasts which, by lowering cake and fruit on the end of a cord, they shared with the two Germans who slept in the room below. The men sent back supplies of chocolates and cigarettes. What sleepless, anxious nights Ada would have spent at Easebourne, if she had known the unholy life Day was leading. The girls smoked their cigarettes at the open bedroom window under cover of the dark, careful to keep the smoke out of the room. A woman who lived opposite reported what she had seen to Miss Harrison. They were lectured for being unladylike; but supervision was light under Miss Harrison's rule. They were allowed to stay out in the evenings until eleven o'clock; and Ada Garner found a young doctor who was willing to certify that they were unwell whenever they wanted a day away from college. Once a week she and my mother took lessons from a handsome riding-master with the handsome name of St. George, sometimes formally in the riding school, sometimes rough-riding over Wormwood Scrubs. A few of the more daring young women took to riding man-fashion, and my mother tried it within the walls of the school, but out on the public highway always modestly rode side-saddle. The riding trousers they wore under their skirts were convenient for playing leap-frog in the bedroom at night. A daytime amusement, 'one of our chief delights', my mother called it, was to walk round St.

Paul's churchyard to buy penny toys, as great a variety as they could find, and to give them away to poor children in the streets. And there was the German Exhibition, the vast Teutonic wonderland set up to outdo the American, Italian, and French exhibitions of the three preceding years, built round a colossal statue of Germania. They often went there, to stare at the reproductions of famous buildings in Berlin, Potsdam, Nuremberg, and Heidelberg, or the castle of Wartburg, where Luther was sheltered, set up on the grassy slope behind the main area where Charlie had seen Buffalo Bill's Indian encampment two years before. They had dutifully gazed at the furniture, pottery, silver, and glass, the hunting trophies sent by Prince Frederick Leopold of Prussia, the Schleswig-Holstein farmhouse, and the gallery of German Emperors. They had glanced once, and once only, at the display of weapons and snares provided by the Duke of Saxe-Coburg and Gotha, and steadfastly refused the invitations of the German lodgers to join them at the beer tables, 'not caring', my mother said, 'for their type of entertainment'. What they did care for, and what became the chief attraction of their visits, was the switchback railway careering between panoramic views of the cities and country-side of Germany.

Ada Garner was in London for much the same reason that brought my mother there. Her parents objected to her friend-ship with a young commercial traveller called Phillip, resident in Leicester. But commercial travellers travel. So it was, that one Saturday in September, when my mother was lying down with a bad headache, Ada pleaded with her to get off the bed and accompany her to the Exhibition. She had made an arrangement to meet Phillip there, but Miss Harrison refused to let her go to the Exhibition alone. 'Be a sport,' she said, a plea my mother always found hard to resist. She got up and dressed herself in a cool green washing-silk patterned with tiny black daisies, put a cream straw hat on her head and a white wrap round her shoulders. A glance in the looking-glass told her she was looking very nice indeed.

Can You Find Me

It was a glorious September evening. Her headache soon vanished in the open air, but she was not looking forward to playing gooseberry and, besides, had guilty qualms about helping a clandestine rendezvous. As they were crossing the Exhibition grounds Ada suddenly grasped her arm. 'There he is,' she said. 'But he's got someone with him. You will have to take him off our hands.' A few more paces and my mother was meeting my father.

He was of those uncertain inches called middle height; short or less than tall according to who was beside him, but sufficiently spare to look well-proportioned. His hair was dark brown, and so were his eyes, the left eye having the trace of a cast, which added, my mother told me, to the attraction of his good looks. They were good, sympathetic eyes, a little brooding and vulnerable until he smiled, but the smile was so complete, so real, she returned it readily. He was just twenty-three. At first she found herself not quite approving of his slight Kentish accent, but it was soon forgotten as they talked and wandered through the Exhibition, meeting from time to time with Ada and Phillip and parting again. What did he tell her about himself, I wonder, on that first evening together? Not, certainly, that his wife had died four months before.

The evening ended with the four of them swooping through the air on the switchback railway. When the time came to part he refused to say goodnight to my mother until she promised to meet him the next day, Sunday, and go with him to evensong at St. Paul's. She promised and they said good night. His name, and how brotherly it sounded, was Charlie. Or to avoid confusion, to spell it as his young brother Walter spelt it in letters that survive, Charley.

Rohleder, the amorous German, was still in pursuit of my mother. Finding himself alone with her one day he dropped on to his fat knees and mustered enough English to propose to her. Before she had time to shape a suitable dignified refusal she heard Pat, Mabel, and Ada Garner stifling giggles outside the partly open door. Already off-balance and nervous she broke into helpless giggles, too. The poor little man was deeply hurt and refused to pass her the salt that night at dinner. By this time the other two Germans were both in love with Pat. Except when threatening to kill each other they were hardly on speaking terms. My mother was glad to get out of the house to spend some evenings each week with Charley Harris, though she was uneasy about what was happening to her (it was about now that she wrote in her letter to Tony: 'I feel almost dazed life seems so strange') and perplexed by his changing moods. Sometimes he would be quiet and depressed, shadowed, maybe, by his lack of means and dead-end job as a builder's clerk, and conscious that Day belonged to a different world from his own. At other times, caught up in his love for her, boisterously cheerful.

Aunt Gussie's agitation had calmed sufficiently for Day to go back to St. Mary's Fields for the Christmas holidays. She went with a troubled mind, knowing how little she had worked at her music, anxious about what the college report would be, and in a confusion of feelings about Charley Harris. She had given him Ada Garner's address, another discomfort on her conscience. A few days after Christmas, when the canal was frozen hard for two miles, she met Ada in the town and was given a letter from him. He asked if he might come down to Leicester to see her. She knew, after the fuss over Will Farmer, that Charley would be even less acceptable at St. Mary's Fields. But Ada Garner, well practised in deception, saw no difficulty. My mother could stay with her for a day or two, and she could meet Charley without anyone being the wiser.

They met in a snowstorm and he asked her to marry him. She had never been so attracted to anyone before, she was sure of that; had never been in love before, if that was what she was. Her thoughts and feelings were whirling like the flakes of snow. Then he told her about his previous marriage and she felt as though he had hit her. That at least was the version she committed to paper, though she had told me at one time that she didn't know of the marriage until after her engagement, too late to draw back. In the written version, which I think is the true one, she goes on to say that he tried to lessen the shock by telling her it had not been a love match, just a boy and girl affair; they had been 'rather unhappy'. She found her affection augmented by pity, and was left uncertain which of the two was the stronger. How long they paced the tow-path of the frozen canal is unrecorded, only that when Charley went back to his hotel and Day to the Garners she had promised to give him an answer before he left the next day.

She hardly slept that night. Her feelings, as she remembered them when she was old, had little to do with passion; they centred on the fact that here was someone who needed her, someone who had been unhappy, to whom she could give happiness, someone lacking worldly goods whom she could take care of and cook for, though she had never attempted to cook anything in her life; someone who attracted her very much indeed. The next day she promised to marry him if he could get the permission of Uncle Willie and her sister Ada.

When she had first got back from London for the holidays she had told Emily ('Teacups') Kettle about the men lodgers at Trebovir Road, and Miss Kettle had felt she must mention it to Willie and Gussie Bates. Gussie's anxieties returned. They were greatly increased when the letter arrived from Charley asking for a blessing on his engagement to Day. Gussie was appalled; even dear Uncle Willie was shaken and concerned. There must be no returning to Trebovir Road. A letter flew off to Bessie and Sidney Bridger asking for Day to be put back into their care. There was talk of making her a ward in Chancery until she came of age.

The outcry only made my mother stick to her guns, 'otherwise', she told me, 'things might have turned out differently'. With a little sympathetic calm she might have considered the unwisdom of what she was doing. Though easily led, she could be pigheaded when crossed. The emerging woman in her wanted to be married, the child in her was unsure, but the child's reaction to opposition played the woman's game.

So, surprisingly, did Ada, which says a great deal for my father's charm, and no doubt for his understanding of the need for redemption. On 27 February 1892, two days before her 'real' birthday (it was leap year), Ada enters in the diary: 'C.H. came to see me. Gave my consent to his engagement with Day.'

CHAPTER ELEVEN

'*Little Mrs.*'

Day found life at Sidcup irksome and depressing after the freedom of Trebovir Road. Bess was pregnant; her first child, Harrold, with a double r, would be born late in July. The three stepchildren, in Day's exasperated opinion based on total ignorance of living with children, were 'perfect horrors'. At Somerville Road she had been the treasured baby of the family, helping, if at all, for the fun of pretending to be useful; at St. Mary's Fields she was waited on hand and foot. The probably quite reasonable amount of work Bess expected from her made her feel like a household drudge. It was a breaking-in to the kind of life which, in the way she imagined taking care of someone, she had looked forward to; and she hated it.

Three days a week she went up to London for music lessons and met Charley Harris afterwards, for the short time between his workday and her return to Sidcup. Getting to know more of one another was limited to talking across the table in a tea-shop. He was living uncomfortably in dismal rooms in Stoke Newington, at a long remove from Sidcup, and this at least could be improved on. Day searched and found him pleasant digs in a house called Hope Cottage (the very name of it was cheering) only a street or two away from the Bridgers. For them, who held the contrary hope that the whole affair would blow over, the move was unwelcome. When Day had first come to them they had made a rule, or Sidney Bridger had, taking his responsibility for a young sister-in-law very seriously, that she must always be back indoors by 9 p.m. As Charley seldom got back to

Hope Cottage much before eight o'clock, when his supper was ready for him, they were hardly better off than when they had met in the tea-shop. One evening Day was late getting back and found the front door locked against her. Sidney from an upstairs window called down to her that the house was shut up for the night; she must look for shelter elsewhere, a curious way of guarding her virtue. Highly indignant she went back to Hope Cottage where the sympathetic landlady made up a bed for Charley on a sofa in the living-room, and Day slept between clean sheets in his bed upstairs. Her indignation melted in the novel feeling of sharing a roof with him for a night and having breakfast with him in the morning, but she was determined to leave the Bridgers and at once wrote off to Uncle Willie to tell him so, and why. Bess, I imagine, understood how Day felt; she certainly had no part in locking her out; and Willie Bates was understanding, too. He paid for her to lodge with a family she liked very much, called Boyce. There was a piano in the house, on which Day could practise and play accompaniments to songs for Charley's tenor voice to sing, or duets they could harmonize together. It was like being back in the old day nursery, playing and singing with Tony.

So the spring and summer of 1892 went by, and in August when Charley had his annual fortnight's holiday he took Day down to Gillingham, Kent, to meet his family. He had described them to her as best he could, and hoped, he said, that she would try not to fall in love with his handsome younger brother, Bert. She felt illogically a certain reassurance in the coincidence of the names, Charlie and Bert; if the youngest brother had been called Hal instead of Walter or Wally it would have been complete.

The three boys had been educated at the Mathematical School, Rochester. Walter was about to go to St. Mark's College, Chelsea – now the College of St. Mark and St. John – to study for a teaching career. Charley must have felt some envy. He had a quick, receptive mind, and to judge by his later success with children at Marwood and Bristol would have made an excellent schoolmaster; but a few years at the Mathematical School was as far as his education had gone, otherwise he might have been spared the depressing years as builder's clerk, the humiliation in Australia and failure on his return. It is very likely that in the five years between his own schooling and Walter's the family cash-box had begun to fill. His father, John Harris, from being a shipwright had been promoted to 'writer' or clerk in Her Majesty's Dock-yards, a humorous, kindly man who, though not at all feck-less (like that earlier clerk at the dockyards, John Dickens), would not, by himself, have taken steps to increase their income. It was his wife, Sarah Ann Skinner, who had the instinct for business and profit. Over the years they acquired eleven small properties in Gillingham and Chatham and each Saturday collected the rents; but at the time Charley left school they were probably putting money by to achieve some capital. At any rate, there was to be no college for him, and on 12 August 1890, three weeks after his twenty-second birthday, he married 'according to the Rites and Ceremonies of the Congregationalists' a girl a year older than himself, Clara Jane Jarvis, the daughter of a Chatham tailor. We can fairly suppose that the relationship began in their teens, since he described it to Day as a boy and girl affair; as soon as he left school he got the job of clerk with the builder in Stoke Newington. He was 'of that parish' at the time of the wed-ding, and took Clara Jane to live there, at 16 Kersley Road, where on 4 May the next year she died of peritonitis after a week's illness, four months before he met Day at the German Exhibition.

The visit to Chatham was something of an ordeal for Day; for Charley, too, no doubt; she feeling herself compared with the earlier bride, he wondering what her response would be to the unfamiliar world of Harrises and Skinners. She would never forget the shock of meeting his grandmother; it severely shook her middle-class prejudices. The old woman came out of her door, a shawl round her head, smoking a clay pipe, and said ''Ad to c'm down to the gate to meet Charley's gal.'

Day, though startled, had the presence of mind to kiss her.

In the first half of the nineteenth century, and doubtless for centuries before, the Harrises were bargemen at Salcombe in South Devon. By family tradition, one of them had been jailed for smuggling and released under an amnesty to mark the accession of William IV. It could well have been my great-grandfather James Harris. He was twenty years old in 1830, and not long after the accession he left Salcombe, making his way along the coast to Chatham to work as a shipwright in the dockyards. A daughter, Elizabeth, was born in Chatham in 1840, and a son John (my grandfather) in 1844, though his christening was postponed until a summer trip to Salcombe five years later. After he married he used to take my grandmother to Salcombe on holiday, or at any rate they were there in 1896, when their son Walter joined them and sent off a letter to his future wife, who was also training to be a teacher: 'I arrived at Kingsbridge at 4.45. After a terribly hard pull my people had managed to get there to meet me and after a beautiful sail of an hour we reached Salcombe again. Of course I had to see the majority of my relations that evening.'

Although Day, to use Tom Fry's phrase, had 'spoiled her chances' of being considered a second daughter to Willie and Gussie Bates, they still remained friendly. On 4 November Ada writes in her diary, 'Day back from Leicester having stayed there a month.' It was her last taste of the joys of St. Mary's Fields for a long time to come. Charley was left in London to get through the month without her; or was he invited for a week-end, perhaps, to suffer his own ordeal of meeting prospective in-laws? Day would have been less than human if she had not wanted to show off the pleasant places she grew up in. If Katie met him it might account for her burst of envy that Day was becoming a 'little Mrs.' first. She vowed to marry the first man who asked her.

It may be that the expression 'little Mrs.', with its pre-echo of Wendy and the Never-Never Land, was no more than a joke, though it holds a hint that Day had no real idea of what marriage would mean, but drifted towards it in a mixture of misgiving and anticipation as she might have approached and mounted a spirited horse.

They were married in the little church of Footscray, in the countryside where recently built Sidcup ended, on 8 July 1893, two days after the wedding of the Duke of York, later George V, and Princess Mary of Teck. In old age, on a sudden impulse or in some now unfathomable mood, she destroyed the wedding photographs. A few details remain printed on my mind's eye, but not nearly enough. Day in her wedding veil, Charley elegant in morning suit, a romantic, handsome pair; two of the bridesmaids sitting on the ground in front of the group, not recognizable as members of either family; and most vividly of all, as though the photograph were in front of me, Charley's mother, 'Nana' as I came to know her, looking very attractive and self-contained (as she always was) in a slipper-bonnet tied with a wide bow under the chin. The rest has vanished from memory, though I used to look at the photograph often enough. Scarcely anyone from Day's family was there. Bess surely was, though expecting her second child, my cousin Noeline, to be born on Christmas Day. Sidney Bridger gave the bride away and signed the register. Ada, whose dear old friend Mrs. Marriott had died the summer before, was at Southbourne. The entry in her diary on that day, after mentioning the wedding, adds: 'Made the acquaintance of Mrs. Flecker Senr.' It could even have been the day when she sat watching the grandson James Elroy playing on the sands.

8 July was hot and thundery. The bridal pair travelled to Llandudno for a fortnight's honeymoon, arriving late in the evening. Willie and Gussie Bates were there, too. They had made their gesture of disapproval by not attending the wedding; now they were prepared to be friendly, and ordered a delectable supper, with flowers on the table and champagne, to be ready for Charley and Day at the end of their journey. In my middle or late teens my mother made one of her very rare and unled-up-to references to sexual matters: 'Your

father was very gentle with me on the first night of the honeymoon.'

The break with the past was gentle, too, for here were Uncle and Aunt, and all the sights and sounds of her girlhood holidays, the minstrels in Happy Valley, the climbing path to St. Tudno's Church, perhaps even an ageing Mr. Arrowsmith conducting his mission on the beach. They had their photograph taken at the Rock Studio, a *carte de visite* by Laroche, photographer to the Queen. It shows them nested among rocks, Charley standing, his right hand resting on a boulder, Day seated, her left hand clenched on her lap to display the wedding-ring. Apart from the ring, and the wide silk tie patterned with Japanese cherry blossom, she might almost be the little girl who was photographed in the Reverend Balgarnie's group perched, ten years before, on the rocks at Raven Hall, tam-o'-shanter, fringe and all.

The honeymoon over, they set up house at 2 Ruthin Terrace, Westcombe Park, near Greenwich Park, a house more substantial than their means, double-fronted, with a dignified flight of steps leading to Corinthian columns supporting a Norman arch and a door panelled with coloured glass. Ada stayed with them for a short time in October; Charley's parents came to see how Day was looking after their son. The visit was unlikely to have given them much confidence: 'At that time,' she told me, 'I couldn't cook dinners.' Her likeness to Copperfield's child-wife is amplified by her having not one pet dog but three, to judge by a charming picture of her taken by Charley on Blackheath, which shows her holding two dogs on a leash and a third in her arms.

It was a hard winter. The gas pipes froze. Brother-in-law Walter was staying with them. When Day tried to thaw out the pipes with a lighted candle she succeeded only in singeing his jacket. Each Saturday evening, with a party of friends, they danced at the Cannon Street Station Hotel until midnight, when they all went back to one or other of their houses and kept up the fun into the early hours of the morning. Day was pleased with being a little Mrs., but equally pleased, and complimented, when at one of the dances someone thought she was Charley's teenage sister, just as she had been pleased when brother Charlie was thought to be her future husband.

The carefree time was soon over. Charley, anxious perhaps to keep Day in the style she was used to, or as nearly as he could manage, had gone beyond the limit of his resources. When my mother talked to me about her early days the events of her girlhood were clear and precise, but her married life can only uncertainly be pieced together from remarks at random which leave all the facts in doubt. Quite early in the marriage she discovered that Charley was 'in the hands of a moneylender'. At some time, probably before they met, he had played cards for higher stakes than he could afford, and lost. Whenever it was, and whatever sum he owed, the clear sky now had a cloud, and before the end of 1894, when Ada spent Christmas with them, they had left Westcombe Park and were living in Lewisham. Since the death of Mrs. Marriott Ada had been homeless again, wandering from one nursing case to another. She had come down to Lewisham from Somersham in Huntingdonshire and returned there when her fortnight's holiday was over. The diary tells us nothing about the visit except that Christmas Day was dark and hot, gaslight needed and the windows open at breakfast time; and on 2 January 1895 she went with Day to Highbury Hill and saw Grandma Hammond for the last time. She died in mid-March, of influenza, six days before her eighty-seventh birthday. Neither of the sons-in-law, Arthur Marshall and Willie Bates, was prepared to take on Raven Hall, and of the three sons, Frank was in New Zealand, Rowland in Australia, and Harry Julius died in 1897. The Hall was sold and turned into an hotel, as Grandpa Hammond had predicted. Into those rooms, which for exactly fifty years had housed the Hammonds, came a bevy of distinguished guests: the Earl of Cranbrook, the Ladies Emily and Katherine Gathorne-Hardy, the Hon. Emily Kinnaird among them. When I glanced at the hotel's first visitors' book one name leapt out from all the rest: Dr. A. Chillingworth of Bedford.

By the strangeness of chance, there he was in 1896, walking
the terrace where Day had sat at her lessons, and seventeen
years later he would recognize Raven Hall in the faded
photographs which hung in Ada's bedroom. From 1913
through almost all my growing up he was to be our family
doctor. Was it the photographs, I wonder, which touched
him to refuse any payment for his visits? Perhaps not, but
the kindness was fortunate, since our money was scarce and
our ailments plentiful.

By January 1896 Charley and Day had moved house once
again, as though pursued by difficulties, this time to Penge.
Day's married life was following the pattern of her earliest
years, when Rowland and Emma had carried the family from
one brief refuge to another. Ada stayed with them in January
and again in February, but the diary for that year has been
reduced to fifteen terse entries, simply stating her geographi-
cal position: 'To Penge, to Finchley Rd (1st time), to Tun
Wells to nurse Miss A., to Mrs. S. at Somersham' etc. She
had good reason to say when summing up: 'An unsettled year
and a most tiring one. Tried my health and strength very
much.' When she visited Penge she must have become aware
of an impending crisis, may have taken part in the anxious
discussions between Day and Charley which ended in their
decision to emigrate. She would miss Day sadly. But whatever she may have confided to her diary at the time, in the
later copying she leaves us only two bleak entries: 'April 21.
Spent the day with Day', and 'May 2. C. & D. sailed for
Australia.' I found an example, later in the diary, of her
elimination of anything expressing emotion. She had glued
sheets of paper over some pages of the original diary and
used them for the résumé of 1907. When I prised off the top
sheet I found this entry: 'A little Bible study, and also B.
reading with Mrs M. My thoughts too full of – ', then a long
phrase which had been scratched out with a penknife – 'to
give my whole mind to my usual happy employment on our
Lord's holy day.'

It is equally impossible to know what Charley's feelings

were about taking off into the unknown, separating himself
from all his family and friends. For Day it was a different
matter, and no doubt she suggested the plan. It must have
seemed to her a perfect solution of their difficulties to join
her brothers and sisters and be reunited with her father and
meet her little half-brother Page. It would be all the more
fun not to tell them she was coming, simply to turn up and
enjoy their delighted astonishment, to sun herself in the
welcome that Tina would get from Tony. Perhaps she managed to infect Charley with her enthusiasm, though he was
not, I think, of the adventurous kind, nor promising material
for a pioneering life; but the thought of making both a new
start and my mother happy overcame what qualms he had.

In all the years Australia had been under the flag they
could hardly have chosen a worse time to go. It seems extraordinary that they should know nothing about what had
happened there, or that no one would warn them. The financial crash in Argentina six years before had helped to bring
about the collapse of the land boom in 1893, with banks,
building societies, every kind of business failing and falling
like a house of cards. Thousands of workers roamed the city
streets and country roads looking for work. Five shillings a
week and food was welcomed as good pay. Unemployed
marchers carried a painted banner showing Christ as a
crucified working man. Burglaries and suicides proliferated.
Charlie and Bert's studio was ransacked, and no one could
afford to buy their paintings. The only people who had any
money were the ships' crews coming in to dock, and for a
time Charlie went into partnership with a man called
Churton, photographing ships and sailors, but not for long.
He came back with Bert from a week's holiday on a farm at
Western Point, to find that Churton had decamped, taking
with him the cameras, the money, and whatever else the
burglars had left behind.

The farm at Western Point, forty miles from Melbourne,
belonged to an elderly man called Ridley who apparently,
however puzzling it is to believe, turned the farm over to

Charlie and Bert, lock, stock, and barrel. Ridley evidently lived nearby and had let the land go to waste. Charlie and Bert harnessed a horse to a cart, loaded up their few remaining belongings, and made the two-day journey through rain and wind to Warrain Farm. It was June 1893. They started off, Charlie wrote, with light hearts and full of hope, to plough the peat land and sow oats and vegetables, but they grew very little except the beards on their chins, 'the only crops that the rabbits and other pests couldn't eat'. Bert had no talent at all for the farming life. Everything he put his hand to, milking, disc harrowing, ploughing, ended in comic disaster; even using the butter-churn. After three hours of hard work, when the butter began to appear, he added too much salt. To wash the salt out he poured in hot water and the contents of the churn poured out through the bung-hole all over the floor. Bert's pet pig went into an ecstasy, slithering and grunting and licking up the butter.

Six months of fighting with nature and farm implements brought Bert to despair. In December Charlie found him sitting beside the fire swathed from head to foot in the black material they used for making a dark-room. He was in mourning for his life. They decided to sell up, and leave what Charlie called the land of misery and starvation, to try their luck in New Zealand.

By the new year, 1894, they were staying with Lil and Jack Staveley and their children at Otaki, near Wellington, N.Z., and here they parted company. Bert, after his recent experience, would never again adventure outside a town; Charlie felt it was useless to stay there, though he was sad to make the break with his brother. He left the family at the breakfast table and set out, as he said, for God knows where, tramping on and on until he came to a place called Akatawara, a settlement of six huts scattered over miles of mountain and bush, the nearest store twelve miles away. Here he fell in with a bushman he called Mad Harry who let him share his Maori hut, called a whare or wharry. Mad Harry carried on animated conversations with the bread and cooking utensils but seldom spoke a word to Charlie. Together they set about clearing an area of the forest, under-scrubbing, tree-felling and 'burning off'. To clear the land they must burn the bush, but it was dangerous. There was danger from the towering trees crashing down the hillside as the fire destroyed the supple-jack vines which held them up. There was danger of being burnt alive if the wind changed direction, as it did one morning. The fire pursued them faster than they could run; but then, as though Charlie's guardian angel had been alerted to the peril, the wind suddenly changed again and the fire retreated. They got back to the whare, exhausted, blackened with smoke, their clothes torn to ribbons.

After a few weeks Mad Harry went off on some unexplained mission of his own. Charlie, shut in on all sides by the mountains and without the sound of Mad Harry talking to the bread, was oppressed and lonely. With a moon at the first quarter he slung his pack on his shoulder and made the long walk back to civilization. For a time he joined 'D' Battery of the Royal New Zealand Artillery, long enough to take part in firing the salute at the Opening of Parliament in Wellington; but he soon extricated himself from the army, and in September was working on the Otakapo Sheep Station, Rangitiki, the oldest and largest in the north island, where he helped to shepherd thousands of acres. In the evenings he sang songs and played what he called his 'harp', though the instrument was more like a zither, played on the lap; or he accompanied the fiddler at clod-hopping dances in the woolshed. He still carried his sketch-book with him, and the life he had led with Bert in the Melbourne studio was seldom out of his mind. The new year, 1895, saw him making his way across the Kaimanawa Mountains with a notion of setting up as an animal painter on the east coast at Wanganui, but he found the market already cornered by a Mr. Fodor. The only brushwork he could get was repainting the lettering on the pediment of an hotel, balanced on the topmost ledge high above the street, which he wryly called 'High art in New Zealand'. By April he was back in Australia, helping to

decorate the inside of Sydney Cathedral, and it began to look
as though he might settle there permanently. He made friends
and started to make some headway with his painting, but
however adroit his guardian angel might be at warding off
death it took small interest yet in the advancement of his
career. As 1895 turned into 1896 a bad drought hit New
South Wales and another spell of depression. By now Bert
had found his way back to Melbourne. 'My affection for
Bert', Charlie wrote, 'took me once more to Melbourne as it
had done from N.Z. in 1886 and from Leicester in 1889.' On
Monday, 13 April 1896, he boarded the 5.15 p.m. train at
Sydney, reaching Melbourne at noon the next day, two weeks
and four days before Day and Charley sailed for Australia.

He found Bert in a studio in Queen's Street 'sitting at his
easel, twirling his thumbs patiently and waiting for something to turn up'. Things were no better in Melbourne, or
very little, than when they had started on the ill-fated farming experiment nearly three years before. Bert was one of
a circle of happy-go-lucky artists and writers, though both
happiness and luck were in such short supply they began to
drift off to look for them elsewhere, as Charlie noted in his
diary:

I made another desperate attempt to make a living by art in
Melbourne although all the wiser ones had left for other parts.
Kept awake at night by the new bells of the General Post Office
clanging out 'Hard times come again no more', 'God bless the
Prince of Wales' 'Home Sweet Home'. I wish God would bless the
poor struggling artist & give him a home, be it never so humble,
& a little prosperity. The Prince of Wales can take care of himself.

It was to this hard-pressed city, which all the wiser ones
had left, that my parents came in the middle of June. The
rough passage of the Bay of Biscay was behind them, and
Day was all-expectant for the amazement and delight of her
brothers' welcome. Instead, there was shock and dismay, a
consternation so complete and abiding that of all the eighteen
months my parents were in Australia, Charlie's sketch-books

of his life record nothing. Every other reunion with his family, even with old shipmates, had been joyously drawn and coloured, but the only acknowledgement he gives that Tina had come more than half-way round the globe to be with Tony is in two photographs, one of my mother, the other of my father, stuck on to the tissue paper between the pages of the sketch-book. His life story was not taken up again until after their return to England.

The misery of the ensuing months can only be guessed from the three or four fragments of memory my mother cared to retain. Reality had so shattered her dream that she never told me of meeting her brothers, or anything about her father. She may not, after all, have met him. His second wife had died and he had gone with his seven-year-old son to live in Adelaide. None of them seems to have been able to smooth her path for her; and the one contact with her family she ever mentioned, the sale to Edith of some of her most precious possessions, was still a source of lament in my boyhood. In 1896 Hal was away with the Anglo-French Expedition exploring the Alligator River in the Northern Territory. Charlie was wandering from place to place picking up work where he could. My parents must often have gone hungry, for my mother remembered all her life the joy of finding a fourpenny piece on the pavement and buying some meat with it.

She had brought from England a small trunkful of treasures, among them the locket holding a strand of Emma's hair which Ada had given her on her fourteenth birthday, and a photograph of herself in her riding-habit. On one desperate day my father said they must raise some money on them from a pawnbroker. She used all her obstinacy to protect her dearly loved belongings, and he lost control. It was the only time he ever showed the least violence. The unexpectedness of it, and the fact that the slightest angry word always distressed my mother, may have made her exaggerate his fury; but harassed and despairing as he was, his nerves jangled by the unfamiliarity of everything about him, he was evidently near breaking-point. He took her by the throat and shook her. She thought he was going to kill her. This one experience of violence in her life was never forgotten.

It was after this, I suppose, that Edith advanced them some money in exchange for the trunk. Day never saw her treasures again, nor ever quite forgave Edith for keeping them, those pieces of girlhood jewelry, no doubt the 'splendid gold brooch from Green that young fellow that was in the boat with us that day', and the photograph she was so proud of, showing her in her riding-habit.

If I had plied her with questions I might have found out more about those grim months of bare survival which reached their culmination in the autumn of 1897. My father had gone up-country searching for work. He left my mother toiling as maid-of-all-work in a lodging house. Early each morning she scrubbed the steep flight of steps at the house front, and at the end of each long day she barricaded herself into her bedroom for fear of the tough male lodgers. There was no knowing when my father would return. Whenever she had an hour off in the evening she would walk to the main cross-roads in Melbourne and stand there looking one way and another, scanning the faces of the passing crowd, hoping against hope that she would see him coming towards her. And then one night, it must have been late September or early October, when she had pushed her washstand against the door and was going to bed, she heard his whistle outside in the street. She went to the window and there he was, standing in the light from the lamppost and waving something held in his hand. His parents had sent two steerage tickets for a boat bound for England.

At some port of call during the voyage home Day was run away with by a rickshaw man and had to be pursued and rescued; and a week before they saw the cliffs of Dover she arrived at her twenty-sixth birthday. They docked on 21 November 1897. The child-wife who had set out with such high expectation nineteen months before had come back a woman.

They went to live with Charley's parents at Gillingham, and except for three or four footprints in the sand I lose all sight of them for the next five years. Ada met Day at Whitstable in January, their first meeting after the return, and again in London in July. Then silence, until on 10 November 1898, nearly a year after getting back, Day went on a visit to St. Mary's Fields. Aunt Gussie had died in April of the previous year while staying at Brighton. Katie was engaged to marry a major, who by the time I knew him had turned into a colonel. Emily Kettle was no longer thought of as the children's nurse who had come to the house a quarter of a century before, but as a valued member of the family. Otherwise nothing had changed. Day woke on her birthday morning feeling that the last three years had been a bad dream. She had sent no word to her brothers since she left Australia, as though she were afraid of touching on wounds; but now at last, sitting in the old day nursery where the Tony and Tina partnership had been born, she was able to write to him.

He replied from 69 Eastern Arcade, Melbourne, on 4 January 1899:

My dear Tina
You are the worserestest kiddy I ever knoed. You say in your letter which I received today, that I promised to write & send photo etc. how the mischief could I write when I didn't know your address. As the Irishman suggested: I ought to have written & asked you for it. I have been waiting all this time for a letter from you & have called at Hammon's but divil a word could I hear of you & came to the conclusion that you were not going to write to me. I thought you would have written as soon as you got back & address to the Fern Tree Gully Hotel. Anyhow I am glad that I have heard from you at last . . .

What a treat it must have been for you to get back to Leicester, I only wish I had been there too. Just fancy Nurse Kettle & West being there yet. And Altie & Cissie separated, their marriage didn't last long. You did not mention what Altie is doing now. Poor Uncle, I do feel sorry for him. He is too kindhearted & people impose on him. I was sorry to hear that you had been ill although not at all surprised. I wonder you are not in your grave . . .

Summer, 1902. My brother has arrived.

My brother at the gate of my birthplace, 65 Sussex Place, Bristol.
Ted Legg's greengrocery shop is on the corner of Ashley Down Hill.

My first photograph,
with Nurse Snow, December 1907

With my father

With my mother and
brother at Combe Martin,
1908

At Minehead in 1910

Myself in 1909

'Little Mrs.'

Ada's diary, usually so quick to report any illness, makes no mention of this one. Day, in years to come, seldom if ever spoke of her health or lowness of spirits, and she may well have been keeping quiet about them now, though she wrote of the illness to Tony, and also brought up the rankling subject of Edith and her trunkful of treasures. She may have thought her brother could retrieve it for her, but he takes her to task in his letter:

You should not consider Edith *mean* for not sending your goods. it is hardly a fair thing for you to expect it, although I know nothing about the business. I presume she lent you money on them and therefore she has a perfect right to keep them & you should consider yourself lucky that *she* has them & not Uncle Sam [here the sketch of a pawnbroker's sign] for if Charley had got hold of them that is where they would have gone & then you would never have seen them again whereas now there is a chance of your getting them back. You should never expect anything more from relations than if they were utter strangers then you will always get on well. relations seldom get on well together because they expect too much from one another. You should feel grateful to her for lending you the money. Never forget a kindness. but for her you might have been stranded in this country & lost your money & jewelry too. business is business & justice is justice, do not think Edith unkind. It is Charley you have to thank for it all, if he had been anything like a man you would never have lost a thing. It was a pity that Chas made himself such a fool out here for there were good things in store for us all if he had only settled down to work like a sensible man. The Country is improving every year & we would have had some fine times together . . .

There is nothing to tell us why Charlie had such a contempt for my father. They were almost of an age; they both could make music and enjoyed singing; each was sensitive and kindly disposed to his fellow creatures. It may be that the Tony–Tina relationship would have put at a disadvantage any husband my mother might have chosen. What kind of fool did Chas make of himself out there? It hardly seems a charitable judgement of a man strange to the country, and a

country in such a state that even Charlie, with only himself
to think about, was finding it hard to keep afloat. He had,
besides, deep reserves to draw on: a natural talent for survival and a zest for life which he had tried and tested ever
since he was sixteen. My father's boyhood was as narrow as
Charlie's was wide.

CHAPTER TWELVE

An End and a Beginning

When my grandfather, John Harris shipwright, aged twenty-three, son of James Harris shipwright, had married Sarah Ann Skinner, aged twenty-one, daughter of Moses Skinner blacksmith, at the parish church, Gillingham, on 18 May 1867, they settled into a little house in Church Path, and there, on 29 July of the following year, my father was born. He had five aunts and two uncles living in Gillingham and Chatham, most of whom I remember in their later days. There was Lizzie Harris, my grandfather's sister, who had kept the accent of her Devonshire origins though my grandfather had not, and who married a man called Clarke. Her son, Jim Clarke, went to Bermuda, became an authority on floating docks, and was later hired by the Australian Government to run one of their dockyards. Her grandson, Ivo, went to Osborne, entered the Royal Navy, and was naval adviser to Noël Coward in the making of the film *In Which We Serve*. And there were the Skinners, my grandmother's brothers and sisters. The blacksmith father, sternly pious, walked five miles each Sunday to preach in a village chapel. The elder brother, Charles, by the time I came to know him, was a highly successful contractor, an alderman, and at some time mayor of Chatham. He lived with his wife Fran in an aldermanly house called Bella Vista in the Maidstone Road. The younger brother, William, married a girl called Lydia Bow, kept a baker's shop in Luton, and died in his forties from eating cockles.

The three sisters, whose names always made me think of the treacle well in *Alice*, were called Polly, Milly, and Emmie.

Polly was enormously stout with a whaleboned bosom that jutted authoritatively under copious black bombazine. I was terrified of being kissed by her; it was like being plunged into the depths of Avernus. Her husband, Walter Hodges, also wore black, with an exaggeratedly high starched collar under a face of gloom. They were Elect Congregationalists, pillars of the Ebenezer Chapel, to which Polly presented an organ. Grandfather Harris maintained that it bore the inscription 'To the glory of Mrs. Hodges and God.'

Milly married a grocer called Dick Bow, Lydia's brother. When some years later Dick went to see Lever's new soap factory Milly wrote to him:

Dear Mr. Bow,
I trust you had a favourable journey to Port Sunlight and that you will learn much about this new soap. We shall be able to sell it in the shop. May God bless you and bring you safely home. The children miss you.

your devoted wife
Milly.

They lived over the shop in Mills Terrace, Chatham, with their three daughters, Milly-Two, Alice, and Mabel, and Mabel's husband Norman Phillips, father of my cousin Alan, who became a foreign-language teacher, a musician, and poet. Dick Bow was an enthusiastic British Israelite, never weary of preaching his faith in our descent from the lost tribe of Ephraim, worshipping at an extraordinary structure called Jezreel's Tower, and predicting the course of the Great War from biblical prophecies.

Emmie, the youngest of the four sisters (my grandmother was the second) and far less concerned about being one of the Elect than either Polly or Milly, married Dick Bow's brother William. They lived very comfortably, largely on the proceeds from what my Grandfather Harris called, with a wink, 'Emmie's Swindle'. This was a kind of hire-purchase system.

She had an arrangement with local shops that certain carefully vetted customers could buy goods on her account and repay her, with interest, in weekly instalments. My grandfather's name for her husband was Bill-bill. They had a feather-brained daughter called Laurie who had an adored, fat, and wheezy pug-dog called Bidgie.

This was as I knew them thirty years or so after my father's boyhood, the same family circle in which as a child he had been haunted by the eyes of God. The God who looked with such evident satisfaction on the Hodges and the Bows made him uneasy and oppressed. In the year that Charlie Hammond was making the forests of New Zealand his cathedral and setting out to find his own world, unbeholden to anybody except the mate of the ship which took him to Hong Kong, Charley Harris was conforming to the life of his elders, binding himself to a clerkship, coming no nearer to the sea and ships, in spite of his bargemen forbears, than the salt of his father's humour and the entries in his father's dockyard ledgers. Whatever *Lebensfeuer* was in him took him no further than a house a few doors away from the Bows in Mills Terrace, where Clara Jane Jarvis lived, the tailor's daughter he wooed and, to complete his conformity, married two weeks after his twenty-second birthday.

It was to this world of his boyhood and early manhood, after his ill-starred venture to break into a new life, that he returned with my mother, demoralized and shaken, in the winter of 1897–8. On the very day of their landing in England, Sunday 21 November, Charlie Hammond's life took a dramatic swing towards success. While my parents were in Australia he had scratched along, with no settled address (letters to be addressed c/o the Fern Tree Gully Hotel), picking up what work he could. He had 'knocked up a cheque in the country', doing some livestock paintings, and sent the money to Melbourne for Bert to put in the bank; but when he got back to town a few months later, hoping they might rent a studio, he found Bert had spent all the money to keep himself going. A Mr. Hitchberg commissioned him to do a series of paintings of ships, advancing enough money for him to hire a studio while the work lasted, but by November he had given up the keys.

Then, at three o'clock in the morning of 21 November, when my mother and father were sleeping their last night on board ship, Bert went racing round to Charlie's lodgings, burst into his bedroom and shook him awake. He came to tell him there was a huge fire at the corner of Elizabeth Street and Flinders Street. Fink's Buildings and the big store of Craig Williamson's were ablaze. Charlie made a diary note of what followed:

A few minutes after Bert had woken me I was sketching the biggest fire in the history of Melbourne. There being no trains or trams running very few people about & no photographers. Monday 8 a.m. Rush about looking for another studio having given up the keys and left the other one, engage cab & at 9 a.m. remove to new studio, unpack materials & start drawing of the big fire, using a box for a table. Finish full page one by noon, run it down to Weekly Times office. Causes tremendous excitement. Nobody else got a picture of it. W.Times just going to press but Editor holds it up for an hour while I make another drawing from across the river showing reflections in the water.

When pay-day came he gave a supper party to his friends, at which Bert proposed the toast of 'Mein backsheesh bruder'. The English magazine *Black and White* also bought a drawing he made of the fire, and after that commissions began to pour in, from *The Weekly Times*, *Punch* (Melbourne), the *Adelaide Critic;* for advertisements, portraits of horses, paintings of ships as they came into harbour. He was a welcome member of a fellowship of artists, journalists, musicians, and actors, who met in the evenings – 'Happy nights in our snug corner', Charlie calls them – at Geary's Café. The meal over, they drew portraits and caricatures of each other and of Bella, the handsome waitress who brought them a brew of strong tea; life was evidently intoxicating enough without alcohol. When Tony wrote his letter to Tina in January 1899 he was still on the crest of the wave:

We have had an abundant harvest, the best for many years so that is a good start then it is very probable that we will get Federation which will be another great stride towards prosperity prospects are very good so far & I sincerely hope they may continue so . . . Am sending you the Xmas number of the Weekly Times with my last drawing in it, 'Christmas in England & Australia' full page. We had a grand Military Tattoo at the Exhibition this year & I made several sketches of that for the Times . . .

But the burst of success, which Bert presented him with on the night of the fire, had brought about a coolness between them: 'Hal is still up country doing well. I very seldom see E.B.H. he is rather jealous of me starting in the same line as him he is awfully afraid I am going to cut him out.'

As far as I know, nothing of Bert's work has survived, only two photographs: one a self-portrait, showing him sitting on his horse Baron, and the other a painting of the champion steeplechaser Domino, the last picture he did; but it may not have been just fraternal partiality that made Charlie write, years after Bert had died: 'Bert was a *genius* at painting a standing horse. He had made a thorough study of the subject and was master of it. No other artist could compare with him. I always liked painting horses and riders in violent action. The two styles were characteristic of our temperaments.' But Bert had little success, and it must have fretted him to watch his young brother's popularity while he got further into debt, and illness overtook him; not that Charlie's troubles and wanderings were over yet. For a second time he came back from holiday to find that a partner had sold all his pictures, collected the accounts, and disappeared. His resilience was beginning to wear thin. He made off to the peace of the countryside at Glen Huntly, and for two months 'studied' irrigation and fruit-growing. In September he was back in Melbourne taking part with his friends the Fritz Kricheldorffs in founding the Australian Literature Society.

It was the last year of the old century. October brought the outbreak of war in South Africa and the sequence of British defeats which went on into December. In England Ada ended the century with two terse entries in her diary: 'Dec.29. Influenza in the house. Dec.31. I caught it.'

The twentieth century came in without any apparent likelihood of my ever being born to see it. After six and a half years of marriage Charley and Day had to make do with visits from Bessie's children: Harrold, Noeline, and three-year-old Bernie. They had a home of their own again, at 34 Kingswood Road, Gillingham, and by some means, no doubt with the help of Grandpa and Nana Harris, Charley had been set up as a builder and contractor, with his brother Bert as partner.

The new century brought an almost immediate change in the fortunes of war in South Africa, with Lord Roberts as Commander-in-Chief, none the worse for the fourteen years portrayed on his knees in the reredos at St. Agnes, Bristol; and as Chief of Staff, Lord Kitchener, whose ichthyoidal, guilt-provoking eyes were to glare at us from the hoardings fourteen years later. On 15 February General French relieved Kimberley; it was Charlie Hammond's thirtieth birthday. He was staying on a friend's farm at Drouin, Gippsland, and two days before had been fighting, all day and half the night, a bush fire which threatened the homestead. On 28 February Sir Redvers Buller relieved Ladysmith. When the news reached Australia Hal rode over to the farm in great spirits and took Charlie off with him to spend the week-end at Haunted Hill. A family called Stocks lived there, father, mother, three sons, and four daughters, May, Minnie, Eva, and Ella. Hal was in love with Ella, and Charlie painted a portrait of her for him. She sits, demure and fascinating, in blue riding-habit, side-saddle on a grey horse.

By the end of March Charlie was back in Melbourne, at work in Fritz Kricheldorff's studio illustrating sheet music covers for Boer War songs: 'When Britain Calls her Sons to Duty', 'When War's Shrill Trumpet Note is Sounding,' and

'When our Boys come Marching Home Again'. Ada notes in her diary that on 31 March Uncle Tom's twenty-four-year-old son, Jack Fry, had sailed for South Africa with the Imperial Yeomanry. Sixty years later I was to dedicate a play, *Curtmantle*, to him and his wife Nancy.

Charlie's fine flow of success had abated a little: 'Fred Murphy fails to pay for painting of horses. Bretnall's book a failure, so get nothing for illustrating it. Newspaper work very strenuous and uncertain. Health and nerves in bad state, decide to join partnership with Roland Bishop in photography and give art a rest for a while.' But he was well enough, on 7 May, to be in Gippsland again, officiating as best man at Hal's wedding to Ella Stocks, and afterwards to dance, as he said, 'till the cows came home'. It was ten days before the Relief of Mafeking. When the news came he was back at the Kricheldorff studios, and on Saturday 19 May, the day when Melbourne went wild with an excitement described in the headlines next day as 'unparalleled', 'extraordinary scenes' and 'frantic revelry', he did a half-page picture for the *Melbourne Times* of the firework display erupting over the city.

Mafeking Day was noted by Ada, but not celebrated. She had caught cold at a drawing-room meeting, and the cold turned into influenza and a painful finger. On 24 June she wrote: 'Bertie 36. My finger very bad. Proved to be blood poisoning from influenza.' She still had no settled place to live. In the second half of this year she moved from Sutton to Bickley, where she saw Bess for the first time in three and a half years, from Bickley to Sidcup, from Sidcup to Fleet. It was not until the following summer that she came to rest in furnished rooms at Langton Green, near Tunbridge Wells.

In the first month of the new year, 1901, Queen Victoria died, and Ada put on her blackest clothes and wore them for several weeks. The diary records that on the day after the Queen's burial at Frogmore a heavy fall of snow buried the countryside a foot deep. After that she found nothing in the world worth noting, except to remember that she and Percy had been confirmed twenty-five years ago on 5 May, until she comes to 4 June when she writes: 'Day had a slight operation.' Nine months later the nine childless years of marriage ended; on 6 March 1902, at seven o'clock in the evening, Day gave birth to a boy, my brother Charles Leslie. The blessedness of that spring and early summer was caught by Charley in a photograph he took in the garden of 34 Kingswood Road; Day sits peacefully sewing in the sun beside a high, elegant baby carriage. She seems unaware of being photographed, content and preoccupied; and I sense Charley's pride and love as he stood watching her, the sleeping baby at her side.

During my school-days, on the few occasions when my mother touched on these years in Gillingham, she evasively called my father an architect. She still harboured a slight feeling of having lost caste, though she seemed otherwise quite unconscious of class distinctions. I grew up believing my father had designed as well as built the house for his parents in Saxton Street, but in fact it had already been built a year before the return from Australia. It stood detached and double-fronted at the upper end of Saxton Street, and seemed to me to make an island of itself, with the rest of the street as a causeway. The rooms, though small, were full of light, and gave a feeling of solid worth and unassuming comfort, like Grandpa and Nana Harris. They called the house Homedale.

Ada gives no reason for her decision to settle at Langton Green that summer. She was very much alone, barely even in contact with her family. Years could go by without seeing Bessie, and there had been no visits to Charley and Day since the early years of marriage. In 1897, while they were in Australia, she had 'heard' that her father, ERH as she called him, had been on a short visit to England (it was soon after the death of his brother Harry Julius) and also that he had married for the third time. And now, at the end of June 1902, she 'heard' that Bertie had also been in England without

visiting her. The purpose of his visit, or how he had raised
the money to come, is unexplained; he may have come to
consult a medical specialist; perhaps Uncle Tom paid his
fare. It must have saddened Ada to know that he had come
and gone without her meeting him. She scarcely ever moved
from her couch now. While she was at Easebourne a doctor
had told her to lie down as much as possible, advice she never
afterwards forgot for very long. She had 'ventured' out for
ten minutes at the end of May, but that was the last time for
more than a year. She had nothing to do but 'mark the
Gospels', write letters, entertain occasional visitors ('Miss
Twinch and Miss Battams called', 'Miss Twinch to tea') which
usually tired her very much, and enter her peculiar indis-
positions in the diary: 'Internal neuralgia. Coronation day',
'A prickling in the side', or, mysteriously, 'I quite ill from
outside circumstances as well as physically'. To make a little
variety she would count the number of fine days in the
month: 'Sept.25. Heard ERH was divorced. 19 fine days this
month. Charley & Day had my organ.'

The organ was a mahogany parlour organ, or harmonium
de luxe, which had been left to her by her old friend Mrs.
Marriott in her will. It bore a brass plate on its ornamental
pediment to say so, and two small circular trays on brackets,
to right and left, to carry candlesticks. After my father died
it stood in the corner of the dining-room at Homedale, and as
soon as my legs were long enough to reach the carpet-covered
pedals, without my slipping off the sloping mahogany organ-
stool, I delighted in the altering sounds to be made by pulling
out or pushing in the ivory-faced stops. My favourite two were
called Celeste and Tremolo, Tremolo because it seemed so
anxiously grateful to be used, and Celeste because it was the
nearest, I supposed, to the sound made in Heaven. In the
thick, red volume of *Hymns Ancient and Modern*, with tunes
above the words and 'C.J.Harris, Gillingham, Kent' embossed
in gold on the shiny cover, the grubbiest page from constant
use gives the hymn 'There's a Friend for little children'. The
fifth verse runs:

> There's a song for little children
> Above the bright blue sky,
> A song that will not weary,
> Though sung continually.

That was the meaning of the Celeste stop. The only comparably thumb-marked page bore the hymn:

> Every morning the red sun
> Rises warm and bright;
> But the evening cometh on
> And the dark, cold night.

When the organ arrived at Gillingham in October 1902 the sun was still rising bright. For three days at the end of the month, the weather, Ada wrote, 'was so warm enjoyed open windows'. My brother Leslie (for though he was later called by his first name, Charles, he was Leslie for many years to come) was growing sturdily. Day had taken him to Herne Bay for an August holiday with the Bridger family, and Charley joined them there, recording the holiday with his camera. He was a popular uncle with the Bridger children. Harrold, when he was an old man, still remembered how eagerly they watched his hand go to his pocket, where he kept a supply of fruit, sweets, and coloured marbles, like a walking shop.

Ada had not so much as set foot outside the door since she had gone for her ten-minute walk in May, and didn't attempt it again until the end of July 1903, fourteen months spent in lying on her bed or the sofa. The diary was languishing, too. She found very little to record in 1903, except that in September Archibald Marshall's brother Noel had been presented to Edward VII at Malta during the King's first state visit to Europe; and on 7 October 'Mr. Chamberlain began his Tariff Reform speeches at Glasgow.' With nothing to think about, and no company except occasional social calls of acquaintances, she was an easy target for her sniping nerves. Thoughts of Emma's illness and death, never far from her mind, were intensified on 20 October: 'Had a very bad attack of pain in my side.' She underlined a sentence in her Bible from Revelation 2:10: 'Fear none of those things that thou shalt suffer', and wrote the chapter reference on the flyleaf.

One of her occasional visitors, a Miss Harding, invited her to spend Christmas Day in Tunbridge Wells, but she felt too unwell to accept. Her only approach to festivity was on 22 December when Miss Twinch came to spend the whole day with her. On the 25th she wrote: 'Dull & grey but fairly warm. Quite alone.' And then before she turned to 1904 she makes one of those almost imperceptible breaches in her reserve: 'The year ended with trouble and anxiety.'

The trouble was yet another defeat for Charley, the collapse of his building business. My mother remembered it long afterwards as painful and humiliating; it repeated, to a lesser degree, the disaster in 1872, the sell-up at Islington when she was a year old. My brother was a year and eight months. But *then* the fault had all been Rowland's; now, or so she maintained, the trouble was due to Bert Harris's slack ways and the wickedness of a solicitor. She was always quite definite that my father was in no way to blame, but for him it was the culmination of ten years of unsuccess. Once again he had to be extricated, as from Australia, with the never failing, if anxious, help of Grandpa and Nana Harris, or so I suppose since there seems to have been no question of bankruptcy – except in Charley's hope of worldly prosperity. That end was dead, and he was forced to find his true self, to explore the path which he was best fitted to follow.

He was an active member of St. Luke's Church, New Brompton (Gillingham), a tenor in the choir and occasional organist. In a photograph of a choir outing, taken during the summer of 1903, he looks relaxed, even debonair, in his panama hat and white tennis-shoes, and though he was then still builder and contractor he seems already to know where his heart was. It was a natural step when the business failed to turn to Mr. Tozer the vicar for acceptance as lay reader. A springtime of study brought him through an examination in simple theology and Bible knowledge, and before Mid-summer day he had the bishop's licence in his hands. It soon became clear that it was not so much the dogma as the doing of Christianity that filled his thoughts. In one of his earliest sermons he said:

We are most Christian when we look around for the wounds and miseries of our friends and neighbours and do our best to heal them . . . And if I were asked for a proof of the power of Christianity in the British nation I would point, not to its hundred or two hundred sects, who will not pray together because they do not spell prayer the same way, and not to our noble cathedrals and numberless churches, I would point to its magnificent and catholic charity, hospitals, infirmaries and dispensaries . . .

As though heaven smiled on his new career, the last week of June was fine and warm. Ada was tempted to go out into the fields for the first time since the previous autumn, and then began carefully to number in her diary each walk she took. On the 29th she sat by an open window writing the last letter she would ever write to Bertie, and early in July Charley, Day, and Leslie came to stay at the hotel in Langton for two nights, Charley as free from any feeling of unworthiness as at almost any time since his wedding-day. After entertaining them at Fairholme, the house where she lodged, Ada went on to the Green with them after tea and back to the hotel for an hour without even feeling tired. It was 'Walk no.3.' All through August and into September the little walks went on, never very far, to the Post Office or to see a friend to the top of the road, while events took a mournful course in Australia. On 24 August Ada wrote: 'Began to be anxious about Bertie . . . 8th walk', and on 10 September: 'Mother's 77th birthday. Out on the Green. 10th walk . . . In the evening heard of ERH's death.' All the unforgiving years since Rowland's disgrace were overtaken by earlier memories, when dear Papa had taken her to watch cricket at Lord's and to buy early morning fish at Billingsgate.

Two days later she got a letter from Bert, enclosing his

photograph. On the 14th, his last day of life, friends drove her over to Tunbridge Wells to stay the night, the first time she had been out of the village since she came there. On 21 October she received from Uncle Tom three letters which Bert had written to him, 'the last one showing plainly what was amiss'. In her newspaper on the 24th she read that the Baltic Fleet had fired on North Sea fishermen, and then at noon came a message from Uncle Tom, 'the news of the sad death of poor Bertie'. She writes nothing in her diary for the next three days, until on a day of sunshine when the trees blazed with gold against the blue sky, she went out on to the Green, 'feeling too upset to settle to anything. 11th walk.' At the month's end she wrote: 'The last week the saddest one since Mother died.'

It was only as sadness, not horror, that Bert's tragedy was told to me, and in Charlie's sketch-book it is shown as gentle as the water-colours it was painted in. On 14 September Bert goes to Sandringham, where sixteen years before he bought his plot of land and schemed with such excitement to build a house looking out across the bay; he sits writing a last message on the sand, and as the sun is setting he shoots himself. In the sketch-book no gun is shown; the truth was too harsh to be set down. But the facts were recorded in the Melbourne *Argus* on 16 September 1904. The body was found lying near a tea-tree. A double-barrelled shot-gun, its barrels pointing upward, the muzzle a few feet from the sand, was bound firmly to the tree. A revolver was tied to the dead man's right wrist and hand, as though to make death doubly sure. A stick three feet long had been wrenched from the tree, peeled and trimmed with a penknife at its forked end, and used to press the gun trigger. Its other end was ragged and fibrous and soaked in blood. The top of the head had been blown away by a charge of shot entering the mouth. In a penny notebook, found near the body, Bert had drawn the act of suicide, the gun tied to the tea-tree and himself falling to the ground. The book was filled from cover to cover with disjointed messages, explanations, and reflections, and the notes spilled over on to a heap of loose sheets. He had come to the beach two evenings before, the day he bought the gun, but it had been too dark when he got there to make the preparations. The newspaper goes on to describe what happened when he returned to the beach shortly after midday on Wednesday:

After fixing the gun he had lain writing for five hours. He assigned exhaustion, ill-health, and over-work as the reason for his suicide. 'If we must die, let's die gamely,' he wrote, and quoted (from Adam Lindsay Gordon) –
> 'Whatever you do, don't change your mind
> When once you've picked your panel.'

The disjointed character of the entries, some of which were written twice – once on a scrap of paper and once in the book – pointed to a derangement of mind. The last words written in the book were – 'I sink with the setting sun.' On one of his visiting-cards was written a message fixing precisely the moment of his death. It ran: 'I saw the sun go down at Sandringham, 6.35 p.m. Goodbye. 13 [*sic*] Sept. 04.'

A mystery remains. Police Constable Scammel, who was fetched by the man and boy who discovered the body, said he had made enquiries and found that the deceased was about 38 years of age (he was 40), resident at Armadale and *was a married man*. But neither Ada nor Charlie in the diaries, or anyone in the family at any time had spoken of a marriage.

At the beginning of Charlie's third sketch-book he has inserted this inscription:

To my dear big brother Bert who has shown so much sympathy and taken so much interest in my welfare from early childhood; who has influenced my life more than anyone else; who first taught me to tell the time by the clock and East from West by the compass; who gave me my first lessons in art, photography and other useful studies; who shared with me many happy hopeful days before the collapse of the land-boom in Melbourne 1893 and battled through the years of the depression which followed. To him I affectionately dedicate these books of our adventure through life.

Life's adventures and uncertainties, illness, death, and world unrest continued to remind Ada that here we have no abiding city. Her diary from January to May 1905 seldom relents. In January Port Arthur surrendered to the Japanese, two friends died, and two thousand people were killed in St. Petersburg. In February twelve-year-old Noeline Bridger, who was getting over rheumatic fever, became worse with pleurisy and pericarditis. Day and Leslie came to Langton for a day while Charley was preaching at East Grinstead, but they all caught cold in the bitter wind; Aunt Louie Marshall died from cancer; Noeline had a relapse and developed St. Vitus's Dance; Duke Sergius was assassinated in Moscow. In March and April she was worried about Day who consulted a specialist in Bedford Square and was weak and overtired. 14 May: 'Charley Harris ill with pneumonia after influenza . . . Dark & thundery. Close hot nights caught cold twice. My side swollen.'

It is like going out of a casualty ward into the open air to turn to June, when the Bishop of Exeter issued the lay reader's licence for the move to Devon, and to know that Charley, Day, and Leslie have reached the eighteen months of peace and happiness at Marwood. Noeline, whose recovery had several times been despaired of, was getting better. The diary is comparatively free of deaths, only four in the next twelve months, though the pages have a sprinkling of accidents and awesome acts of God: the roof of Charing Cross Station falls in; an electric tram car accident at Highgate, three killed, twenty-one injured; an eruption of Vesuvius and earthquake shocks at Valparaiso. Even the quiet of Marwood was not quite immune from intimations of the darker powers. The earth trembled and spewed out a rat which ran through the cottage and alarmed my four-year-old brother. But the warm sunshine in the second half of July and for almost the whole of August 1906 even got into Ada's diary, though the building of a new house opposite brought on a bad attack of neuralgia from want of quiet. The glorious weather coincided with a month's holiday spent by the Bridgers in Marwood. They arrived just after Harrold's fourteenth birthday and in time for my father's thirty-eighth. Before preparing the birthday picnic, which Charley scarcely had time for between Sunday-school and evensong (it was Sunday), Day sent off a picture postcard to Ada: 'Thought this sheep-shearing photo would interest you. Can you find me . . . We had a slight Earth-shock here on Wednesday.'

They were all happy; happy in the friendliness of the villagers and the peace of the Devon hills, happy in my father's success, his 'especial power in addresses to children', happy drawing the water from the spring and jogging along the lanes in the pony-cart. In two photographs the cottage doorway is the frame to their contentment, my mother sewing in the sunshine, and my father sitting on the step, one muddy-booted foot pressed against the door jamb, the only picture of him with a really carefree smile. When Bess was back in Sidcup after the holiday she sent the postcard to Ada of the picnic in the woods, with her words of praise for Fred Bindon, 'have seldom met a nicer fellow'. She posted it on 25 September, just a month before Ada got the news of Charley's decision to make the move to Bristol, with all its unhappy consequences.

Day's health gave an immediate signal that the change to city life was to be regretted. Anxious messages began to be passed between Charley and Ada soon after the move to Sussex Place. In December Day showed some improvement, and for lack of any other dismal news the diary, on 19 December, a year less a day before my appearance, records: 'Education Bill died', killed by the Lords. On Boxing Day there were six inches of snow, and on the 27th: 'More snow. Froze hard. Day ill with influenza.' She continued unwell far into January when Ada 'heard that school did not agree with Leslie' (he had lain unbudgeable on the pavement outside) and a spell of intense cold set in, the windows thick with ice.

It was a troublesome time for Charley, already faced with the pressures and poverty of an urban working district. But by the time the worst of the winter was over Day was better; Leslie was settled into a new and happier school, kept by a Miss Bartlett, who looked remarkably like Ada; and Charley was deep in an unsparing devotion to the parish, more abundant than his strength. The full tale of the good he did is buried with him, but long after his death my mother still spoke with a kind of awe of how he carried off his supper to the hungry, of whole nights spent with the dying; and she treasured a letter of condolence from a parishioner which quoted from *Abu Ben Adhem* to describe him: 'Write me as one who loved his fellow-men.' In the sermons he preached at Marwood he often spoke of the need for compassion. 'Without love a man has no moral worth,' he said; and certainly he was ungrudging in his concern for people. 'His thoughts', someone wrote to my mother, 'seemed ever expanding out to those who were in trouble and distress.'

The Marwood parishioners kept in touch. A postcard survives, posted a year after the move to Bristol, a photograph of one of the farm workers, F. J. Kelly, ambling along a lane on the back of a farm horse. By the side of the picture he wrote: 'Do you recognise this took by Mr. Bridger just below No Mans Land as the horse was walking. (quite unexpected)', and on the back of the card: 'Sent off hamper & Bag to day trusting it will arrive.' My mother, at this time, was trusting that I would arrive, too; November came and went, and women in the parish turned up their eyes at my disinclination to be born, terrifying my mother with tales of late arrivals being born 'monsters'. Her fears weren't allayed until the doctor had carried me to the window and expressed his approval of my head.

So there I was, in a state of life, learning to focus on what was round me, knowing light and dark, exploring the differences between near and far, attuning to sound, distinguishing one sensation from another; the threat of approaching storm, the benediction of the secure hearthrug beside my father's boots; carrying within me who knows how much of the lives of the past, the attorneys, the churchmen, the Quakers (I hope), the bargemen, the shipwrights, the bishop who got into Johnson's *Lives*, the auctioneers, the blacksmith, the yeomen, the carpenters, whose existences meeting and begetting gave place to the term of consciousness which I call my own.

CHAPTER THIRTEEN

The Man in Black

On 29 February 1908 Ada had a real birthday, her fifty-second measured by years. The couple she had lodged with at Fairholme were about to leave Langton and she had recently taken rooms with a Mr. and Mrs. Woodgate. A friend sent snowdrops and Miss Twinch came unexpectedly to tea. Hal's birthday letter said the heat in Victoria was 110° in the shade, a record; but there was snow on the ground in Langton, and the cold went on well past Easter. At the end of April Ada was writing: 'Heard from Day. Baby still has whooping cough, but better . . . Thick snow. Paper gave accounts of snow all over England and on the Continent . . . Naval disaster in the Channel owing to blinding snowstorms.' And 5 May was 'very unlike the lovely summer day in 1876 when Percy and I were confirmed'. Then quite suddenly the weather changed to excessive heat; Ada was kept awake all night by a cockchafer in her room, making, she said, a tremendous noise for such a small insect; and in Bristol on the last day of the month I looked up from my pram and saw the threatening sky, and lightning struck the cross on St. Agnes Church. Three days later, at three o'clock in the afternoon, the worst storm that Ada had known for many years brought hailstones like marbles and flooded the shops in Tunbridge Wells. She travelled in a friend's carriage the next day to inspect the damage. But then the lengthening June days grew comfortably cooler, and she went into the fields to gather ground ivy, to make into an infusion for bathing her eyes which were weak and inflamed. 'Unsatisfied women', she added, 'had a meeting in Hyde Park.'

During these first months of my life the weather, even the solar system, was behaving capriciously, blowing hot and cold, breaking calm days with frequent storms. At the end of June there was a partial eclipse of the sun, and on 1 July the diary recorded: 'Very hot. Heard from Uncle Tom about their tour in N. Italy. So light that I went to bed by daylight at 10 p.m. There was a midnight sun. Day and family went to Combe Martin. Baby had 2 teeth at 6 months.'

The photographs of the Combe Martin holiday seem to breathe a contentment like that of the Marwood days. The sea-breeze flutters my mother's skirt as she lifts me laughing up into the air, and twists my scant hair into a jaunty curl on the top of my head. I found life very satisfactory, to judge by the apparently unfailing chuckle, and my father's arms a particularly pleasant means of transport. 'You were devoted to him,' my mother used to tell me; and it may have been here at Combe Martin, or soon after on our return to Bristol, that I experienced the glow of warmth and happiness as I crawled on the hearthrug, my first remembered sensation of love.

His health may already have been causing anxiety. In April we had moved to a house up on Ashley Down; in October we moved again, to 78 Sefton Park Road, and this may have been the move my mother told me about, made because the hill climb was a strain on his heart, though there was yet another change to come, to 6 St. Nicholas Road. At any rate in April 1909 Ada was writing in the diary: 'Day wrote that Charley will not be able to work for 3 months.'

She had been charting her own bodily condition with a growing intensity, worrying about the pain in her side, bathing her eyes with essence of ground ivy. By Christmas she had taken to her bed, living on sips of cold water, and in January Mr. and Mrs. Woodgate asked her to leave, 'owing to extra work when not well'. If she had stayed on at Langton Green her nerves might have made an end of her, but in Tunbridge Wells, where she found a tiny room in Monson Terrace, she had many acquaintances to amuse her, not least among them Miss Twinch. On 1 July 1909 she wrote: 'Out in morning. Met Miss Carpenter. Trimmed a hat I bought in February 1899. After tea, on the Common with Mrs. Westley. Met Mrs. Caley, and Miss Twinch returning home . . . Heard from Day at Woolacombe with P.P.C. of the chicks.'

The picture postcard was one of several photographs my father took of my brother and me, standing in the water of the moat we had dug round our sand-castle, or with wooden spades at the slope standing guard on the rocks, while my mother, a third child on the way, sat enjoying this last untroubled summer. 'Day wrote, all pleased with Woola-combe', the diary says. It was the end of my father's con-valescent time. At the beginning of August he was back to all his work at St. Agnes, the men's club, the children's services, the sick visiting, the entertainments, the meetings to call attention to poverty and unemployment, activities now gone beyond recall, visible only in a folded leaflet and a few photographs; a glimpse of him singing a good-night song with a group of little girls in night-dresses carrying candle-sticks in their hands, or with older girls on an 'outing', straw-boatered in a hayfield.

October came, with my first introduction to Aunt Ada, the day on Tunbridge Wells Common, and a week later my mother's miscarriage. Her distress at destroying the new life, the haunting thought that she had somehow murdered the baby, may have caused her to wish the responsibility on to my father, to blame him for letting her carry me downstairs.

The sociability of life at Tunbridge Wells had almost com-pletely taken the place for Ada of doctors and ground ivy. On Christmas morning at midday a cab, or 'fly' as she called it, drove her to a boarding-house called Sunny Mount where she picked up Miss Twinch and two other friends and they all went on together to spend the day at Cranwell House with a Mrs. Westley and her little dog Jet. (The dog was soon to become an almost daily companion on her walks.) 'An enjoy-able day,' she wrote of this first Christmas in nine years not spent alone. 'The others left at 10. I stayed to sleep.' And not a mention of feeling tired. Since retrimming her old hat in July she had begun to take an interest in her appearance. On New Year's Eve she went into the town and bought a new jacket, 'my 1st new warm one since the autumn of 1894'; the excitement gave her a restless night. Ten days later she bought a new hat.

It was the January of the 1910 election, brought about by the Lords' rejection of the People's Budget, a rejection which threatened financial chaos and a Liberal show-down with the Upper House. Ada went into the town to hear the announcement of the local results. Captain Spender Clay had won, with a majority of 3,210, and she stood and listened to his speech from the balcony of the Conservative Club. Whether my father voted Liberal, or, perhaps unknown to my mother, Labour, he would have felt the Kingdom of Heaven had suffered a set-back in the results of the election. The Liberals lost 104 seats and would have to depend now on the support of the Irish Nationalists and Labour. 1910, the last full year of his life, was going to be a troubling one, both for him and for my mother. Physically he was in poor shape, with not much flesh on his bones ('terribly thin', my mother told me), and increasingly dependent on brandy to drive himself on. It was some time during this year that he went up to London to consult a specialist, and stayed for two nights with his youngest brother Walter, (then a master at Morden Terrace School), at 181 Algernon Road, Lewisham, a house from which in my early teens I began to explore London. Walter and his wife Annie, or Nance, had two children: Jack, a year older than my brother, and Nora who shared my year of birth. Jack has one memory of my father's visit. He made them all laugh by telling how my two-and-a-half-year-old self imitated people, particularly – or most tellingly – my father, which bears out that we parody best what we love best. This year, when everything was going wrong for the rest of the family, seems to have been my brief heyday, the year of my anti-war demonstration when I dropped my brother's lead soldiers into the simmering jam, the year I won praise from a visiting pianist for beating time to his playing, changing the beat as the tempo changed. A miniature baton arrived a few days later, 'for the budding composer'. It was the year when I stole a pair of scissors and cut off a little girl's hair in the greenhouse, and in a rage hurled a fork at my brother. It is likely to have been the year when I sat watching a visiting clergyman who talked with an unrelieved solemnity, and said to him, when he came to a pause, 'Now laugh.' According to my mother I had a gross appetite for laughter at the time, and when feeling too serious tickled myself under the chin to produce it, not a commendable trick, but as I was quite soon to find life less of a joke it may be excused.

While I went happily on, exchanging my petticoats for short trousers and my long curls for short hair (taken to the barber's by my father, while my mother wept to think of me so changed), my brother, now eight years old, was perhaps unconsciously affected by the tensions beginning to build up. He may sometimes have sensed a strangeness in our father, that difference by which our mother could tell when he had been drinking; at any rate he was ill at ease with him, even a little fearful of this man so loved by other children and by me. When I went to my brother for his memories I found that the iniquity of oblivion had not just blindly, but comprehensively, scattered her poppy, leaving no trace of my father, except of being taken by him to see a primitive moving picture of the American Civil War, which scared my brother out of all enjoyment and gave him nightmares. Otherwise he remembers only a paternal guidance in the matter of reading, and still has on his shelves the well-illustrated children's editions of *Ivanhoe*, *The Talisman*, and *Robinson Crusoe*. No comics were allowed into the house. They were read by my brother *en tapinois* in the school playground.

My brother had bronchial asthma in February, bronchitis in March, and diphtheria in April. On his eighth birthday (6 March) the King, tired and worried over the fuss about the Lords, travelled to Paris on his way to Biarritz, attending next day a performance of Rostand's *Chantecler*, which he

found stupid, childish, and like a pantomime. The Théâtre
de la Porte St. Martin was so dreadfully hot that he caught a
chill, and on 6 May he died from cardiac bronchitis. 'Everyone', Ada wrote two days later, 'seemed to be in black', and
on 20 May, the day of the funeral:

Very hot. Brilliant sunshine . . . The King buried at Windsor.
8 foreign Kings besides numerous princes followed. Procession 1½
miles long. To Sunny Mount at 10. Took Jet out . . . At 1.30 I
went to the Town Hall to see the local procession start for Trinity
Church. I was the only lady upstairs . . . Went round to the church
to meet Miss Twinch . . . I took Jet to see procession leave Trinity
Church.

The first anniversary of that day, 20 May 1911, was to
know another funeral, my father's.

It would be overstating things, at least I hope it would, to
say of my family in 1910 that 'everyone seemed to be in
black'. On the surface life went on as before. We all went on
holiday together to Minehead in June. My father took a
photograph of us sitting in the woods, not unlike the picture
of the happy picnic at Marwood before I was born; but there
was already a touch of doom in the air. The coils of the
double-headed snake, of illness and drink, were tightening
round my father, wrestle as he might. In one of his sermons
he had urged with a deep anxiety that a man should take
heed of his besetting sin before its power was too strong to
escape. He was secretary to the Temperance Society and
chairman of the Band of Hope, but the hope for him was now
as blind as the picture by G. F. Watts which hung in our house.

On 6 August Ada writes in her diary: 'Called at Sunny
Mount for Jet. Tried unsuccessfully to get rooms for Day';
and a month later she notes that Day had taken 'the chicks'
to Gillingham. Is it reading too much into this to think she
needed to talk about her anxieties, or at least to get us away
from Bristol for a while? Was it now that she was so disturbed
by what she felt was my father's over-reliance on Florrie
Briggs, my godmother, daughter of one of the parish council?

So disturbed that she would still speak of it a dozen years later. Florrie Briggs was a pleasant-looking young woman with soft brown hair – we had a photograph of her in my boyhood – and a valuable social worker in the parish. I believe it may have been this as much as anything that my mother was jealous of. Even if she had not been occupied looking after house and family she was shy of strangers, and retiring, a little ill at ease at social functions, or so I remember her, though by then she had no pretty hats and dresses to give her confidence. Whether the relationship between my father and Florrie was simply a common interest in the parish, or at the most an affectionate friendship, the parishioners no doubt gave it their closest attention, reason enough for my mother to feel unhappy.

In October came the almost inevitable end to any object of Ada's affection, as the diary tells:

Oct. 6. Thurs. Hot. Revolution in Portugal. About 12 o'clock dear little Jet fell out of Mrs. C's window at Sunny Mount and died early in the evening.

7. Fri. Connie came early to tell me of Jet's death. I to Sunny Mount after dinner. Miss Twinch very upset about Jet.

8. Sat. Out a little. Missed my pretty little black companion.

9. Sun. Not at all well.

The pain in her side returned, but she continued to go to prayer meetings at Sunny Mount unless it was raining, as it was on the 20th, the day Harrold Bridger sailed for Australia. He was off to join his uncle Charlie Hammond in his photographer's studio in Raymond Street, Sale, Gippsland. In 1889 when Charlie had made the voyage in the *Riverina* he had taken two months and a week to reach Adelaide; Harrold, in the S.S. *Persic*, did it in one month and nine days. When the ship touched at Albany on 26 November he wrote in his journal: 'The first thing we did was to rush to the only barber's shop in the place . . . here we were able to get a newspaper to read, and I suppose the thing that struck me most in the news was Count Tolstoi's death.'

Ada spent most of November on her bed, too ill and weak to go out now that she could no longer look forward to walking Jet on the common. There was another election, in December, but she felt none of the interest she had felt in January, when there had been 'dense crowds and deafening noise'. Captain Spender Clay's majority dropped by a thousand, but the Government's position remained practically unchanged, the number of their seats not enough, Lord Hugh Cecil considered, for the introduction of any 'revolutionary' legislation.

But a week later there was news which interested her greatly: the appointment of a new Dean of Lincoln. He was Thomas Charles Fry, sprung from the vast Somerset clan. Her great-great-grandfather was his great-grandfather's brother. Confused by the number of Peters in the family, she believed the relationship to be nearer.

The Dean had been Headmaster of Berkhamsted School, and gets an unfavourable mention in Graham Greene's autobiography; and in 1915 he was to write a letter to *The Times* newspaper suggesting that the War Office should be given powers to drive night-clubs out of the Thames Valley, as a concomitant to driving the Germans out of Belgium. He caused a sensation in the early 1920s, when he was in America on a fund-raising tour for the cathedral, by calling the story of the Flood a myth or allegory. I remember it as front-page news in the *Daily Sketch*. If Ada was still alive to read it, which I think she was, she would have wondered why she had carried the news of his Deanship with such pleasure and pride to Sunny Mount and Miss Twinch on 14 December 1910. She would have felt as shocked as the Bible belt had been. To her the scriptures were God's Word, and God spoke with the voice of a historiographer, not of a poet.

The year 1911 began for her with a prophetic event: 'Jan 31. Read that Sir John Jackson had signed agreement for the irrigation of the Mesopotamia Valley. Evidently the first step to the building of Babylon the Great.'

For my father the greater prophetic event of 1911, marking a step in 'the working out of the Kingdom of God upon earth', would have been the passing of the National Insurance Act. But his concern with this world was almost at an end. On 28 March Ada notes that 'Day, Charley and baby had influenza.' As soon as we were better my mother, brother, and I went on holiday to Minehead. My father took his last photograph of us before we left, standing outside the front door of 6 St. Nicholas Road with a neighbour's dustbin in the background. Instead of the brazenly cheerful look I always before had presented to his camera, I seem anxious, even startled, and cling to the hand of my brother as though the world had become less trustworthy.

We probably left Bristol during Holy Week; at any rate we were settled in lodgings at Minehead before Easter Sunday, 16 April, when my brother came down with measles. On 28 April Ada recorded that Leslie had recovered but I was not well, and adds, 'Charley ill at Bristol and unable to go to them.'

The days of the next fortnight are full of imponderables; the truth is hard to find, in some of the details impossible, and the versions passed on to me range from the incomplete to the demonstrably false. My mother's friend Louie Chandler, mother of the little girl whose hair I barbered, believed that the illness which prevented Charley from joining us at Minehead was a touch of delirium tremens. The last time he read the lesson in church, she told me, had been a fiasco; he had been incapable of finding his way through the words; but the post-mortem report made no mention of any sign of alcoholism, and as she also said that he was found dead on the moors little faith can be put in her reliability. It does seem likely that after we left him alone in the house, tired and ill as he was, iller than my mother could have realized, he may have been drinking. But early in May, though just when I don't know, he had pulled himself together and joined us, and shortly afterwards set out on what my mother always called 'a walking tour'. At the inquest it was said that he left us on Monday 15 May, to spend a day in Ilfracombe and return the same night; the parish magazine said he was returning to Minehead from a short visit to Devonshire; but he was away long enough to send my mother a postcard, so she told me, to say she needn't buy provisions for the week-end because he was bringing back a chicken.

The walking-tour notion is the more puzzling since he started his journey by train. My mother saw him off. Louie Chandler thought they quarrelled on the platform, but that was not at all my mother's story. Perhaps she tried to dissuade him from going. As the train drew out of the station she had such a feeling of loss and dread that she found herself running down the platform, as though the train were dragging her with it.

Where was he going, and why was he going? If to visit his old haunts and friends at Marwood he would certainly have seen Fred Bindon, and Bindon told the coroner he hadn't seen my father since July 1909, when we were all on holiday at Woolacombe.

Wherever he had been, and for however many days, he reached Ilfracombe on the afternoon of Monday 15 May. At three o'clock in the afternoon he went to a public house in the High Street called the Posada, kept by a man called Lionel Gadyn, and introduced himself as an old acquaintance of Mr. Gadyn's father. He said he had missed the Minehead boat and asked if he could have a bed for the night. (At the inquest Lionel Gadyn told the jury that he had taken him in 'more as a guest' because he had known his father.)

The next morning he came downstairs at 9.30, refused any breakfast except some egg and milk, and made no effort to leave. He lay on the sofa for most of the day, taking no food or drink either at lunch or tea-time. He said he was feeling very tired. At nine o'clock he went to bed. Mr. Gadyn was uneasy about him, and at 11.30 went to his room. My father was dead. He was forty-two years old.

It would almost seem that he had left Bristol to see us for the last time before going away to die with the least disturbance to my mother. What were his thoughts through the hours of that last lonely day?

On Wednesday 17 May, my mother, brother, and I were in the little front sitting-room of the house where we were lodging at Minehead. I remember looking out of the window and seeing a man dressed all in black coming up the path from the front gate. In my memory he is wearing a top hat, but it may have been the flat, wide-brimmed black hat of a parson. I recall no more of him than the glimpse as he came through the gate; perhaps the landlady had told my brother to take me into the kitchen before she opened the front door. When the visitor had gone she picked me up in her arms and carried me back to the sitting-room. She stood just inside the door, still holding me, my brother at her side. It was a very small room; a sofa filled the whole of the wall between the door and the shallow bay window. My mother was lying on it, her face turned away from us, resting on the sofa's head, and she was crying. I only remember how strange it was to see her there where she had thrown herself down in such grief, but my brother remembers her saying 'I want to go home, let me go home!', desperately, like a child left alone among strangers.

We travelled back to Bristol that same day, in a carriage marked Reserved, so my brother remembers, either because he was still infectious from measles or to give my mother quiet. The next day Grandpa and Nana Harris travelled from Gillingham to be with her. It was the day of the inquest at Ilfracombe. Someone had sent for Fred Bindon to come up from Marwood to identify the body. Mr. Gadyn thought the deceased had been suffering from a nervous breakdown. The post-mortem examination, by a Dr. Langridge, revealed a considerable amount of fluid in the pericardium, the heart was large and dilated, and the lungs intensely congested. The cause of death was heart failure, the result of pericarditis. The jury returned a verdict of death from natural causes.

On Friday the 19th Bess travelled down from London to be

with Day, and Ada wrote a valedictory poem of four verses beginning:

> The Worker slept. And duty called in vain,
> And failed to wake him to his work again.
> So weary was he, and so fast asleep
> That nothing would disturb that slumber deep.

She had it printed 'In Affectionate Remembrance', with a heavy black border.

He was not brought back to St. Agnes for burial. Arthur Rashleigh, the vicar, travelled to Ilfracombe to conduct the funeral service. The *In Memoriam* in the parish magazine said that some of those connected with the Lake Street Mission were there, and a few people from Marwood, perhaps F. J. Kelly who sent off the hamper in 1906, certainly Fred Bindon and his sister. Grandpa Harris and my father's two brothers, Bert and Walter, were the only representatives of the family. Nana had evidently stayed in Bristol to help Bess look after my mother who was too badly shaken to face the funeral. A weight of loss, bewilderment, sorrow, regrets, self-reproach even, seems to have crushed her. It was ten days before she was well enough for my grandparents to take us to live with them at Homedale. She had one more hurt to come from that death: on my father's gravestone in the Ilfracombe churchyard the Harrises added the name of his first wife, Clara Jane Jarvis.

The last beleaguered months of my father's life seem to have outweighed for Arthur Rashleigh the four and a half years of devoted work that had gone before. His pastoral letter in the magazine mentions the death with pious triteness: 'We are feeling the loss in the parish of one of God's workers – our brother Mr. Harris, who has been called away in the midst of his labours. But we have faith to believe that God's work will go on, and that He will provide fresh workers to take the place of those whom He calls to Himself.' One of the parishioners, in a letter to my mother written on the day of the funeral, spoke more from the heart:

The last photograph
my father took of my
brother and me, 1911

With my mother, brother, and Aunt Ada at Gillingham, 2 January 1912

Myself modelling goldfish in plasticine at the Froebel Kindergarten,
Bedford. The girls were called Rita and Connie.

Aunt Ada, with hat and me, in the
Clapham Fields, Bedford, 1914

My mother in 1939

The Man in Black

He was to very many of us a real comrade in the fight. His winning personality & ever present thoughtfulness for others, did those who came in contact with him a great deal of good. His thoughts seemed ever expanding out to those who were in trouble and distress; even in his last illness despite the fact that he himself was too weak to get out of bed, his thoughts were rushing about to see if this or that person was prepared for – did Mr So & So have his attention, or did Mrs Cannock feel tired or any & every soul was present in his heart. We shall miss him very much at St. Agnes.

When my mother was eighty-one, her memory failing, only the good things of the marriage remained in her mind. She came across the exercise book in which she had written down her recollections, and against the description of the first chance meeting at the German Exhibition she scribbled: 'As things turned out I could not have married a better man . . . my dear husband . . . we were very happy.' But a year or two earlier she had destroyed the photographs of the wedding.

There is no way of knowing how soon after my father's death I completed my memory-picture of him. At Minehead on the night he died? Or at St. Nicholas Road during the week or so after? I was sleeping in a room with my mother. This suggests that we were still at Bristol. At Homedale my brother shared a bedroom with us; but I remember only two beds almost filling the room: my own, near the door, and close beside it my mother's. It must have been fairly late at night, for my mother was in bed and asleep. I woke to the feeling of an approach, of the darkness bringing something to me. I think the door was shut, and yet the place where the door was seemed very deep, like a tunnel, and it was bringing something to me with a kind of taut deliberation or slow emphasis. Then I saw my father standing beside the bed, faintly lit by the tiny paraffin lamp or night-light. I called out to my mother 'Daddy's here, daddy's here', but my mother, barely awake, simply murmured to me to go back to sleep. I remember feeling puzzled and sorry that she wouldn't wake up properly or believe me, and by then I had lost sight of my father.

CHAPTER FOURTEEN

Interval at Gillingham

My father made no will. There was nothing to be willed. We had been living from month to month on his small salary and my mother's tiny income from Emma's legacy. The grandparents Harris had no doubt or hesitation about what should be done; we must go and live with them at Homedale. Grandpa was 67, Nana 65. It was no small matter to have two children, particularly a three-year-old, invading their peace. There were only three bedrooms of any size; one was regularly let to a sequence of naval officers on spells of duty in the dockyard, who with their families also occupied the sitting-room; the fourth bedroom, hardly bigger than a cupboard, was slept in by the maid, Ellen Earle. The grandparents gave up their front room to us and moved into a smaller one at the back. Their kindness was unfaltering, and Nana's serenity pervaded the house, a quiet shattered only once while we were there; a swift retribution overtook me for speaking pertly to my mother. I was suddenly snatched from the dinner-table by an angry grandfather and carried screaming and struggling upstairs where I was dumped on a bed. The experience of being helpless in a whirl of physical strength was as shocking to me as my father's attack on my mother must have been to her, or indeed as this occasion was to her, too.

By July she had sufficiently shaken off the numbness which followed my father's death to begin thinking about the future. Thankful as she was for the refuge of Homedale it could only be a temporary measure. She was all the time uneasy about our being a nuisance, constrained in her relationship with us,

and longing for a home of her own. On 28 July 1911 she took
us to Tunbridge Wells to visit Ada, setting out quite early in
the morning and spending the whole day with her on the
common until she saw us off on the 6.08 train. While my
brother played with me in the sunshine my mother broached
the question of whether Ada would be willing to join us in
Gillingham; by pooling their resources they might together
be able to afford to rent a house. Another help towards
independence, though exactly when or how it came about is
uncertain, was the rent from two or three houses. I have
mentioned how Grandpa and Nana Harris over the years had
acquired a number of cottage properties in Gillingham and
Chatham. Each Saturday Grandpa would go round with a
black leather bag collecting the rents, and he and Nana would
then sit at the dining-table separating the coppers from the
silver and making entries in an account book. The rents from
two or three of these were evidently being paid to my mother
by the end of the summer, if not before. The sum was small,
and the cost of keeping the cottages in good repair, particularly in later years, made the weekly sum even smaller,
but it was enough to enable her to propose to Ada a home of
their own.

Ada was living at Tunbridge Wells as cheerfully as she had
ever lived anywhere since Emma's death. She had her circle
of friends, and days were kept lively by prayer meetings at
Sunny Mount, Dr. Ussher's sermons, an occasional cantata
at the Free Church, and playing unspecified 'games' with a
Mrs. B. All through a blazing August, too hot for Miss
Twinch to go out, when the chief topic of conversation was
the railway strike, Ada debated with herself about bidding
all these joys farewell. But there was also the welcome
thought that Day, for the first time, needed her, not only for
the help her annuity would bring but the companionship
too, and a share in training the chicks to be good Christians.
It was 4 October before she finally decided to throw in her
lot with us, and the next afternoon she called on all her
friends to break the news. She filled the next fortnight with

tea-parties, suppers, and sermons, and on the 17th Miss
Twinch helped her to pack. She had meant to spend the whole
of the following day at Sunny Mount but instead waited all
through the morning and afternoon for a man to fetch her
boxes. It was six o'clock before she was free to hurry round
for a last meal with the ladies. The next morning Miss Twinch
accompanied her as far as Tonbridge and my mother met her
at Maidstone. She was to go into lodgings until they could
find a house. 'Got to my rooms in Gillingham at 3 p.m. Very
tired and giddy,' Ada wrote.

For two or three months she seems to have been contented.
She was always made welcome at Homedale for dinner or
tea, had her first ride in an electric tramcar, attended the
Naval Hospital Church on Sundays, and helped my mother to
search for a home. On 21 November she writes: 'Looked over
more houses. Dissatisfied women broke windows in London.'

I was beginning to be less of a bonny little chick than she
had once thought me. The easy acceptance of life which had
carried me through my first three years began to dwindle
after my father died. I spent my fourth birthday in bed, but
I was better by Christmas, and on 2 January 1912 the four
of us had our photograph taken at the Parisian Studio in the
High Street. My mother is looking severe and strained in the
black silk blouse and hard white collar and cuffs which had
been her uniform since she had given up wearing widow's
weeds; and Ada looks exactly as she continued to look for the
rest of her life: the frizz of hair across the top of her expansive
forehead, the bumpy Hammond nose underlined too immediately by the wide mouth, the cheek with the deep incision
turned away from the light, the bodice of her black dress
decorated with beads of jet. The only frivolity is a jabot of
white lace under the chin. The white lace was for 'best'; at
other times its place was taken by a bow of ribbon, often
cherry red. She was fond of these little flaunts of cheerfulness.
When she lay dying in the Bedford Infirmary she wore a
scrap of blue ribbon in her hair which she fondly imagined I
had given to her.

Interval at Gillingham

At the end of January 1912 we moved into our own house, 53 Marlborough Road. It looked out across an open space of grass called The Lines, enormous to my eyes, meeting the sky where the ground dropped steeply away to Chatham and Rochester. It was the way my brother went to school. On our first coming to Gillingham he had been sent to the local elementary school, rougher and tougher than anything he had yet had to deal with. My mother turned in anxiety to Bessie, whose two boys were now off her hands, and Bessie was now paying for him to go to a private school in Rochester run by a Mr. Tonkin. We could watch him walking into the distance, getting smaller and smaller until he dropped over the edge; and in June we had a grandstand view from our windows of Admiral Sir Robert Poors taking the salute at the Military and Naval Review. It was the summer when Admiral von Tirpitz and the generals in Berlin increased their influence over the Kaiser after the failure of the Haldane mission, and Winston Churchill brought our battleships from the Mediterranean to make a third battle squadron in home waters. The cloud was as yet no bigger than a man's hand, but it held a greater threat than the brimstone sky I had seen from my pram.

It was soon clear that life with us at Gillingham was not suiting Ada so well as the peaceful companionship of Miss Twinch and the other ladies. As early as 17 January, when she sent a copy of *The Stones of Venice* to one of Edith's sons in Australia, she complains of two attacks of sickness; and by April the strain of living in a house with two children was beginning to tell. 'A day of strumming [on the piano],' she writes. 'Nearly ill with the noise.' To give her a rest from me a decision was suddenly taken to send me to school, not at the beginning of a term but towards the end, on 8 July, when I was four and a half. I stayed there for ten minutes. They had taken me down area-steps into a dark basement room full of children, all older than I was, sitting at desks very close together, and left me there. I was put into a desk in the front row. An unsmiling woman placed an exercise book in front of me and moved on without speaking. The other children – most of them girls – stared at me and nudged each other. What chiefly frightened me was that I had no idea what I was to do with the exercise book or why it had been put in front of me. I looked at its mottled cover (red, black, and white; I can still see it in my mind's eye), my heart thumping. The next moment I was out of the room, up the area-steps and into the street. The teacher caught up with me on the pavement; I have a confused impression of that alarming moment, but somehow I must have got the better of her, and somehow she got me home, perhaps leaving the school to look after itself. The next thing I remember is sitting crying on the side of my bed; Ada kneels in front of me sternly taking off my socks, while my mother stands beside her quite as unhappy as I. After that she must have come to an understanding with Ada about who was in charge; at any rate it was the last time I remember being punished. The next day Ada made one more effort to overcome my resistance. The diary merely says she took me 'to see the children play' on The Lines, but it was really a plot to reintroduce me casually to the schoolmistress and her flock. As soon as I caught sight of them in the distance I struggled to get my hand out of Ada's firm grasp, and fought so hard that she took me home again. It was forgiving of her not to mention it.

She was not happy. As 1912 wore on the entry 'I out alone' made a regular appearance in the diary, and reports of illness increased. All through September and on into October she lay on the sofa each day, 'Pain constant'. In the first week of October she wrote: 'Scarcely able to stand these days but managed to get downstairs every day', and a week later: 'Got worse. Wrote to Dr. Fairweather. Bessie & Noeline moved to Bedford.'

That last sentence contained our future, and this is how it came about. On 19 September – 'the 27th anniversary of Mother's death', the diary reminds us – Bernie Bridger had sailed for Australia to join his brother Harrold, after coming down to Gillingham to say goodbye to us. As soon as he had left, Bessie began to make arrangements to live separately from her husband. The family reticence kept the facts well shrouded, but years afterwards my mother told me Sidney Bridger had brought, or suggested bringing, another woman to live with them, a fellow church worker. Her choice of Bedford may well have been because a cousin, Gertie Linsell, daughter of Rowland's sister Henrietta Selina, lived there with her four children, Aubyn, Hugh, Iris, and Ralph. If it were Gertie who sought and found for Bessie the little house at the northern limit of the town, 120 Gladstone Street, she set the scene for all the years of my growing up.

Ada summed up 1912 on New Year's Eve: 'A noisy day. I very overtired and glad to go to bed.' And then, on a line to itself, her back-sloping handwriting increasing in size: 'A year of disappointment.'

After only two months at Bedford Bessie decided to give her marriage another chance and went back to Sidney Bridger at Beckenham. She wrote to my mother describing the house in Gladstone Street, rented for £20 a year, and told her what excellent schooling the town provided. On 18 January 1913 Ada wrote in the diary: 'Daisy nearly decided to go to Bedford', and on the 25th: 'Daisy decided to live at Bedford.'

CHAPTER FIFTEEN

Bunyan's Town

On the last day of March we were all up at half past six to get ready for the journey. The day was gloomy and wet. Ada was feeling weak and sick. What were my mother's feelings? Was she relieved to be starting afresh or anxious about what lay ahead? We were met at Charing Cross by Sidney Bridger. London was under a dense pall of fog. While the cab carried us through the shadowy streets to St. Pancras the bell of St. Paul's Cathedral was tolling for the funeral of Lord Wolseley, the Sir Garnet whose triumphant entry into Cairo Emma had referred to in her letter to Bessie thirty-one years before. Then thirty years before, on another day of rain and fog, she had brought eleven-year-old Day to St. Pancras and put her into a carriage 'with only one little boy, going to Bedford'. My mother could draw some cheer from the old station, so familiar, filled with memories of the days when she and Katie used to travel up from Leicester with Uncle Willie to hear the Christy Minstrels, or to see Charles Wyndham in *David Garrick*.

Bess and Noeline met us at Bedford and took us to 138 Foster Hill Road where we were to lodge for two or three nights. The next day they went back to Beckenham, leaving us to get acquainted with 120 Gladstone Street. Ada's first impression was of 'a pretty, clean little place, but rooms small'. Pretty it was definitely not, but Bess would certainly have scoured and scrubbed it until it shone. It was towards the top of a long street divided into two by a road crossing at right angles called Stanley Street. Below Stanley Street was Lower Gladstone Street, workmen's cottages, their front rooms opening straight on to the pavement. Upper Gladstone Street began with a butcher's shop, the floor freshly scattered with sawdust each day, and from that point the houses became semi-detached, with a narrow passage to the left and right of each pair, leading to the back gates, and a foot or two of space between the front window and the railings, too meagre to be called a garden. The topmost house in the street, the last house in Bedford to the north and six doors above us, was double-fronted and faced an unmade-up road which ended at the cemetery gates and the park. Beyond the double-fronted house were allotments, a path going up beside them to a stile and Cemetery Hill. The whole long street was like a ladder of tenuous social differences. It would never have crossed our minds that we could know anyone in the lower half. Once you were over Stanley Street and past the butcher's shop (it was called Day's) the possibility of acquaintanceship began, though I don't remember knowing anyone, even by sight, until nearly half-way up to the top. Mrs. Thorne behind her privet hedge at 106 was the real beginning of our social world, and from there on the houses seemed increasingly conscious of the double-fronted house, the apogee. All these subtle gradations have vanished now. The front railings were taken away during the Hitler war, the fascia wood under the eaves has rotted away, new streets have buried the allotments and the double-fronted house has lost its pride of place.

But on 3 April 1913, when the furniture arrived, we were quite prepared to agree with Ada that the house was pretty. Bess had done her best to make it so. She had cut large yellow and green chrysanthemums out of wallpaper and pasted them on the panels of the front sitting-room door. Varnished over, they had a liverish look. This front room was to be Ada's sanctum until by the pressure of circumstances she was banished to her bedroom. This was where, lying on her horsehair sofa, she taught me my lessons until I went to school. The lesson books of her own childhood were brought out for my instruction, and the stories she read me were those she had read to my mother, *Jessica's First Prayer* and *Nellie's Memories*, the book she had been reading at the Forest Hill farm when Emma was dying. Another was an extraordinary story about two children walking about inside a gigantic human mouth and being drenched by the springs of saliva. But when we came to the uvula, like a giant slug attached to the back of the cave, I lost interest and never learned how the adventure ended. And yet she had a way with children; I was always quite happy, at this age, to be with her. She taught me to sing a song called 'The Muffin Man' while I rang the gilt handbell banded with blue enamel which lived on the mahogany sideboard. We played paper games together, one of us drawing a head and folding it out of sight for the other to add a body; and Consequences, and I-Spy-with-my-Little-Eye. She discovered to me the secret of how to leave only one marble on the solitaire board. I always hoped the triumphant one would be my favourite, a marble of pure crystal with fine rainbow threads caught inside it, clear, full of light, an angel among the earthbound others.

Ada's fern case stood in the window on a bamboo table. Under a glass dome a moist forest of ferns grew round a ruined castle, heart's-tongue, maidenhair, and tiny seedlings, the children of the forest. When the sun shone through the window in the mornings it glittered on the drops of condensation on the glass, and when I came to know the Arthurian legends it was into this forest the knights came seeking the Holy Grail.

The only other furniture the moving-men brought into the front room on that April day was a dining-table, which we covered with a flower-patterned plush cloth, and four chairs. These, with Ada's sofa and the sideboard, left no space except the hearthrug to move about in. But the back room was even smaller. Four flimsy Edwardian chairs, the upright piano and a piano stool filled it. The front of the piano was inlaid with a pattern of roses and sprouted two candle-holders. The top of the piano stool, covered in mustard plush, was slightly convex. When turned upside down it became my boat. I sat inside, holding two of the legs, and rocked to and fro, voyaging like my mother through the Bay of Biscay or some perilous sea of my imagining. Above me, hanging over the piano, was a sepia print of Holman Hunt's *The Light of the World*. The eyes in the picture followed me wherever I went in the room, moving their gaze as watchfully as the eyes of God haunting my father's childhood.

The kitchen was where we spent most of the time and had our meals, except Ada who had hers on a tray, lying on her sofa in the front room. Through the kitchen was a little scullery and the back door. In the scullery was the coal cupboard, the larder, a mangle, a pump with a curved iron handle to draw up water for the tap over the sink, and a brick 'copper' in which we heated up the water for baths. There was a bathroom at the head of the stairs, but the only way of filling the bath was to carry pails of hot water up from the scullery. I had my bath in a tin tub in front of the kitchen range. While my mother towelled me down she sang a sad song about 'Ten dirty little fingers and ten dirty little toes'. Perhaps the owner of them died; certainly the tune had a melancholy sound, and death was something that happened to children in songs and in some of the books Ada read to me. I preferred to think that the hero of another song, the Little Boy Blue whose toys waited so unavailingly for him, had simply grown up and gone away.

My mother's favourite music-hall song (we sang it together during her last illness forty-four years later) was 'Daddy wouldn't buy me a bow-wow (*bow-wow!*)', and she had two rhymes which she used to recite to me with never-failing enjoyment to both of us. One was:

> Three little ghostesses
> Sitting on postesses
> Eating buttered toastesses,
> Greasing their fistesses
> Up to their wristesses.
> Ugh! *dirty* little bistesses!

The other, which no doubt came to me all the way from Emma and the days at Some Vile Road, began

> Two little dogs went out for a walk
> And it was windy weather.

They tied their tails together so that they wouldn't be blown apart, but the wind, 'as sharp and keen as a carving knife', cut the string; and then my mother's voice took off with zest, her eyes twinkling brighter than ever, for the climax:

> Away, away, like kites in the air
> The little dogs flew about
> Till one of them was blown to bits
> And the other turned inside out!

The two tunes I loved most of all, and the words too, were evening hymns: 'The day Thou gavest, Lord, is ended, the darkness falls at Thy behest' and 'Now the day is over'. Whatever it was that needed assuaging in me they assuaged; they had the same perfection as the rainbow marble on the solitaire board. 'Now the darkness gathers, Stars begin to peep' – and the first and brightest of the evening shone over the piece of waste ground in front of our house, where the house-building on the opposite side of the street had stopped short. 'There is Daddy's star,' my mother would say.

The first half of April was wintry with sleet and snow. For three nights Ada lay awake because of the cold. But as the days passed into May the barometer was rising for all of us. My brother did well in the entrance examination for the Modern School, and a year or so later won an Exhibition which paid his fees, £4.4s. a term, for the rest of his schooldays. Ada wrote in the diary that she had made '1st friend for 18 months', though perhaps no one would quite replace Miss Twinch, and the new surroundings had put new life into her. She could walk the mile or so into the town without feeling tired, even when she lost her way and found herself in the cattle-market. She bought herself a remarkable hat which balanced on her head like a piled-up tray on the splayed fingers of a waiter, the whole thing surmounted on the left by a black brush which exsufflated defiantly into the air. The hat stood a quarter of her own height, a symbol of her reanimated spirits. Proudly wearing this, when my lessons were over, she would take me for a walk in the fields above Cemetery Hill, where we picked the subtle quaking-grass to put in a vase in her room; or on Saturday mornings to the market in St. Paul's Square. Here Ada would buy her week's supply of fruit drops, and as we walked back along the High Street she would open the bag and give me one to suck, until the morning it stuck in my throat. After that I had to wait until we were home. It was a long way to go for a bag of fruit drops, but perhaps Ada enjoyed the bustle of the market as much as I did. We never failed to join the crowd at the crockery stall for the entertainment of seeing the trader juggle with plates, three at a time, while he kept up a flow of raucous patter which made us laugh.

St. Paul's Square, brooded over by the statue of John Howard the prison reformer, chin in hand, was still the heart of the town, as it had been seventy-five years before, on another summer's day, when a small boy called William Hale White, who grew up to be Mark Rutherford, was brought there to an open-air feast to celebrate Queen Victoria's coronation on 28 June 1838. Bedford was all flags and bunting then, he remembered, and so it was on 24 May 1913, Empire Day. We hung a Union Jack out of the front bedroom window. (On the same day Berlin was *en fête* for the wedding of the Kaiser's daughter.) It was a hot Saturday, and my mother, my brother, and I watched a cricket-match in the Modern School playing-field. We could have watched it almost equally well from our back bedroom window. What we called our garden – a square of tired gravel edged with London Pride – was separated from the north-east corner of the field only by a ditch and a hedge. The practice-nets were near that corner, and on summer evenings we heard the sound of play through our open windows. When I was seventeen, in a poem called *The School Field*, I wrote:

And heard the crack of bat and ball contesting
Cold as an ice-drop on our warm content.

In 1914, when the Army took over this part of the field and
built a firing-range, the sound we heard was the crackle of
rifle-fire. But we lived in great quiet in 1913. According to
the season of the year children bowled hoops or spun tops
in the middle of the road, undisturbed except by the horse-
drawn milk-float in the early morning, or old Charlie the
firewood man trundling his cart and calling 'Wa a'yee
woo'?' through his cleft palate, or the knife-grinder treadling
his machine. Occasionally a barrel-organ came our way and
I would run out to give the man a penny. Otherwise, apart
from bicycles (Gell's bicycle shop in Harpur Street was a
thriving business), I remember scarcely any traffic at all, not
even an omnibus. Everybody walked or cycled. Even as late
as 1925 I could stand with Mr. Nightingale the art-master
right in the middle of the High Street and quietly contemplate
the bright cumulus cloud towering above Hockcliffe's book-
shop. In 1913 the local hunt met on St. Peter's Green at the
northern end of the High Street. Ada took me to see it and
we stood admiring until the pink coats and the baying
hounds streamed away up St. Peter's Street.

There was always some excitement to look forward to that
summer. In June Ada bought The Hat, Grandpa and Nana
came to stay; we took them to watch the Modern School
rowing races on the river, and to see John Bunyan's birthplace and the old Moot Hall at Elstow. In July Grandpa and
Nana's maid, Ellen Earle, who slept in the cupboard-like
room at Homedale, came to spend her holiday with us.
Though she always called Grandpa 'the Master' she was more
like one of the family. She was small and dark, unfailingly
cheerful and funny, and I loved her dearly. While we were
living at Homedale I would come down the staircase, where
my eyes were level with a large framed print of the return of
Lord Kitchener after the Boer War, which hung above the
hall hatstand, and make straight for her kitchen. I thought

her the wittiest person in the world. If I scuffled one of the mats on the kitchen floor she would say 'Mind my Brussels!' She had a comedian's sense of timing and tone of voice, and without knowing what it meant I found it unforgettably funny. She read a weekly paper called *Home Chat*. In its pages there was always an advertisement for a kind of soldering material called Fluxite. Each week it had a new comic drawing illustrating a rhyming verse which told the adventures of the Fluxite Twins. I wonder now how an advertisement for solder could give me such pleasure, unless Ellen added her own improvisations, but it stays in my memory as my first lively response to literature and art.

She was with us for a full month in that almost cloudless summer of 1913, a holiday which started with the town regatta and went on through days of picnics in the park, a visit to the Trades Exhibition, boating on the river, and watching – Ada, Ellen, and I – Graham White circle his aeroplane five times above the Grammar School playing-field.

On 19 September – the twenty-eighth anniversary of Emma's death, as Ada did not fail to note – I went to school. My mother had decided to send me to the Froebel Kindergarten in The Crescent. This meant paying fees, and to meet the extra expense she took in a lodger. She and I moved from the front bedroom to the back, and the room where the piano was became his sitting-room. He was a thin, grey, remote man called Mr. Hunt. None of us took to him. My mother had another bed to make, another meal to serve and clear away, more washing-up. Ada's part in the domestic scheme was to help my brother with his homework, teach and entertain me, and to carry her tray to the kitchen at the end of a mealtime. The rough work, such as scrubbing the floors and the front step, was done by Rose, surname unknown. She was slow, heavy, and kindly, and sometimes brought with her a slow, heavy, and brooding young son called Stanley. The skin of her face and hands was etched with a black network of ingrained dirt. We got on well with her for some years, until during her menopause she went a bit crazy and threatened to attack my brother, a great favourite with her up to that time.

My mother's devotion to duty had the weakness of never teaching us to help her in any way. We took her labours for granted. I saw her self-control break for a moment on only two occasions: once when I must have been more than usually exasperating, or she was more than usually tired. She suddenly chased me round the kitchen table as though to hit me, and as quickly regained her calm. And several years later when my brother, with acute appendicitis, was being taken to hospital in an ambulance. She had put on her hat and coat and was lacing up her boots. I tried to comfort her, and she bit my head off to stop herself from crying. She was over eighty before I saw her let her deep feelings break surface again. There was a great deal of Emma in her, the apparently cheerful acceptance of what life put before her, but also on occasions a touch of the rebel and a stubbornness which may have been Rowland's. I once caught a glimpse of what her fury could be when roused. She had fetched me from school and we were walking up Lower Gladstone Street. Through the window of one of the cottages we saw a woman hitting a child and heard the child yelling. My mother burst open the front door, raged at the woman for her wickedness and promptly left, slamming the door behind her. I was astounded. My mother, who never raised her voice, who could bear no altercation of any kind, so shy and self-effacing with strangers, suddenly transformed into a whirlwind of passion! We walked back to our house in silence, both a little shaken. Ada could sometimes stir the rebel in her by reproving her for letting the housework interfere with church-going. It was exasperating, with all there was to do, to be reminded by Ada of the story of Martha and Mary:

But Martha was cumbered about much serving, and came to him, and said, Lord, dost thou not care that my sister hath left me to serve alone? bid her therefore that she help me. And Jesus answered and said unto her, Martha, Martha, thou art careful and troubled about many things: but one thing is needful: and Mary hath chosen that good part, which shall not be taken away from her.

Having made her point Ada-Mary would retire to the good part she had chosen of lying on the sofa to continue her Bible study, filling the margins with copious notes in a microscopic handwriting.

After my rejection of schooling the year before, they were probably apprehensive about how I would behave on my first day at the kindergarten. There was no need to be. The light alone reassured me. I found myself in a big room as bright as the open air. All down one side, at child-height, blackboards were fastened to the wall. A friendly teacher suggested I might like to draw on the blackboards with coloured chalks and left me to get on with it. Later that morning, my confidence established, I turned my attention to what the other children were doing. The diary simply records with relief that I liked my first morning very much; and the liking continued throughout the five years I stayed there. There was an upper school for older children, the whole place part of a training college for student-teachers. The name of the Principal was Miss Walmsley whose air of no-nonsense overlaid a sympathetic heart, and who rescued me, when at eighteen I left the Modern School, by inviting me on to the staff until I could make up my mind what I wanted to do, and paid for me to have shorthand lessons. The Vice-Principal, and largely in charge of the kindergarten, was Miss Spence, who first brought words into vivid life for me, as I shall tell. The Froebel system of education as practised at The Crescent sixty-five years ago had reached an excellence not lightly to be challenged, in spite of the proliferation of theory since. I was happy, I was interested, I learned fast. The world of school was a spacious, airy, bright world, disciplined without punishment, full of play, laughter, activity, and music. We started each day, appropriately enough, by singing 'All things bright and beautiful', and then marched away to a tune played on the piano by a teacher. One morning Miss Spence pretended there was no one there who could play, but she had heard, she said, that I had composed a march tune. In some curious untaught way my fingers had been able to find chords and tunes on the keyboard from the moment I could reach it, that rapt strumming which had so tried Ada's nerves at Gillingham. My most recent opus at the time was called 'The Lovers' Quarrel', played entirely on the black notes, but I had also invented a piece called 'Pharaoh's March', with a heavily emphasized pom-pomming bass. This I proceeded to play while the children marched off in good order.

Since leaving Gillingham I had lost touch with the Fluxite Twins. Their place had been taken by the political cartoon in Ada's *Daily Express*, drawn by Strube. Lloyd George was always accompanied by a mangold-wurzel and a pheasant. The mangold-wurzel had little arms and legs and a grin, the pheasant a long craning neck and an anxious look. The reason for these companions, never explained to me, may have been given by Lloyd George himself when he came to Bedford on 11 October 1913, to speak about land reform, but our choice of entertainment on that day was something different, my first visit to a theatre, the County Theatre in Midland Road, close to the railway station. The play was *Peter Pan*. My mother may have wondered uneasily whether the crocodile, Captain Hook, and the pirates would give me one of the nightmares which often visited me, but I found them very funny, particularly when Smee tore the calico and Hook thought he had split his trousers. It was the tension at the end of Act I that I found almost unbearable, when the children were flying round the nursery before following Peter out through the window. I longed for them to get away, to reach the freedom beyond the four walls, before Mr. and Mrs. Darling came back and stopped them. I covered my face with my hands, dreading to see the grown-ups coming in at the door.

My second theatre visit, early the next year, was to see the pantomime of *Dick Whittington*. One inspired moment stayed for ever in my mind. The scene was the deck of a ship which seemed to be rolling on a high sea. A teddy-bear steward came on, carrying a tray on the tips of his fingers, a napkin over his arm. As he stood there, swaying with the ship, his face gradually turned green; and though I had never been to sea or experienced seasickness, memory vividly recorded my delight, while everything else, Dame, Whittington's cat, transformation scene, vanished completely away.

On my sixth birthday Ada gave me a dressing-gown; and from somewhere came a toy theatre, too expensive, I should think, for my mother to have bought me, perhaps second-hand but strong and handsome. The base was a grooved wooden stage, two feet wide, and into the grooves you fitted the proscenium, the scenery, and the actors. It was a model of the London production of *Peter Pan*, the actors coloured photographs of the London cast. As I see them now in my mind's eye they seem to have been Gerald du Maurier as Captain Hook and Pauline Chase as Peter. When my mother moved from Bedford sixteen years later neither my brother nor I was there to guard our possessions. The theatre was thrown out or given away, along with my brother's collection of lead soldiers.

Ada was not altogether approving of fairy-tales, though she made a place for fantasy, if instructive, as in the story of the children inside the mouth; and allegory, as in *The Pilgrim's Progress*. I ran to find her one day in great excitement, to tell her how I had just seen an elf in the grass. I was so sure of it, had seen it in such detail, her sharp rebuke amazed and deflated me. I stood beside her bed (she was resting as usual) while she explained to me what a low opinion Isaiah had of those who believed in wizards that peeped and muttered. It was not the only time the pictures in my head got me into trouble. I went to tea with a friend called Tommy Cartwright and mentioned to his assembled family that I was born in India. When my brother heard about it, from

Tommy's elder brother Joe, he took me to task. How could I lie like that, he said, when I knew my birthplace was Bristol? I was puzzled. Yes, I did know I was born in Bristol, but I also felt quite sure I was born in India, and it seemed to me I could clearly remember the domes and white buildings to prove it.

Though my belief in the elf was taboo, belief in Father Christmas was encouraged. He made a breathtaking appearance at the kindergarten's breaking-up party each winter term. After games and tea and carols we sat in an expectant half-circle on the floor. There was no light except the candlelight from the high tree. Two student-teachers stood by carrying wands tipped with damp sponges to snuff any wandering flame. We were told to be very still and listen. Then we heard sleigh-bells gradually coming nearer. I felt a mysterious distance of snow and ice, and half expected the cold to come into the room. Now the bells were close outside and stopped, and out of the shadows came the friendly, awesome man himself, solicitously attended by Miss Walmsley. She hoped the journey hadn't tired him. What stays in the memory is not the moment when my name was called to go to him for my present, but the bells approaching out of the distance, the darkness charged with anticipation, as it had been before I saw my father standing at my bedside.

The sensation of a region of snow and ice outside the walls was keener, and so in a way more real, than my everyday experience. Many years were to go by before the magic of the natural world found its way to me, though details caught my attention: the smell of may blossom in the park, and the large white and pink trumpets of convolvulus which climbed the chicken-wire in the allotments. The almost black hollyhocks in Paddy Mortimer's garden were good for an experiment in ink-making when crushed and mixed with water; laurel leaves as parchment to scratch secret words on, which became visible when left in the sun. Surroundings were simply the space containing my activity. But I got a surprise from water. A teacher had taken a group of us to study pond life, in other words to catch tadpoles and sticklebacks. I took a step on to what I thought was the grass verge and it gave way under me. Instead of scrambling out again I felt a power in the water, like the strong pressure of a hand forcing me further in, and I was up to my waist before the teacher got me out. Like Hal, when he had fallen into a pond on 3 June 1878, I 'returned home soaked'.

But it was usually at night that unconsidered things became considerable. I was taken for a long summer's afternoon in a punt on the river. That night when I closed my eyes I was looking into the deep, glycerine-smooth water where the reeds and lily-stalks tilted with the current. Fish darted and pierced the body of the river, and the river and I seemed to become one life, my body insubstantial, transparent like the river, and the fish were swimming through me. Even after my mother had come to me, hearing me cry out, the river-nature was slow to pass, until at last I sank through it into sleep. It never happened again, though I spent innumerable days on the river during the next twelve years.

In one other way I was not immune to the natural world. The touch in the air of the seasons changing made itself felt, if not in 1913 then soon after, particularly the first dank smell of autumn which set me tingling and vibrating from the chest to the feet as if I were being brushed by teazles.

It was the custom, in that last full year of the old world, for the wives of Modern School masters to pay social calls on the parents. If they were out, cards were left. If my mother was in her workaday clothes she would hurry upstairs, leaving Ada to do the honours, and stay immured in the bedroom for the twenty minutes or so, the measure of the formal call. But then the call had to be returned, a great trial to my mother who usually took me with her for support, and I can remember the relief we both felt when the person called on was out and we cheerfully turned our heads for home. Ada delighted in these goings-on. Etiquette was one of her accomplishments; she knew exactly how many visiting cards to leave and when to turn the corners down, and she answered invitations to at-homes in her best third-person style.

One of the callers and called-on was the wife of a master called the Reverend Tubby Evans who, nine years later, began to give me private lessons in Greek (I had thoughts of being a clergyman), which started with the memorable jingle:

> Alpha, beta, gamma, delta,
> Knock a woman down and pelt her,
> Epsilon, Zeta, Eta, Theta,
> Pick her up again and beat her.

Mrs. Evans was very tall, skeleton-thin, and wore a large-brimmed flat hat, which gave her the appearance of a walking Γ-square. She overstepped the limits of kindness and anxiety to help, by bringing us a bag full of old meat bones to be boiled down into soup. 'Does she think we are paupers?' my mother said indignantly as she shut the front door at the end of the visit. Our penurious gentility had to be guarded, and Ada did her best to keep us up to the mark. When I went walking with her I was not allowed to point, even at in-animate objects, and the half moons of my fingernails were of as much concern to her as the rings round Saturn to an astronomer.

She was liking life in Bedford, taking part in our interests, making friends, and she walked one day with my brother and me across the fields to Clapham and back by the road, the greatest distance she had gone on foot since her girlhood. On Sunday 16 November she writes: 'Day, 2 boys & I to school service. Rev Farrar preached on Re-incarnation nothing said to help either Christians or sinners.' The service for the boys from the Modern School was held every Sunday afternoon in St. Peter's Church. Outside the church was the statue of John Bunyan. He stood massively with his back to St. Peter's Green, a finger between the pages of a book, maybe the Bible, though I always thought it to be his own book, *The Pilgrim's*

Progress, written in Bedford jail. My acquaintance with the adventures of Christian was already well advanced. Even before I could read I was allowed, on Sundays and holy days, with washed hands, to turn the pages of the copy inscribed on the fly-leaf 'Ada with Papa's love. Xmas 1865', and study the profusion of engravings by H. C. Selous, Esq., and M. Paolo Priolo, while Ada explained them to me. There were a hundred and two pictures in the book, and I came to know every detail of them by heart, as well as the ornamental borders which framed the text on every page, of shells and grapes, manacles, skulls and bones, angels, serpents, acorns and roses, apples, doves and devils. Christian's gesture of appeal as he sank in the Slough of Despond, his combat with Apollyon, Giant Pope gnawing his nails, the man sweeping the room full of dust, the shepherds of the Delectable Mountains, and the ninety-seven other pictures were as surely engraved on my mind as on the pages. The print was so large and handsome that I was very soon, with Ada's help, reading the words for myself. The book stands on my shelves now, as good as new except for a slight scuffing on the cover, after 112 years of use.

As I was writing this I began to wonder whether the flight from the City of Destruction had anything to do with a recurring nightmare which began to afflict me about this time. I made no such connection in my mind then. In the dream I was certainly, like Christian, escaping from a doomed city; but my path was the keyboard of a piano, and flight was made more difficult by the necessity to walk only on the black notes. I knew that the city at my back was going to be blown up in a mighty explosion. The urgent need to escape, and the care wanted to keep my foothold, always woke me up in a sweat of terror before I had progressed very far.

On Christmas Day 1913 Ada broke her rule of eating alone: 'Hard frost early, then sunny. Heaps of presents for everyone. I alone to church. All dined together off chicken. Had tea together.' And on New Year's Eve she wrote: 'On the whole a better year. Able to do more, and no real illness since April.'

We woke on the first morning of 1914 to find the windows opaque with frost-flowers, and the water in the jug on the washstand, and the urine in the chamber-pot, crusted with ice.

CHAPTER SIXTEEN

The War

Early in the year there was a death in our street. At 112 lived the James family: Mrs. James, a widow, three sons, and a girl, Kathie, about my own age. The eldest boy, Walter, died of consumption on the last day of March, and four days later his funeral went past our house. All our blinds were tightly drawn as though the house could not bear to look.

On Sunday afternoons during term-time I was taken to the Modern School service in St. Peter's Church. The school sat in the centre pews, the parents and families at the side. I always sat next to the aisle, my mother and Ada beside me. One afternoon a senior boy, in the pew level with ours across the aisle, fainted during the singing of a hymn. Two other boys carried him out. He had red hair, and his face, which came close to mine, was paper-white. I thought he must be dead, like Walter James; this was what death looked like; and in spite of my mother's assurance that he would quickly recover, the image of that unconscious body made the afternoon services hard to endure for some time to come, and increased in meaning over the next four years.

Ada had no real birthday in 1914. February ended on the 28th; but she had lived for fifty-eight years, and on 10 March she wrote in her diary: 'I am as old today as Mother was when she died', though she teased me by saying she was not so much older than I was, because of the missing birthdays. I was beginning to feel very uncertain anyway about the dependability of the facts of time and space. One morning when I was marching with the other children out of the school hall after morning prayers suddenly I felt removed, as though I were only fractionally part of what was going on, or rather as though I were in the future looking far back to the present, a feeling I later got used to as nothing extraordinary, a physical quirk. But it was more difficult to get used to what sometimes happened at night. Space, time, sound, and bodily movement would all change their natures together. The change would begin with the distance between the bed and the window. Instead of being two or three yards away the window receded to a distance of thirty or forty yards, or even further, as if I were looking through the wrong end of a telescope. The lace curtains, filtering the light of the street, made a milky square at the end of a dark tunnel. This was the signal for sound to take on a frantic urgency. The gentle ticking of the clock beside the bed became drastic – faster, louder, more metallic. If I turned over in bed, moving with slow deliberation, the movement was like a wild rush through space, the rustle of the sheet like a dashing wave. Even the careful bending of a finger took on a dynamic importance. The only way I could break free from this overcharged world was by calling for someone to talk to me; then things gradually returned to their normal state. Reality was sometimes as undependable as the green fringe of the pond which betrayed me to the water. So, too, was the balance of power in Europe.

There was a tropical downpour on 16 July when we went to watch the town regatta, but all was fair on the 27th, a day we awoke to with excited anticipation. The famous hero of the reredos at St. Agnes Church was about to be seen in the flesh. Lord Roberts had come to Bedford, and in the morning would inspect the Modern School Officers' Training Corps. My brother was the youngest, and smallest, member of the O.T.C. I remember watching him that morning polishing his buttons and binding his legs with khaki puttees. 'The town gay with flags,' Ada's diary says. 'Prizes given in the Corn Exchange by Mr Black, M.P. Afterwards the parents went within the school railings to see Lord Roberts inspect the cadets.' I clung to the railings supported by my mother and peered between them at the little man in silk hat and frock-coat walking beside the tall figure, also top-hatted, of the Headmaster, Mr. Kaye. They moved along the khaki ranks lined up in Midland Road, and then, wonder to behold, the Field-Marshal, Earl, Knight of the noble Order of the Garter, paused in front of my brother and asked him how old he was. That evening he addressed a crowded meeting in the skating rink. He urged the need for an increased defence force to protect our islands against invasion. Few took him seriously. The next day a student of nineteen shot the Arch-duke and Archduchess Franz Ferdinand of Austria at Sarajevo.

On the 31st my mother, brother, and I went on holiday to Lowestoft, leaving Ellen Earle to keep Ada company. We were joined at Lowestoft by Grandpa and Nana Harris, my Uncle Walter and his wife, and their children, Jack and Nora. There were a few days of building sand-castles and popping the pods of bladderwrack, a few visits to the Sparrows' Nest to watch the Pierrots, and then the world began to fall apart. At home Ada was noting it down:

3rd. Mon.	Bank Holiday. Read that Germany had begun war with France & Russia. Thunder & lightning in aft.
4. Tues.	Banks to be closed till Fri: so could not get any change. England's navy mobilized & army to follow suit today.
5. Wed.	Ellen brought in a paper at 9.15 p.m. English had sunk a mine layer & taken a German ship.

At Lowestoft I was taken on to the pier to hear a brass band concert. Through the gaps between the boards I could see the waves spinning their foam under our feet. Things felt precarious. While the band played I looked across the North Sea to the mist on the horizon. The Enemy were hidden in that mist. At any moment I might see them looming out of it, like the storm which came out of the bruised sky and struck the weathercock on St. Agnes Church, like the man in black who came up the path with my father's death on his lips.

The brazen sound of the band was part of it. Electric shocks went through me as though I were smelling autumn.

We travelled back to Bedford on the 14th, taking a horse-cab from the railway station. The smell of the upholstery and the smell of the horse were indistinguishable, warm, tangy, and ripe, and together with the sound of clopping hooves made one of my favourite, though rare, sensations. We found Ada waiting with the news that a soldier was to be billeted in our house, a Seaforth Highlander. Sixteen thousand of them were coming to the town. She and my mother lay on their beds all night without undressing. There was confusion on the railways, trains arriving hours late. The soldier came in the early hours of the morning, a small, nineteen-year-old Scot from Wick, called Robertson. On the 18th Ada writes: 'I called Robertson at 4 a.m. No quiet. Bagpipes, voices, drilling, etc. Our army said to be safely in France.' Robertson's broad Scottish way of talking was hard to understand. He often lapsed into the Gaelic. It seemed to speak for the whole unintelligible state of affairs.

Ellen Earle took me into the park to play, but there was no playing, no hide-and-seek in the two round areas of grass surrounded by shrubbery, which we called the Pancake and the Frying Pan; no rolling down the steep bank below the Bowling Green. The park was full of soldiers, horses, and mules. Mules were a new animal to me, and not pleasant. One kicked out a soldier's eye, and Ellen hurried me home. Within a month the military had taken over the corner of the field where the cricket-nets had been, over the hedge at the bottom of our backyard, and built a brick rifle-range. There was even less quiet for Ada, marksmen cracking away all the day long.

By the time the school term began, on 18 September, the first flurry of disturbed excitement was over. I had been moved out of the kindergarten a year ahead of my age and joined the older children. Ada's teaching had given me a flying start. She had taught me to read quite easily at five years old, so the kindergarten really was child's play, spiced with instruction in such practical things as how to bake a loaf of bread (a very small one), and I remember practising to tie bows with pale blue tape on a wooden frame, and at last tying my own shoe-laces. But now I began to sit at a desk and had books to work with: a book of poetry, green with a pattern of paler leaves, and a French primer called *Le Livre Rouge*. For Geography we used a sand-tray to build the canals and dykes of Holland, the country which neighboured brave little Belgium now trampled over by the Huns, though the war was never mentioned at school; indeed any physical compulsion was unheard of. The teachers were not allowed even to push us gently into line when we were forming up to march into Prayers. But outside the school there was no getting away from the war, not only because of the soldiers in the street, banging away in the field at the back, digging trenches in the Cemetery Hill fields, but every morning there were the pictures in the *Daily Sketch*, and a growing list, faithfully kept by Ada, of cousins who had joined up, in England, Australia, and New Zealand: Jack Fry and his brother, a number of Hammonds, Hugh Linsell, Bess's two boys, Harrold and seventeen-year-old Bernie, and Lil's son Bob Staveley. Hal was enlisting recruits at Maffra. We put up a map of Europe on the kitchen wall, and my brother stuck the flags of the nations into it to mark the front lines.

On 13 November Ada notes: 'Day's 43rd birthday. Heard that Bernie was in the Australian infantry. Lord Roberts taken ill after reviewing Indian Troops in France. 14. Sat. Lord Roberts died 8 p.m. from a chill.'

My birthday party was much enlivened by the soldier who had taken Robertson's place a week before. He was Harry Stevens, the son of a farmer at Crockham Hill. I had never understood what this Kentish-born young man was doing in the Seaforth Highlanders until I read David Garnett's *The Golden Echo*, where he tells how his father, Edward Garnett, persuaded a Scottish farmer called Stevens to let an empty farmhouse at Crockham Hill to some Armenians, the Nazarbeks, refugees from the Turkish massacre of 1895, who so disrupted the neighbourhood that 'if Mr. Stevens had not turned them out . . . there might have been a massacre of Armenians in the Weald of Kent'.

Harry Stevens made a great hit with me. There was no need to say 'Now laugh', either to him or to myself. In each other's company we were always laughing. One of his tricks, when we were sitting at the kitchen table after the midday meal, was to smile, showing a full set of teeth, then quickly to smile again to reveal a front tooth missing, which returned to its place at the next grin. It was like the magical disappearance and return of flakes of paper which came and went from the fingers to the chant of 'Fly away, Peter, fly away, Paul, come back, Peter, come back, Paul!'

The Seaforths left for France on May Day, 1915, a year which had begun with the death of Miss Twinch. I was taken to where they were forming up to start their march to the railway station, carrying in my hand a bunch of forget-me-nots to give to Harry. 'We chatted with Harry as long as possible,' Ada wrote. I had expected them to march off to the skirl of bagpipes, but instead they were played away by the band of a Lancashire regiment. The sound churned my stomach. Ever since the August day on Lowestoft pier military band music had seemed like a giant whistling in the dark, awesome and somehow vulnerable. All through May and June news came in of the killing of soldiers we had known, but Harry was not one of them. He had written to my mother that he was 'happy in a barn near the firing line'. Harrold and Bernie Bridger, we heard, were in Cairo, on their way to the Dardanelles.

Bess's daughter Noeline, nicknamed 'Kid' by her brothers, erupted into our lives that May. She was Titian-haired, freckled, brusque, noisy by our standards, and very excitable. Her enthusiasm was something of a trial to Ada who wrote in the diary a year later: 'Noeline rushed about excited. Engaged for farm work.' She was always Noeline to Ada, but soon became Kid to us. In spite of a weak heart, the result of the rheumatic fever of her childhood, she joined the

Women's Land Army and put Ada's patriotism to the test by
appearing in breeches and leggings and a knee-length smock.
I don't know why she came to stay with us in 1915. The house
was already overcrowded. Harry Stevens had been succeeded
by two men of the Royal Engineers, George Randall and
Percy whose surname I have forgotten. When they were off
duty we had sing-songs round the piano. (The piano was
wounded sometime during this year or the next; a shot went
through it when a soldier was fooling with his revolver.) The
star of these musical evenings was Miss Killick, the elder of
two sisters who lived next door. Their father looked very like
Edward VII, whose picture, and Queen Alexandra's, decorated the biscuit tin on the kitchen mantelpiece, a tin kept
filled with my favourite Pat-a-cake biscuits. He rode a
tricycle, wore Norfolk breeches, and when he was dying he
saw Jesus waiting to receive him; at least, Miss Killick said
he did. She was thin, highly strung, and performed a humorous monologue to her own piano accompaniment, which we
thought brilliant. But one evening, when we were all crowded
into the tiny room, eager for the piece to begin, she had a
crise nerveuse and fled from the room in tears. I was so
unused, both at home and at school, to grown-ups showing
any emotion whatsoever, the scene astounded me. I have
wondered since whether, perhaps, she had grown fond of
George Randall, who was sturdy and kind and soon to be
killed, and found his presence beside the piano too much for
her. We tried to put life back into the evening by singing
'Jingle Bells', 'Riding down from Bangor', 'Clementine', and
'Polly-wolly-doodle', four of my favourites in the song book;
and when my bedtime came we sang 'Now the day is over',
to put me into a suitable state for sleep. My mother came up
to the bedroom with me to hear me say my prayers –

> If I should die before I wake
> I pray the Lord my soul to take –

and to read me the passage for the day from a small red book
called *Little Pillows*, the fellow of a small blue book called

Morning Chimes. The reading was meant to insulate me from the nightmare of escaping out of the doomed city. When she was tucking me up I said that a boy at school had told me I had come out of her stomach. She was very indignant and hotly denied it, but offered no alternative suggestion to account for my arrival.

1915 was the year when the eyes of God which haunted my father's childhood, the reproachful eyes of *The Light of the World* above the piano, were as nothing to the glaring eyes and pointing finger of Lord Kitchener on all the hoardings demanding volunteers: You, and you, and you. It was the year when the last rays of the Edwardian sunlight drained out of the landscape and the warring nations sank into mud. The flags in the map on the kitchen wall remained unshifted, and after a time the map was taken down. We were given a game to play called 'The Silver Bullet'. By dexterously tilting the box this way and that the bullet had to be negotiated along a complicated maze, called the road to Berlin, without dropping into the holes on the way. When very occasionally I controlled my hand enough to bring the bullet safely to its goal, I hoped I might have helped our soldiers to advance a little.

Ada was recording in her diary a growing national hysteria. After the sinking of the *Lusitania* in early May mobs attacked shops trading under German names. Members of the Stock Exchange set fire to the *Daily Mail* building because the paper had criticized Lord Kitchener. The German master at the Modern School, Mr. Tischbrock, was sacked. I took a dislike to Prussian Blue in my paint-box, a paint-box which George Randall gave me on my eighth birthday at the end of the year. We spoke always of 'the Huns'; what they did was called 'frightfulness'; the drawings in the papers showed them to be ape-like men in spiked helmets, far worse than the picture of Giant Pope gnawing his fingernails in *The Pilgrim's Progress.* The Christmas before, when the British and Germans had sung 'Silent Night' – 'Heilige Nacht' – together before killing each other again on Boxing Day, they had still been comparatively human, but now they were the Beast and nothing would kiss them back to humanity again except Victory. The Kaiser was the Devil, as the waxed points of his moustache clearly showed. But when people began to call the fighting Armageddon we knew they were wrong, we had Ada's word for that, and Ada was an authority on the Last Days. The margins of her Bible when it came to the Revelation of St. John the Divine were black with notes in her tiny handwriting. Armageddon was to be the Great Tribulation at the time of the three-and-a-half year reign of Antichrist at Babylon the Great. The phrase 'a time, times and half a time', she explained in the margin, dipping her steel-nibbed pen into the ink with confidence, meant '1 year, 2 years, and $\frac{1}{2}$ a year $= 3\frac{1}{2}$ years'. It was some comfort to us to know at any rate that the war was not Armageddon, though my belief in what she could prove from the Bible had recently received a check. I came back from school one day with the information that the earth travelled round the sun. Ada told me I must put any such thought out of my head, because Joshua had commanded the sun to stand still on Gibeon, and the sun *stood* still; as Galileo had also been told three hundred years before.

Just as the winter term was about to begin, the news came that my twenty-year-old cousin Hugh Linsell had been killed in action, killed on the same day as the fiancé of another cousin, a nurse with the Red Cross, Nellie Hawley, who later was drowned when the ship she was on was torpedoed. In November the second son of the widowed Mrs. James, whose eldest had died soon after we came to Bedford, died of wounds. He was given a military funeral which passed our house on the way to the cemetery. These slow processions up Gladstone Street happened so often that even now when I hear the pounding notes of the funeral march, the thuds of the opening bars followed by that aching effort to lift the notes higher, I also hear the rattle of the gun-carriage and the irregular clatter of the reined-in horses. It puzzled me why the band on the way back from the cemetery should be playing a cheerful tune and the soldiers marching so briskly. Ada said it was because we knew the dead soldier was now happy in a better world, but I was still offended by it, feeling they had turned their backs on him, glad to get the ceremony over.

The better, happier world for me was The Crescent, our name for the Froebel Training College; the rooms were big and full of light and air, even if the walls were not made of jasper, and though we had no harps we sang a great deal, songs taught to us by Miss Walmsley's niece, Miss Huntingdon. The three I best remember were Kipling's 'Big Steamers', 'The Camel's Hump', and a skittish, tinkling song about airy fairy pipers underneath the silver moon. But even more clearly, as vividly as if it were yesterday, I remember the morning when Miss Spence opened my ears to the life of words. We were in what was called the Lower Hall, where the Christmas party was held, acting the scene from *The Water Babies* where Mrs. Doasyouwouldbedoneby tells stories to the children, 'such things as [Tom] had never heard before in his life'. Miss Spence was Mrs. Doasyouwouldbedoneby. What stories she read to us as we sat at her feet I don't remember (they are not in Kingsley's book), but suddenly words were not only sentences but individuals. She gave each word so exactly its proper weight and meaning, yet so lightly, I felt I could hold the words like coloured stones in my hand. Perhaps because my ears were alerted, so were my eyes. I can still see the light touching the golden wood of the polished floorboards where we were sitting.

Such small things open windows in the mind. We were acting the story of the Burghers of Calais. I had a tiny walking-on part, one of the crowd of citizens. I was given a bucket to carry and told to wander through the street, going about my lawful business, until my attention was caught by what was going on. The realism of it astonished me. It was a real street, where people lived; history had really happened. The leading parts I played have left me, but I know exactly where I entered with my bucket. Thirty-five years later Miss

Spence told me I wrote a play at this time for the other children to act; she still remembered a line or two from it, but my memory had rejected every trace to make room for the silent water-carrier of Calais.

Memory is a great eccentric, hoarding random moments, trivial anxieties: as when I was sent by one of the teachers to find out the time from the kitchen clock. The school kitchen was a small, dark room with a brick floor, never used as far as I know for cooking; a big clock with a short pendulum was above the fireplace. I had set about my errand quite confidently, but now the clock-face high above my head confused me. I stood on the tips of my toes, not to get nearer the clock, but because I always stood on the tips of my toes when worried. At that moment Joseph, the man-of-all-work, came into the kitchen. He wore a long grizzled beard, and when I first came to the school I had an idea that he might once have been the Virgin Mary's husband. He told me what the time was, and I carried the information back to the class, uneasily accepting the teacher's undeserved thanks. Maybe the episode stayed in the mind because school was usually so free of trouble; which makes another occasion as hard to understand now as it was at the time. We were being taught in a class-room at the top of the stairs, a room smaller and not so filled with light as the others. Miss Spence was taking the lesson, so whatever it may have been it was certainly pleasant and interesting. All was well with me one moment, the next I was caught in a storm of distress, as though the room and all of us in it were suddenly in great danger, invaded by some inimical presence or threatened like the doomed city in my dream. Perhaps, as in the dream, I tried to get away, because I next remember being out in front of the class, Miss Spence pressing me against her to try and stop me shaking. I imagine it was all soon over, and if I could relate that morning with other events I might even find a cause, but it left me believing, from time to time, in the ever possible chance of being ambushed.

Towards the end of that year 1915 I was given my first

press notice. Ada cut it out and put it between the pages of the diary. The occasion was the school Christmas-tree party. 'A lithe and shapely lad of tender years', wrote the *Bedfordshire Times*, 'danced the hornpipe as cleverly as we have ever seen it done.' I was wearing a white sailor-suit with bell-bottomed trousers, and round my neck on a cord a whistle, which Ada begged me not to blow anywhere in her neighbourhood. The suit was an extravagance we could ill afford. My mother wore the same clothes year after year. It was a considerable event when Jack Fry and his wife Nancy called in 1925 to take her on a shopping expedition. She came back with an expensive dress, and a hat like an inverted flowerpot with a feather. My brother and I thought the hat unsuitable, if not eccentric, and so, I think, did my mother, though she bravely wore it for a month or two. In 1915 she wore a small plain hat with a black veil twisted into a tight knot under her chin. The spots on the veil seemed to make her grey eyes twinkle more than ever.

On 31 January 1916 Ada entered in the diary: 'At 9.15 p.m. all lights went out. Zep raid over Midland counties. 59 said to be killed & 101 injured.' I saw one of these slow, ghostly bringers of death in the crossing of searchlights, and another coming down in flames far off in the western sky.

The spring came in with the German attack on Verdun; April brought the Easter Rising in Dublin; but my first clear memory of the year begins on a June morning. I had been kept away from school because my brother had mumps. Kid Bridger offered to take me shopping with her. We walked down The Crescent to a little wool shop in Bromham Road. The woman behind the counter talked in a shocked voice about the headline news in the morning's newspaper. Lord Kitchener had been drowned on his way to Russia. 'What terrible days these are!' she said. 'Where is it all going to end?' It was a few days after the Battle of Jutland, made noteworthy for me by a full-page drawing of sixteen-year-old Jack Cornwell standing to his gun though mortally wounded. And then on 20 June Ada wrote in the diary: 'At 9.30 Miss

Killick ran in to ask me to go to Mrs James who seemed half out of her mind.' She had received a letter from an army padre to say that her third son, Aubrey, was dead. I was playing in the street and saw her come out of her house, raving, sobbing, throwing up her arms, her grey hair in wild strands and wisps. She was lurching about as though she wanted to escape somewhere, but there was nowhere to go, and two neighbours were trying to persuade her to go back indoors. Five years before at Minehead my mother had begged to be taken home, but now Mrs. James was struggling to get away from her house.

Eleven days later, on 1 July, 20,000 of Kitchener's army were killed on the first day of the Battle of the Somme. A man who lived across the street took part in the battle. When he was invalided home I watched him trying to walk along the pavement, his wife supporting him. He had no control of his legs; they kicked out sideways while he tried to move them forwards. After the war, when we were staying with my uncle Bert Harris, who was then mayor of Penryn in Cornwall, the ducklings in his garden had a disease called the sprawls; they reminded me of the small, frail man in Gladstone Street.

In August I was given a second-hand bicycle. My cousin Jack Harris was staying with us, and taught me to ride it along the unmade-up road which led from the top of the street to the cemetery gates. The only building on the north side was the Pumping Station which fetched up the water for our needs with a throbbing, chuffing sound. The road at this point had three deep furrows in it, and before long I discovered the pleasure to be had from riding at speed from the cemetery end and using the furrows as a switchback which bounced you off the saddle. The bicycle was something of a blessing. I was getting too little exercise, spending too many hours hunched up indoors drawing and writing and reading. The myth of my father having strained his heart in the gymnasium was engraven on my mother's mind. When I went to the Modern School in 1918 she refused to let me take part in gymnastics; and because I had once had gastritis or enteritis or both, I was not allowed to bathe in the river or to eat apples and plums from a neighbour's trees. In consequence these things became as obsessively tempting as the fruit of the Tree of Knowledge, the tasting of which would be death.

There was a morning of excitement on the last day of the summer holidays. An aeroplane roared over our roof, almost knocking the chimneys off, and landed in the school field. People came running down the narrow passageway beside the house and climbed up on to the iron bar which fenced the ditch, holding on to our garden wall and each other's shoulders while they peered over the hedge. Part of the wall came down. When the aeroplane took off again it struck the wire fence near the firing-range and crashed. It was nearly nine years since Blériot's accident on the day I was born, but aeroplanes were still extraordinary things. The locals scrambled through the hedge and broke pieces off the machine as mementoes. My brother got a small piece of aluminium piping to add to what he called his Museum, a portable chest of drawers in which he kept a button from a dead Turkish soldier's jacket, a piece of a Turkish sandbag, some Egyptian tram tickets (all supplied by Bernie Bridger), a franc note, Maundy money, pieces of coral, and a boomerang sent from Australia by Hal.

On my mother's forty-fifth birthday, when influenza had kept her in bed, news came that forty-six-year-old Charlie was going to take a bride. In the autumn of the year when my father died (1911) Charlie had turned over his Gippsland photographic studio, in a quixotic gesture of generosity, to Harrold Bridger, and gone back to Melbourne, breaking his journey at Maffra to visit Hal and Ella and their twin daughters. He had rashly thrown himself back into the struggle to make a living, and it was more than a year before his guardian angel took notice of him again. By then he was living at Malvern and took his meals at a nearby café where another regular customer, a man called Thomas Alfred William Kerr, a pianist, often sat at the same table. They got on well together and Kerr invited Charlie to spend a fort-night's holiday at his week-end bungalow at Belgrave. Of all the places Charlie had visited in the world Belgrave delighted him more than any other, and Kerr wanted to sell three blocks in the very position he admired most, but they were already on offer. In a letter to my mother years afterwards Charlie described what happened:

I wanted one of them badly so he said that if he did not hear from the man by Saturday I could have one. Saturday post came but no letter! I bought all three (2½ acres). On Monday a letter came to say the man would take them all. I had beaten him on the post! On account of ill health for over a year and having given away my wonderful business in Gippsland I was down to my last shilling. Being unable to carry on any longer in town I had brought all my paintings up to Belgrave and hung them on the walls of the dining room at the Coffee Palace. Belgrave was then only a small bush township visited by a few tourists and week-enders. I never for a moment expected to sell any pictures. So imagine my surprise and joy when I sold £85 worth in the first week and was thus able to pay the balance off my land and start to build a bungalow.

My land was just a rough unfenced bit of native bush that had never been cultivated since Australia rose up out of the sea millions of years ago. It was a tangle of undergrowth and fallen logs. I started to clear it with axe, mattock and cross-cut saw. And, with the exception of a few days when a friend came and helped me jack heavy logs off the fencing line and to split some fencing posts, I cleared it single handed ... I had never done any building before but I built most of the house and all the outbuildings unassisted, also seats, arches, summer arbours and garden ornaments; lined, papered and coloured the interior and made the furniture, all in spare time ...

When he started to make his garden he felt sure his guard-ian angel must be lending a hand. Every time he set his heart on some plant or shrub or tree, or a dark-blue wild orchis, seen on a walk, which he knew would not bear trans-planting, he would find it a few days later on his own land as he went on clearing the scrub.

You and I [he wrote to my mother] were the only gardeners in the family when we were children at home. Do you remember Hal's caricature of us two bending over a diminutive apple tree watching for a new leaf to grow? And the collection we made of all the weird insects we found? And how other people's cats used to come and scratch up our precious seedlings?

As though to plant his own childhood there in the bush he called the bungalow Winscombe, after the village under the Mendip hills where his grandfather Fry had built Springfield nearly sixty years before, the village where in 1262 the vicar had bought the family's freedom. Here, after the wedding on 18 November 1916, he brought his wife, Augusta Frances Cecil, a distant connection, he told us, of the English Cecils. He made a life-sized statue of her to stand in the garden, and lived, as he said, a honeymoon life with her for the nineteen years until she died.

January 1917 was very cold, the coldest winter, the papers said, since 1895, the year my father and mother had set off for Australia. The taps all froze, and a water jug broke with the pressure of the ice. I was ill in bed for two or three days, protected from draughts by a Victorian scrap-screen. In the centre of the leaf nearest to me was a large coloured print of a beautiful young woman holding a lighted candle in a candlestick. Her hair fell on to her naked shoulders and the swell of her breasts lifted her thin white night-dress like hills under a sprinkling of snow. The golden candle-light explored the structure of her face, casting soft shadows above her cheeks. The word under the picture was 'Goodnight'. She was a great comfort to me. Was it she, I wonder, who entered into my pencil a few years later, so that whenever I doodled it was a woman's breasts my pencil drew, even filling the margins of my school books, until the boy sitting next to me said I would get into trouble; and was it a regression to infancy or an approach to manhood, if indeed there is any great difference between them?

At the beginning of the winter term I was told to go to Miss Walmsley's study, and there she introduced me to a pretty young woman called Miss Coleman who was to give me private lessons in elocution; no one had asked me if I wanted them, but I got very fond of her and enjoyed what she taught me. When Miss Walmsley had left us alone together she told me to lie down on the carpet. She said she was going to teach me to breathe, which I thought hardly necessary since I had been breathing all my life. She made me relax my neck and arms and fingers and legs and toes, an exercise I probably needed. Later she began to talk about the sounds of words, of how round an 'O' was, and how 'I' was a fusion of 'ah' and 'ee'. She gave me Stevenson's 'My Shadow' to learn by heart, the first of many poems we worked on together: among them Kipling's 'Smuggler's Song', Tennyson's 'The Revenge', and much of *Hiawatha*. I particularly enjoyed the bated excitement of:

> Then upon one knee uprising
> Hiawatha aimed an arrow
> Scarce a twig moved with his motion,
> Scarce a leaf was stirred or rustled.

Six lines from the 'Ode on the Death of the Duke of Wellington', given me as an exercise in rounding my 'O's', were a revelation. I had written some verses the year before, not out of my own feelings but in imitation of Wordsworth's 'Written in March' (which was written in April), a jingle of rhymes. In Tennyson's lines the sound increased the sense for me, sound became sight and participation.

> Lead out the pageant: sad and slow,
> As fits an universal woe,
> Let the long long procession go,
> And let the sorrowing crowd about it grow,
> And let the mournful martial music blow;
> The last great Englishman is low.

I could see the many people gravely assembling in the lengthened line about the crowd; in the heavy stresses of 'the mournful martial music' I could hear the firm tread of the soldiers taking Aubrey James to the cemetery; and the first bars of Chopin's march was in the beat of 'the last great Englishman'.

Ada was also enlightened that spring. Among various entries in the diary about zeppelin raid casualties and coastal bombardments she writes: 'Feb.28. Wed. I went to hear Rev. J. Politeyan at St. Cuthbert's. The No. 666 in Rev. Splendid address. Learnt several things.' I have searched through her Bible notes to the Revelation without finding any answer to the problem of No. 666. She would have been surprised to know that the self-styled Beast, No. 666, Aleister Crowley, had been born just round the corner from Milverton Crescent while she and the family were living in Leamington.

Towards the end of August 1917 I was taken on a week's visit to my mother's childhood. The stories she had told me about St. Mary's Fields had always seemed to be about a long lost world, gleams of light at the bottom of a well, and suddenly I was in that world myself. Stedman, who had come first as gardener's boy and saw my mother grow up, worked on in the garden. Sarah, the head parlourmaid, still took up her place at mealtimes like a sentry against the dining-room wall, starched as though to last for ever. She was beanpole thin, and when on duty so expressionless that you hardly noticed a face between the cap and the apron, whereas Cook, who had married Stedman, was as plump and yeasty as the bread she baked, and almost as funny as Ellen Earle. I was delighted to have tea with her off the huge scrubbed table, in a kitchen as big as the whole of our house in Bedford. The grey parrot rattling his chain in the billiard-room cocked his head when he saw me, fumbled in his memory, and said 'Morning, Charlie'. I held out a stick I was carrying and the parrot sidled along it towards my hand. I meant to let him climb on to my shoulder, but my courage failed me as he got close and I dropped the stick. The outraged squawks and fluster of feathers made me hot and ashamed, but when the bird had climbed back on to its perch I tried again, grimly holding the stick until the parrot was almost on my hand, when my hand whipped away of its own accord. I left the billiard-room demoralized, and the parrot, I believe, never called me Charlie again.

Emily Kettle was still there, Nurse 'Teacups' Kettle who had brought my mother up after Emma had parted with her. During this August visit she took my mother into Leicester to see the film *The Birth of a Nation*. When they came back they found me playing in the rock-garden by the goldfish pond, a favourite corner in my mother's memory, secret, hidden from the house and lawns by a screen of trees. 'And they were behind me reflected in the pond.'

On the day we were to leave I went up the wooden nursery stairs to the little sitting-room, the old day nursery, played some notes on the piano and set going the musical box.

Great-uncle Willie Bates stood beside the pillars of the front porch to say goodbye. He gave me a new half-crown piece. Then we caught a time-machine at the station and travelled out of the past back into 1917 and Gladstone Street.

CHAPTER SEVENTEEN

Victory

On 18 October 1917 I had what I considered to be a proof
of the power of prayer. It was some time since any soldiers
had been billeted on us. Their place as lodger had been taken
by a schoolmistress from the girls' High School. It was nearly
a year since Bernie Bridger had come to stay before returning
to the front, more than four months since Harry Stevens, the
day after coming out of hospital, had surprised us with a
visit. As I walked home from school I thought how much I
should like something of the sort to happen again. My
mother, brother, and Ada had been unwell, and according
to the diary I had been waiting on them all 'with a sunny
little face that was cheerful to see', a testimonial I welcome,
as my memory of myself is less flattering. But I must have
needed some fillip to the spirits to make me pray so fiercely
as I passed the butcher's shop that somebody in uniform
would be in the house when I got there. And it was so. God
had supplied Lil's son, Bob Staveley, in the uniform of the
New Zealand infantry; and a friend of his, Arthur Noble,
nicknamed Con, as a bonus. What is more, they came to
collect me from school the next day, wearing the shape of hat
Hal had worn in the North-West Mounted Police. But
though God could bring off the occasional conjuring trick He
was bafflingly unhelpful in larger matters. Before six months
were out, on 23 April 1918, Con watched Bob die in a German
prison camp, with an injured hand and a smashed thigh.

My notion of God was as unlike Ada's as Charlie's had been
unlike Frank Hammond senior's thirty years earlier. Their
God apparently had a right-hand side at which Jesus sat,

and an unflagging interest in routine worship. I thought of Him in terms of space and light, and in certain sounds and words. I remember staring hypnotized at a frosty sky, vexing my mind with the thought of infinity; it seemed that where my imagination failed God began. It was where space in some way entered into everyday life that He seemed close and conversable, as it did in the two evening hymns, and for some odd reason into that moment of the *Te Deum* which never failed to enchant me, when after an overlong preamble about cherubin, seraphin, saints, prophets, apostles, and the Holy Church throughout all the world, the chant magically modulated to a minor key for 'Vouchsafe, O Lord, to keep us this day without sin'. The *Nunc dimittis*, too, held the feeling of distance, a cool breeze at the end of a hot day. Lung-pleasure could be got from singing hymns like 'Onward, Christian soldiers!' but they gave me no feeling of God. As for those Sundays when I was unlucky enough to have to kneel through the claustrophobic litany, God seemed to withdraw to the outer limits of space.

So I was happy when my mother sometimes let me join my more pagan friends for a Sunday on the river or a picnic in the park. Ada said nothing, except to her diary. Resentments were seldom spoken of in the household, or so delicately hinted they crept past unnoticed. In this way, though a kind of peace reigned, we could wound each other without being aware of it. After Ada died my mother tore out and destroyed the last four years of the diary because of hurtful comments about her, and no doubt about my brother and me, though she never told us what they were; perhaps more in the style of the entry about my romping on a Sunday: 'He is too young to realize that those who take God's Day for [illegible] pleasure shut His blessing out of their lives.' Or this, on another churchless Sunday, about my mother, who had little enough time for relaxation and was suffering at the time from what Dr. Chillingworth called 'internal varicose veins': 'D & 2 boys to tea at Mrs Mortimer's. Day depressed. No wonder when pleasure takes 1st place.'

The pleasure was a very occasional visit to a moving picture, the theatre, or a school function. It was odd that Ada, who found any housework too exhausting to venture on, had so little conception of what my mother's working day was like; and there were quite as many Sundays when she stayed away from church, too unwell to get off the bed. But equally we little understood what *her* life was like, dependent on our very casual affection to ward off loneliness, her nerves still haunted by Emma's death. When the High School mistress came she was banished from the light front sitting-room to the dark little back one (the piano was moved for a time into the kitchen); and when my brother became head boy of the school in 1919 and needed somewhere quieter than the kitchen to do his work in, she had no place to be except her very small bedroom. It had a stale, yellow smell, a smell the colour of the faded photographs of Raven Hall hanging just inside the door, which took kind, dapper Dr. Chillingworth so by surprise when he first saw them, the place where he made his holiday in 1897. Ada spent many hours of the day in this room, pursuing her Bible studies, copying out her diaries and gluing the new pages over the old ones. She started to write a story, or series of stories, called 'Sum Peeple', and gave herself the *nom de plume* 'Hal'. When she had finished a chapter she would read it to me. I found the opening of Chapter One when I was prising apart the glued pages of the diary. The heroine, though young, paralysed, and illiterate, was perhaps not unlike the way Ada pictured herself:

Jane Ann with her small white – but always smiling face spent her days sitting propped up with cushions by the window that overlooked the street. Very little of what went on, or of what was said by the neighbours and passers by escaped the quick eyes and ears of the interested observer . . . Jane Ann dearly loved bright faces and cheerful voices and had an intense longing that the other kind of person should find out why they were not better and happier.

She sent the story to Will Palmer, the editor of the

Bedfordshire Times, and proudly wrote in the diary that he had thought Jane Ann 'a ripping little character'; but he made no offer to print it. When he printed a childish effort of mine not long after she showed nothing but delight.

We accepted her interest in us as a matter of course. She played chess with my brother, helped us both with our school work, read to me and played paper games with me when I was ill, and closely followed, and recorded, my brother's successes in cricket, rugger, and fives. But as the months went by our world included her less. Even in 1916 she was writing in her diary: 'Leslie confirmed. Day & Noeline went. Although I was his godmother I was not even asked to go.' Not asked, perhaps, because for the past three Sundays she had felt too unwell to go to church; but a confirmation service meant much to her. The diary, not long before, had celebrated the fortieth anniversary of her own and Percy's confirmation. That morning in May, when the sun shone and Percy had given her flowers, was still the supreme day of her life. (What had happened to Percy? The last news of him in the diary is in November 1904: 'Heard that Percy has 3 grandchildren.')

The vigour with which she had met the first year or two at Bedford, sharing in most of the things we did, had left her now. 'I went shopping 1st time for 8 weeks', she writes on the first day of December, and Christmas Day has a bleak entry: 'I sat in front room all day as Daisy & 2 boys had dinner & tea with the Rosses. Oxo & tapioca for dinner. Not like Christmas. No one went to church.'

When Bernie Bridger came back to England on leave in February 1918 she wrote: 'I hardly saw Bernie. The young people do not want an old one.' And the next day: 'Bernie left at 8.30. Did not even know he was going so soon.' She had made a great effort on the first Sunday of the year and gone to church on a bitterly cold day, '1st time since Sept 30th', to attend an intercession service. There seemed to be no way out of the interminable war, no hope of breaking through on the Western Front. 'Over there', as we called it, the various cousins were hidden from us in a cloud of gun smoke. The *Daily Sketch* printed a picture of the drowned Nellie Hawley. On 11 February, two days after Bernie left us and two days before his twenty-first birthday, Ada writes: 'Noeline flew in excitedly to say Harry B. Hammond was reported missing & one of the Frys dead. (No truth about the latter).'

At the end of the month she took me to the Blind and Crippled Girls' Flower Show, to see them making paper flowers, and my mother and I went back secretly later in the day to buy a bunch to present to her on her unreal sixty-second birthday, as she mentions unenthusiastically: '28. Thurs. No birthday. Oxo, jelly, & a spray of flowers from the Show.'

March had begun, that fearful month when 59 reduced British divisions faced 81 German divisions, poised for Ludendorff's offensive. If the war should last two more years, which seemed quite possible, my brother would be of an age to be called-up. On his sixteenth birthday (6 March) Ada gave him a copy of Bunyan's *Holy War* and a book by George Macdonald. On 21 March the Germans launched their mighty attack on the British Fifth and Third Armies from the Somme to Cambrai. Ada makes no mention of it, but concentrates on the school steeplechase two days later, in which 'Leslie . . . to his delight came in 4th'. By then the line of the Somme had gone, the British Fifth Army smashed. General Foch was given supreme control of operations in France on the 26th, preventing the demoralized Pétain's proposal for a French withdrawal on Paris. The next day Ada recorded that my brother had come first in his heat in the mile, and I had recited part of *Hiawatha* at Miss Walmsley's at-home. It was not until the news came, on 1 June, of the German ten-mile advance towards the Marne that she noted 'War news bad'. By then Bob Staveley had been captured and had died, though it was early November before we heard of it.

I had been at The Crescent a year too long. All the boys of my own age had left. It may have been the need for a change of scene which made me invent an island to live in. I drew a map of it, started to work out a language and taught a boy in the next street to speak it. The island was not entirely in our heads; to give it some substance we chose a house in Clarendon Road to be the royal palace, the house belonging to Mr. and Mrs. Mortimer, partly because it was double-fronted and had a lawn at the back, but particularly because at a tea-party there Mrs. Mortimer, pretty and elegant, had worn a coffee-coloured dress, exactly the colour of the curtains. So every time we passed the house we smartly eyes-righted or lefted and brought our hands up in a salute. But the new language made conversation slow and limited, and after a while we let the island sink back into the sea. While it lasted it gave me a vague, if unsatisfactory, feeling of escape into a new world, of emulating my uncles in their journeys from Somerville Road to Canada and the antipodes. When the invented language was given up I made my way buoyantly along the pavements, when walking alone, by chanting the noise of metrical lines, in a mixture of real and unreal words, whatever came to the tongue; as it might be:

> Across the hurling of outrageous seas
> Cantankerous in applegrove array
> Flaunts the armada whooshing to the shore, etc., etc.

If this game drew startled looks from passers-by I was unaware of it.

There was a growing feeling that we had come through the worst days of the war. By the end of July, when my brother at the term's end came home with prizes for Divinity, Geography, and the Archaeology prize for an essay on Bromham Church, the Germans were slowly falling back in the Second Battle of the Marne. On 9 August Ada was writing in the diary: 'Nora's parents arrived about 3 p.m. War news better.' It was a temperate way of describing what Ludendorff later called the black day of the German army.

My cousin Nora had been staying with us since the beginning of the month. We were the same age and got on well together, singing and play-acting and going for long walks, so far one day (to Clapham and Bromham) that my brother was sent off on his bicycle to search for us. To celebrate her parents' arrival we put on a performance in Miss Killick's sitting-room in aid of Dr. Barnardo's Homes. 'The children acted well,' Ada wrote. 'The collection amounted to 6/-.'

I had left The Crescent at last, coming home with an honours certificate in drawing from some national art society; '1st child in the school to pass this division at the 1st attempt', Ada said. Miss Killick's brother-in-law, who was a Sunday painter and had started going to evening classes at the local art school, came to the back door to ask if he could take me to the life class. My mother was as scandalized as if he had asked to take me to a brothel. When he said that the men wore bathing-slips she retorted indignantly that in her opinion it was the women who should wear them. The daring of her student days, when she had smoked cigarettes and tried riding astride, had not made her less shy of the human body. A year or so later she looked over my shoulder when I was turning the pages of a borrowed copy of *The Studio*; I had stopped to look at a painting of a naked nymph lying supine on a swirl of vapour, her legs slightly apart and dangling towards us. My mother said it was wrong of the artist to have painted her in such a position; in consequence the picture became imprinted on my mind. The blameless picture took its place with the information, dropped into my ear by a schoolmate, that the little girl who lived near the cemetery gates was willing to take down her knickers and show you her anatomy. The sin which we asked the Lord to vouchsafe to keep us without, evidently included more than telling lies and using bad words. I knew two bad words, 'damn' and 'blast'. 'Damn' was particularly bad when coupled with 'you' because, as Ada told me, it consigned, or intended to consign, the person addressed to eternal torment and separation from God; but I never really knew why 'blast' was bad. In my early kindergarten days, walking home from school with my mother, I repeated to her a poem we had just learned which included the line 'The blast it hollow blew'. My mother's mind was elsewhere but her ear caught the word 'blast' and she told me I must never say that word again. Other words which were unacceptable but a necessary part of life were exchanged for euphemisms. Jemima or 'Mima for chamber-pot; No. 1 and No. 2 for the use of it. The buttocks became a sit-upon. 'Belly', even though the Bible made free use of it, was rude but 'stomach' was not. Ada still said 'nether garments' or 'unmentionables' for trousers, though with a faint smile as if she were joking.

But this ridiculous code of speech had an admirable counterpart. No gossip was to be repeated, or people discussed in a way that could hurt them, or anything said that would not be said to their faces. This rule, so well understood, made it doubly startling when my mother came out with one of the two or three remarks she ever made relating to sex. The news-agent's shop was kept by a warm, friendly couple called Butterfield. Mrs. Butterfield was short, plump, cheerful, and motherly; Mr. Butterfield tall, round in the face, and always joking which endeared him to me. When we had left the shop one day my mother suddenly said it was Mr. Butterfield's 'fault' that they had no children. Why she thought so, and why she expressed such an opinion as soon as we had closed the shop door, puzzled me then and mystifies me still.

On 10 September Ada wrote in her diary: 'Mother's last birthday on earth was 32 years ago', and on the 12th: 'The whole Russian royal family stated to have been killed... Heard that Willie Rolfe [a neighbour] had died from his wounds.' But over a week before she had said: 'Acct in paper of our side breaking through the Hindenburg line', and by 26 September, when I sat for my entrance examination to the Modern School, we had all begun to sense a thinning of the four-years-old darkness. I came home, Ada said, happy and excited to be in the same school as my brother, and started next day in the fifth form of the Juniors. I was wearing a stiff Eton collar, a symbol of the new life. On Sunday I wore for the first time the complete Eton suit, a 'bum-freezer' as the jacket was called (but not in our house) and long striped trousers, and took my place in the centre pews at the school service. The memory of the death-white face of the red-headed boy was fading, and it was a long time since I had last dreamed of escaping from the doomed city. But one dream I had about this time, or not long after, a sensation so unlike anything I had known before it was never forgotten. I was in a mysterious underground cave, a cave dimly lit, perhaps by candle-light, and I was naked in a small tub of water being bathed by an enchantress. Her hair hung about her face and shoulders, like the hair of the girl on the scrap-screen, but dark while hers was fair. She was not simple and friendly and comforting like the girl on the screen, but a practiser of dark, delicious magic; and as her hands bathed me I felt electricity going through my flesh, as on the first day of autumn but more poignant, exploring me with an increasing urgency, as though my body were the strings of an instrument, tautening until they would snap in a volley of sound. Whether the mysterious cave was womb or vagina, the newness of the sensation was like a birth.

'Germans surrendering fast this week', Ada noted on 31 October. On the day Austria capitulated (4 November) our rising spirits were checked by a letter from Bess who had just heard, nearly six months after the event, that Bob Staveley was dead. On the morning of 11 November, a Monday, the fifth form of the junior school was being taught by a little clergyman called Shepherd-Smith, known to us as 'Smuts'. We were restless and excited, knowing already the importance of the day. Suddenly the bells of St. Paul's Church started a massive peal, a maroon went off, all the church bells in the town were ringing. We cheered and thumped our desks, bouncing up and down in our seats, quite prepared to run out of the building and into the street. We could hardly believe that Shepherd-Smith meant us to go on with our work, as though the world had not been completely transformed. The world was at peace, a state of affairs I could hardly remember, and at peace perhaps for ever. There would be bonfires, and

flags, and fireworks, and no more death until the time for
death. At some earlier time, about some other good tidings,
I forget what, I had said to my mother, 'There will be nothing
to put right by the time I'm grown up', and she had said
with an earnestness that impressed me, 'You can be sure
there will be only too much.' But for years I went on believing
that *homo sapiens* was really sapient and the future was in
good hands, tending towards the Kingdom of God, as my
father expected, with little room for the establishment of
Babylon the Great and the machinations of No. 666, as
expected by Ada.

One day I went for a walk with a friend, either Jim Murray
the Scot or Mac Gillespie the Ulsterman. We went through
the gate at the top of Gladstone Street into the allotments,
and up the path beside the chicken-wire where the pink and
white convolvulus grew. The path met the Cemetery Hill at
a wooden stile. The wood was the colour of a dark conker,
highly polished and gleaming with light, scored with lines
like an old face, and gently hollowed here and there by
generations of hands and legs. While the other boy climbed
the stile I looked back the way we had come. The sun was
setting. It glared through the chinks in lilac and hot-ember
cloud, sent shafts of pure light in a fan shape above them,
and catching a wisp of detached vapour turned it into gold
so intense it could have contracted into a star. It was as
though the doomed city had exploded into glory instead of
horror. But because the glory was inexpressible and impossible to contain I felt stabs of almost physical pain in my
chest and behind my eyes, a feeling of total inadequacy to
deal with what I saw. It was a relief to be facing the creosoted
fence of the cemetery, to walk on up to the Clapham fields
talking about nothing in particular. But I was left with a
sense of cowardice, of betrayal even, as though in turning
my back to avoid the discomfort I had sinned against the
light, and from time to time the thought returned to make me
uneasy. I knew, or grew to know, a lack in myself, of confidence or determination, which made me turn aside from

anything that threatened to demand a struggle, a too willing surrender to any feeling of insufficiency.

Christmas came, in the warmest December Ada could remember. We could hark to the herald angels singing, without irony now. The statesmen started to make the peace settlement in the Hall of Mirrors, though it was July 1919 before they reached it. Ada came to the school Choral Society concert riding for the first time in a taxi, rather than a cab or fly. The world had changed, not only outside but inside our home. The Victorian world, which had never quite left us, began to fade. *The Light of the World* was taken down from where it had hung above the piano; and the piano itself was made to give out unfamiliar sounds. Instead of Kid Bridger's rendering of 'The Relief of Lucknow', a descriptive piece which introduced 'The Campbells are Coming'; instead of 'The Lost Chord', 'Until', 'The Indian Love Lyrics', a High School mistress lodger played Ravel and Debussy. She let me sit in a corner and listen, spellbound by the strange new fellowship of notes.

Ada had less than six years to live in the peace-time world, and the diary is torn away before the end of July 1920. It must have been not long before she died that I showed her the first scene of a play I was writing called *Armageddon*. It was about a group of men and women who had escaped from a devastated world on to a rocky island, perhaps an echo of the old nightmare of the flight from the doomed city, or part of the reverberations of the war which were not yet stilled in the family. (Bernie Bridger had come through apparently unscathed, and gone back to Australia, but he was to be 'poor Bernie', as his uncle was 'poor Bertie'. Before Ada died the news came that he had walked off into the bush, and was never heard of again.) I had made one of the characters in my play say 'My God!', or perhaps 'Good God!', and Ada anxiously reproved me for using the Name in vain. When she herself used the word it was said on a breath, with a slight tremble, as though her vocal cords were genuflecting. Bodily genuflexion was too High Church to be contemplated, except an almost imperceptible lowering of the head during the Creed. I was impatient of the airless, text-ridden nature of her belief, which seemed so far from the invocation of 'God is a spirit and we must worship him in the spirit and in truth'; and yet I had an uneasy respect for it, a feeling, unworded at the time, that even though so narrowly interpreted it was a deeper valuation of life than belief in a progression of accidents, a phenomenal opportunism beginning nowhere, or than the evasive obtuseness of Isn't-Nature-wonderful?

One night in 1924 my mother woke me to come to her help. Ada had fallen out of bed and lay speechless but conscious on the floor. When we lifted her back into bed she seemed, in her flannel night-dress, almost like a child, so small and dependent. There was no money to send her to hospital; she had to go to the infirmary, and there for a few days she lay with a bow of blue ribbon in her scanty hair, and died, leaving me *The Pilgrim's Progress* inscribed 'Ada with Papa's love. Xmas 1865', and her Bible with the margins mazed with her tiny writing. When Jack Fry came to the funeral he reproved my mother for not letting him know in time for him to pay for proper nursing. She would never have thought of asking anyone for help, but it left her feeling she had failed Ada, and she came as near to crying as I ever saw her.

On the day of the funeral I was in bed with mumps, but soon afterwards I remember standing a long time in what we called the box room, where I slept, a room just large enough to take a bed, a chair, and a chest of drawers, feeling the strangeness of the absence, and knowing what I had never thought of before, that I was fond of Aunt A.

In 1867 when she was eleven years old she had worked a sampler for one of her grandmothers, a list in red stitching of the children as far as Hal. It hangs above my study door:

> Ada Louise Hammond
> Bessie Mary 9 years
> Percy Rowland age 7
> Edith Clara six years
> Helen Schabner age 4

Edwin Bertram 2 years
Harry Beaumont, baby
For Grandmama 1867
with Ada's love

In 1935 Charlie was writing a long letter to my mother. Before it was finished his wife suddenly died. He lived on alone for twenty-two more years, painting occasionally, working in the garden, watching the birds, the grey and scarlet cockatoos on the hawthorn bush, the kookaburras that fed from his hand. In 1939 he sent a series of fifteen small pictures which he headed: 'The three brothers – Bert, Hal & Charlie. Starters in Life's Steeplechase. Illustrations showing our respective positions through the years from the fall of the flag in 1884, when our home in England broke up, to the present time.'

The coloured drawings show them as jockeys, sometimes one ahead, sometimes another, Charlie falling at a fence and remounting, Bert crashing at another and not rising. In the final drawing the shirts of the two survivors have been left uncoloured, though one is shown to have fallen: '19— Which one?'; and at the end of the letter, scribbled on the back, he says: 'And so our steeplechase is nearing its end. I wonder which of us two will be the first to fall? Your ever loving Tony. (You will note the jockeys are riding old style. Not "Tod Sloan" style as they do these days.)'

Then in 1951 he sent a postcard drawing to complete the series showing that Hal had fallen, aged eighty-two. Bess, too, had just died at ninety-three, but Edith, at ninety, and Lil, at eighty-eight, were still alive. My mother and Charlie died, as they had been born, within a year of each other, at eighty-six. The Tony and Tina letters went on almost to the end:

Dearest Tina
Yours with Christmas Greetings reached me in good time . . . You say 'Don't forget Tina will you?' Fancy me forgetting my little sweetheart! . . . Yes, I remember all the mischief we used to

get up to and I daresay I remember a lot of things that you have forgotten such as when the shavings under the nursery floor caught fire and we two were locked in. Mother and Ada came up stairs just in time and called father (for a wonder he was at home). He pulled up the floorboards and put out the fire. That was at Milverton Crescent, Leamington. (You were 2.)

It has been a vile winter here. I long for the sun so I can sit in it and get warm. I am tired now so will go and post this. It may be the last you will ever get from your loving Tony . . . but if I cannot write do not forget that your old Tony is always thinking of his little sweetheart Tina.

In her old age my mother had a dream, so unlike her unvisionary self that it stayed in her mind. There was a great storm at sea, like the storm in the Bay of Biscay when the captain decorated her with the button from his uniform, like the storm which had brought the S.S. *Rockabill* limping home on the day I was born. A white horse descended slowly out of the heavy clouds. As it touched the angry waves and sank out of sight the sea was instantly as tranquil as a mill-pond.

FAMILY TREES

THE HAMMOND AND FRY FAMILIES

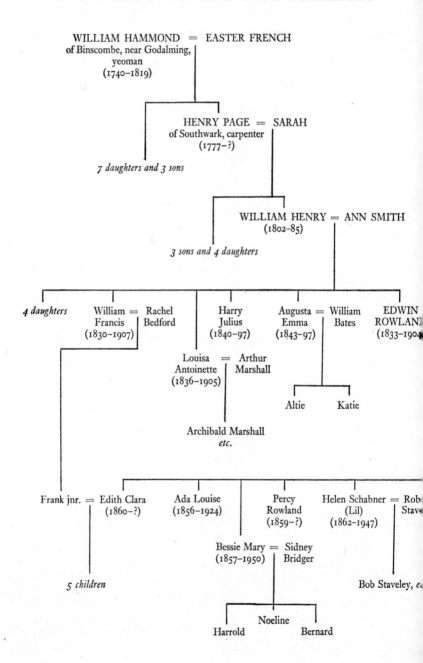

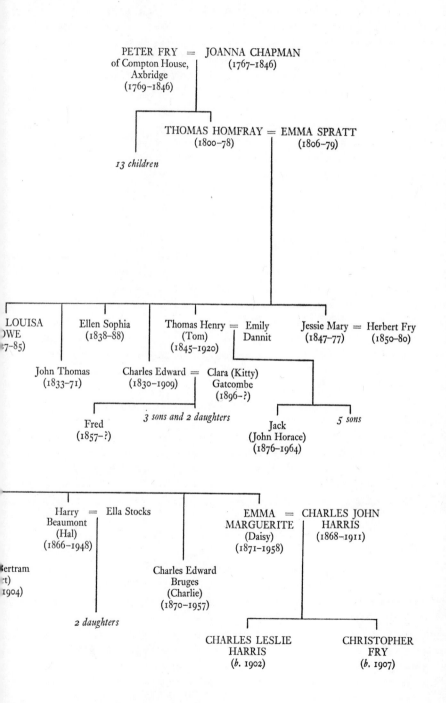

PETER FRY = JOANNA CHAPMAN
of Compton House,   (1767–1846)
Axbridge
(1769–1846)

THOMAS HOMFRAY = EMMA SPRATT
(1800–78)   (1806–79)

13 children

LOUISA   Ellen Sophia   Thomas Henry = Emily   Jessie Mary = Herbert Fry
)WE   (1838–88)   (Tom)   Dannit   (1847–77)   (1850–80)
7–85)   (1845–1920)

John Thomas   Charles Edward = Clara (Kitty)
(1833–71)   (1830–1909)   Gatcombe
                                   (1896–?)

        Fred   *3 sons and 2 daughters*   Jack   *5 sons*
        (1857–?)   (John Horace)
                                                          (1876–1964)

        Harry = Ella Stocks   EMMA = CHARLES JOHN
        Beaumont   MARGUERITE   HARRIS
        (Hal)   (Daisy)   (1868–1911)
        (1866–1948)   (1871–1958)

                    Charles Edward
                    Bruges
                    (Charlie)
                    (1870–1957)

ertram
t)
1904)

        2 daughters
                                    CHARLES LESLIE   CHRISTOPHER
                                    HARRIS   FRY
                                    (*b.* 1902)   (*b.* 1907)

THE HARRIS FAMILY

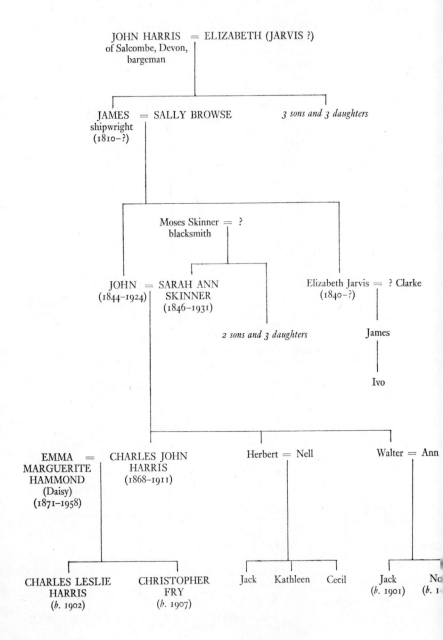

JOHN HARRIS = ELIZABETH (JARVIS ?)
of Salcombe, Devon,
bargeman

JAMES = SALLY BROWSE   *3 sons and 3 daughters*
shipwright
(1810–?)

Moses Skinner = ?
blacksmith

JOHN = SARAH ANN   Elizabeth Jarvis = ? Clarke
(1844–1924)   SKINNER   (1840–?)
(1846–1931)

2 sons and 3 daughters   James

Ivo

EMMA = CHARLES JOHN   Herbert = Nell   Walter = Ann
MARGUERITE   HARRIS
HAMMOND   (1868–1911)
(Daisy)
(1871–1958)

CHARLES LESLIE   CHRISTOPHER   Jack   Kathleen   Cecil   Jack   No
HARRIS   FRY   (b. 1901)   (b. 1
(b. 1902)   (b. 1907)